CW01649718

ST IVES 1975 – 2005

Art Colony in Transition

Peter Davies

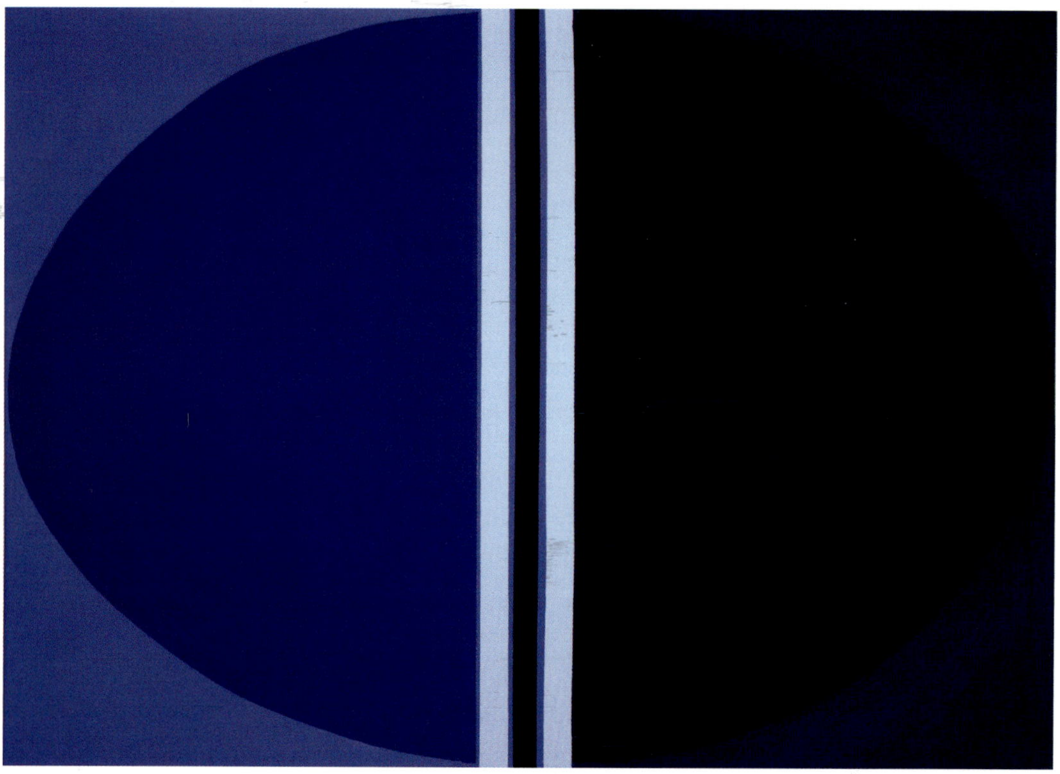

ST IVES 1975 – 2005

Art Colony in Transition

Peter Davies

St Ives 1975 – 2005
Art Colony in Transition

Front Cover: *Noon 2003*
Morag Ballard (oil on canvas)
courtesy of England & Co.
Frontispiece: *Hello Blue*
Sir Terry Frost RA
courtesy of Michael Cane

Cover Design: Simon Bishop
Typesetting/Layout: Tobi Carver

Printed & Published by:
The St Ives Printing & Publishing Company,
High Street, St Ives, Cornwall TR26 1RS, UK

www.stivesnews.co.uk

ISBN: 978 0 948385 45 6

CONTENTS

FOREWORD

CORNWALL boasts one of the most exciting and vibrant contemporary art scenes in Europe – and who better to convey a flavour of its wide and varied nature than the distinguished art critic, painter and printmaker, Peter Davies, with his well informed blend of documentary journalism, art history and contemporary art criticism?

The period covered by this book is one that Peter has lived through and witnessed. He personally knows the majority of the artists represented and for some twenty years has been reviewing their exhibitions in *The St Ives Times and Echo*. He has compiled for *The Independent* the obituaries of many of the senior members of the St Ives Schools, such as Sir Terry Frost, John Wells, Wilhelmina Barns-Graham and Alex Mackenzie.

Peter also has an eye for spotting emerging talent and has encouraged many a young artist through his perceptive catalogue essays and exhibition reviews.

I first met Peter in 1998, when I exhibited his paintings at Whitstable Museum & Gallery, a service run by Canterbury Museums. When I came to work at Falmouth Art Gallery Peter helped in a great many ways, generously sharing his encyclopaedic knowledge of Cornish art.

When the Secretary of State allocated *1933: Study of a Head* by Ben Nicholson to Falmouth Art Gallery in lieu of inheritance tax, it was Peter, through his enthusiasm, who communicated to the media and decision makers, not only the importance of the painting, but of the 'landmark' decision to house the work in Cornwall rather than in London.

Peter also advised on the ground-breaking *Surrealists in Cornwall* exhibition, in which Antony Penrose chronicled a holiday in 1937 at Lambe Creek on the River Fal by Roland Penrose, Lee Miller, Eillen Agar, Max Ernst, Man Ray, Paul Eluard and Henry Moore. As a critic he gave his support to the *Portscatho: Portrait of a Cornish Art Colony* exhibition curated by Chris Insoll and including the work of Trevor Felcey, Lynn Golden, Grace Gardner, Chris and Anthea Insoll, Michael Stone and Eric Ward.

Peter has worked closely on this current book with the editor and publisher of *The St Ives Times and Echo*, Toni Carver. Like Peter, Toni has done much to encourage Cornish art, and together, as writer and publisher, they make a formidable team.

Of course a survey of contemporary Cornish art is an impossible task and talented artists are inevitably going to be not included. It would require several volumes to include everyone of merit. In mounting exhibitions I know the problems of selection only too well.

Nevertheless, Peter Davies is not afraid to take on this difficult task and to make tough selection decisions. For this reason his portrayal of an art colony in transition makes fascinating and illuminating reading. Peter has an 'edge' to his passionate affair with Cornish art, which makes this an intriguing and thought provoking book that will be treasured by collectors and art lovers for many years to come.

Brian Stewart
Director
Falmouth Art Gallery
July 2007

Chapter One

INTRODUCTION

a. The Legacy of Hepworth and the Coming of the Tate

During the late winter and early summer of 1975 the large community of artists in St Ives, loosely termed a 'school' or, less problematically, an art 'colony', lost three of its most illustrious 'members'. During February the painters Bryan Wynter and Roger Hilton died aged fifty-nine and sixty-three respectively. In May the death of seventy-two year-old sculptor Barbara Hepworth registered to an even greater degree the growing feeling that the modern movement in Cornwall, which had peaked between 1939 and 1964, was drawing to a conclusion.

Settling with her family in Carbis Bay in September 1939, a refugee from war-torn London, Yorkshire-born Hepworth later became – the example of her highly focused yet curiously eclectic and restless husband and collaborator Ben Nicholson notwithstanding – the pre-eminent St Ives artist. The wartime sojourn in Carbis Bay demonstrated a removal of Hampstead modernism to the Atlantic seaboard where what the London critic Lawrence Alloway later termed its 'thirtyish purism'[(1)] softened in response to an irresistible local landscape. After Hepworth's split from Nicholson and her move into 'Trewyn Studio' in the heart of St Ives – where she lived for the close-on thirty remaining years of her life – the sculptor dominated the machinations of both local and, in her later capacity as Tate Gallery trustee, national art politics.

Hepworth became an OBE and CBE in 1958 and 1965 respectively. Local, national and international obligations attended this success. Her career flourished during a post-war era of reconstruction, egalitarianism (she was a churchgoer and Labour Party member), civic responsibility and new international co-operation through the agency of the United Nations. The two important public sitings of sculpture in Hepworth's later career – *Single Form* outside the U.N. Building, New York City (1964) and *Dual Form* in front of St Ives Borough Council's Guildhall (1968) – symbolised perfectly the ethical, moral as well as aesthetic dimension of her project. Among the numerous tributes in the wake of her death nothing struck closer to home than Frank Halliday's recollection of Hepworth as a 'busy member of a working community . . . on terms

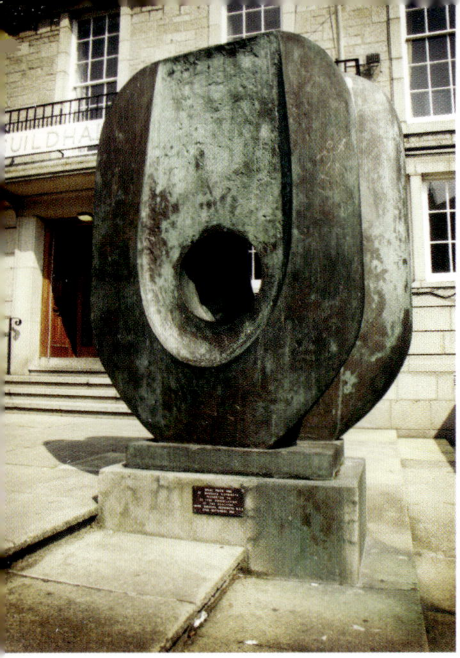

Barbara Hepworth
Dual Form 1968
photograph: Tobi Carver

of easy friendship with people from all sections of the community'.[2] Despite this her assistants often found her personally distant and to the public a mystique developed behind the high Trewyn walls. In her early days at least blessed with the looks of a Hollywood actress and receiving distinguished visitors to her studio Hepworth brought glamour, prestige and celebrity to the workaday aspect of the town which, in a pre-celeb' culture era, was earnt and real. The exoticism of the plants and trees among which her monolithic bronzes nestled merely added to this image.

During the early Trewyn years this space was relegated to a masonry yard but, encouraged by friends like the musician Priaulx Rainier and Will Arnold-Forster, one-time owner of Eagles Nest and author of *Shrubs for the Milder Counties*, Hepworth turned the area into a horticultural haven as well as sculpture garden. After receiving the Freedom of the Borough of St Ives in 1968 Hepworth occasionally opened the garden to townsfolk who, before the property became the Barbara Hepworth Museum in 1976 and was taken over by the Tate Gallery in 1980, were pioneer samplers of this magical and unique environment of shrub, flower, plant and monument.[3]

The posthumous fate of studio and garden saw a convergence between the management of her estate and the expanding enterprise of the Tate Gallery. Her son-in-law, Sir Alan Bowness, who was Tate Gallery Director between 1979 and 1988, oversaw this collusion. Brian Smith, Hepworth's discrete and trusted secretary, supervised the early period of the new museum. It was not however until 1993, under the directorship of Bowness' successor Sir Nicholas Serota, that Tate Gallery opened its seaside branch at Porthmeor. The early Tate years under curator Michael Tooby were characterised by retrospectives featuring leading St Ives artists, some of whom were still active but nearing the end of their careers; these were interspersed between displays that were unconvincing, if well-intentioned, sops to second generation or contemporary artists. Under his successor Susan Daniel McElroy this policy mutated into contemporary exhibitions by non-Cornish artists among them the notorious and ill-conceived YBA exhibition *Real Life (2002–3)* that seemed to depart from Tate St Ives' founding principle 'Modern Art in a Cornish Context'.[4]

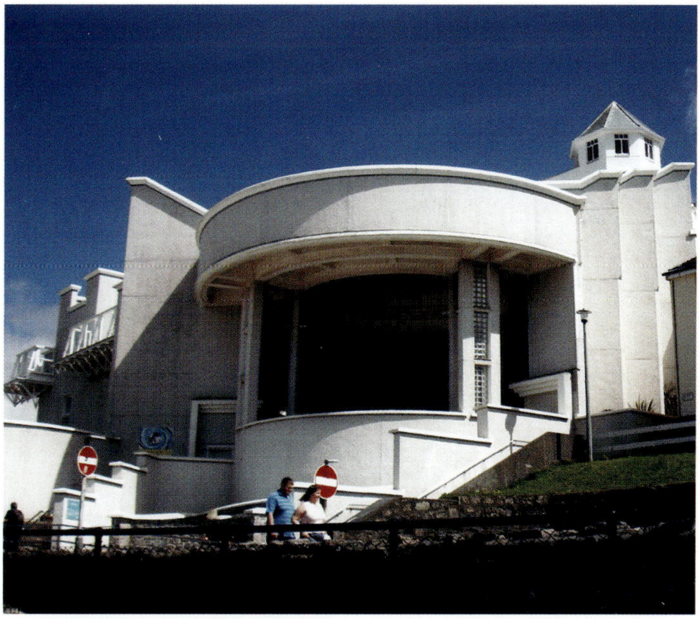

Tate St Ives
photograph: Rosie Osborne

Exhibitions of Barbara Hepworth and Terry Frost (1993), Bryan Wynter (1994), Guido Morris and 'Porthmeor Beach: A Century of Images' (1995), Christopher Wood and Mark Rothko (1996), 'A Quality of Light' (1997), a 90th birthday retrospective 'The Fragile Cell' for John Wells (1998), W. Barns-Graham (1999), Peter Lanyon, John Virtue and Sandra Blow (2000), Patrick Heron and Roger Mayne (2001), Richard Long, Ian Hamilton Findlay and Naum Gabo (2002), a huge Barbara Hepworth Centenary exhibition, Terry Frost (again) and Alan Davie (2003), Karl Weschke (2004), W. Barns-Graham and Denis Mitchell (2005) and Paul Feiler and Roger Hilton (2006) told a curatorial story of consolidation, historical reappraisal and speculative and inappropriate indulgence into contemporary metropolitan trends. Though smashing projected audience figures – by 1998 the gallery had reached the million visitors landmark – the Tate was less than popular among sizeable sections of the general public, whether tourist or townsfolk, which frequently complained of abstract bias (shades of Hockney v Norman Reid 1978), elitism, curatorial obscurantism and wasted wall space. Bungled proposals first to expand the gallery by demolishing adjacent flats then by annexing Barnoon car park incurred local wrath which compelled a retreating Serota to look at alternative venues as far afield as Hayle.

b. A critical re-evaluation

The catalyst in the rising fortunes of modern St Ives art, marking its ascent from its 1970's doldrums, was the broad survey 'St Ives 1939 – 64' at Tate Gallery, Millbank (now Tate Britain) in early 1985. Roughly a midpoint between Hepworth's death and the opening of Tate St Ives the exhibition was both popular and a critical watershed. Curated by David Brown whose chronology for the New Art Centre exhibition 'St Ives 1945 – 55' (1977) anticipated this re-evaluation, 'St Ives 1939 – 64' offered a thoroughgoing critical re-assessment while providing a springboard for the successful transformation of the post war modern movement into a fin-de-siecle revivalism which provided continuity through the accommodation of a new generation.

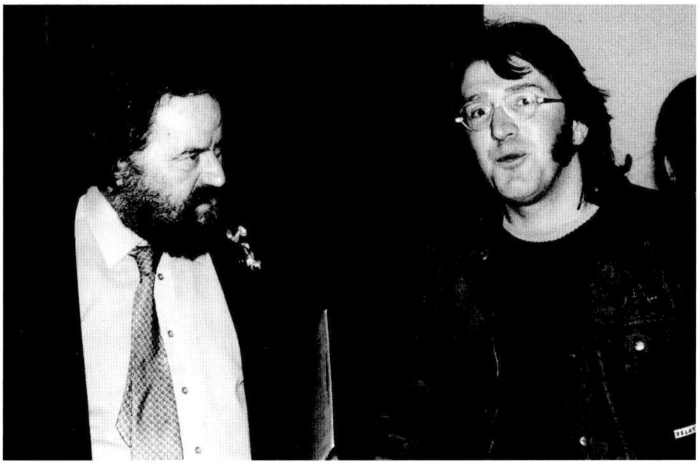

David Brown with Peter Davies at the Tate opening Feb. 1985, London

This critical re-assessment was undertaken, in national press and specialist art magazine alike, by the bright 'sparks' of contemporary art discourse. Michael Shepherd's *Sunday Telegraph* headliner 'St Ives Has It' was challenged by *The Guardian's* more sceptical Waldemar Januszczak who referred to the 'hopelessly minor artists' accompanying the major core exhibitors.[5] The latter's sweeping, ill-informed review was followed, nearly twenty years later, by his 'snide' and controversial *Sunday Times*[6] review of Mariele Neudecker at Tate St Ives, a review engendering a *St Ives Times and Echo* headline article in which Mayor Harry Isaacs, a one time Leach Pottery employee, invited the critic back to town to look more closely and less dismissively at the town's cultural heritage.[7]

Both the Art & Language critic Charles Harrison and Peter Fuller saw the modern movement in St Ives as historically contingent on broader national and, ultimately, international imperatives. Harrison' observation that St Ives 'may only accidentally have been the site of the artistic developments we associate with it'[(8)] chimed with Fuller's view that 'ultimately St Ives became a kind of crucible in which so many of the significant issues affecting the Fine Arts were tried and tested.'[(9)] As part of his romantic retrenchment (a rejection of high modernism he shared with Lanyon) Fuller endorsed Patrick Heron's October 1974 *Guardian* articles defending St Ives against exported American culture as 'one of the most revealing art critical essays of the last decade'.

Harrison's definition of St Ives in terms of an arbitary artistic grouping sharing close geographic, social and historical links (sanctuary, camaraderie, salubrious environment, cheap rent, clear light, ready-made former fishloft studio space etc.) led to his conclusion that in both wartime and post-war Cornwall 'an unadulterated modernist culture could only continue in rustication.' For Fuller this factor was vindication rather than vice, the critic applauding St Ives' representation of 'the best aspects of British taste, tradition and sensibility.' Fuller's markedly moralist position in which 'achievement in art almost always involves an element of refusal of modernity' led to an endorsement of Lanyon's so-called 'Higher Landscape Painting' above the 'repetitive outpourings' of Heron, Wynter and Frost some of whose work 'purported to rely on visual sensation alone'.

c. Revival and retro chic: an ongoing 'constructivism'

After the late modernist hiatus of the 1970s, the so-called decade that fashion forgot, a new generation of artists, students, dealers and collectors associated itself with St Ives. New painters capable of extending the achievements of Gabo, Nicholson, Wells, Lanyon and Hepworth did so with an eye on the universal geometric possibilities of pure abstraction linked to landscape or other 'romantic' source material. An intermediate generation, among it George Dannatt (b. 1915), Michael Canney (1923–99), Paul Mount (b. 1922), Denis Mitchell (1912–93) and Roger Leigh (1925–97), led to a younger group that included Morag Ballard (b. 1961), Vanessa Gardiner (b. 1960), Patrick Haughton (b. 1942) and Jeremy Annear (b. 1949).

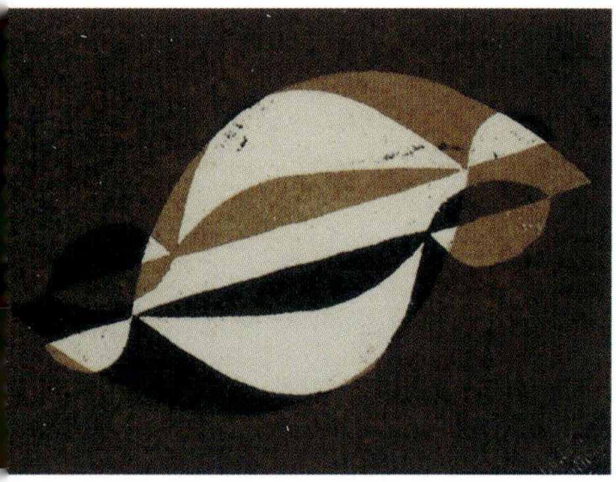

John Wells
Shell Form
Linocut
photograph: Belgrave Gallery

The influence of John Wells (1907–2000) on each of the above was historical rather than contemporary in nature. Wells' output had diminished during the 1970s, the artist reduced to rehabilitating or restoring old paintings and constructions – many of them classics in more ways than one – in cobwebbed corners of the Newlyn schoolhouse studio he owned and shared with Denis Mitchell from 1969. *Vol de Nuit* (1985) rekindled earlier interests in flight while an 80th birthday exhibition in July 1987 at the Wills Lane Gallery, St Ives – whose owner retired borough architect H.C. Gilbert was one of the few gallery proprietors the reclusive and suspicious Wells would deal with – was a prelude to the valedictory Tate exhibition 'The Fragile Cell' (1998). And when *The Independent* critic Iain Gale featured Wells and Mitchell in a 1992 article[10] he took a misleadingly backseat role. Socially interactive with trusted colleagues (the younger painter John Emanuel drove him around in later years) and supportive of respected fellow artists (he bought a small white relief now belonging to the Kent-based St Ives collector Peter McMasters from Michael Canney's 1983 exhibition of recent work at the Newlyn Art Gallery) Wells continued to send small original Christmas cards in the honoured St Ives tradition, the linocuts *Circles and Squares – Black* (1971) and *Circular Study* (1974) revealing undiminished deftness of touch and articulation of

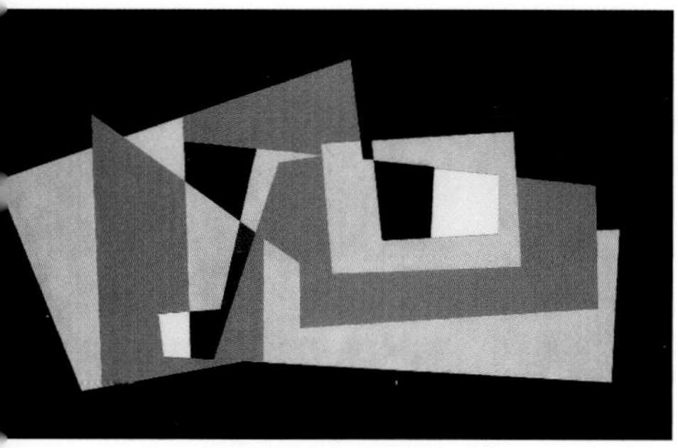

George Dannatt
Grand St Malo
– Citadel Version 6 2003
Oil on Medite Board
photograph: Osborne/Samuel

segmented geometry in space. After his death the studio was absorbed by the Borlase Smart Trust, which became the Borlase Smart – John Wells Trust.

Wells' uncanny mix of mystical, poetic and scientific (medical) sentiments inspired his friend George Dannatt, an amateur painter in the constructivist tradition, connoisseur and notable St Ives collector. A small exhibition of their work at Southampton City art Gallery in the early summer of 2007 celebrated this friendship. Dannatt's professional background, like Wells', informed the nature of his work, his practise as a Chartered Surveyor and music critic for the *News Chronicle* during the first post-war decade giving his work a lyric precision. The interpenetration of coloured planes – split, overlapped or divided – create counterpoint or unpredictable harmonies of a musical kind. There is a dichotomy in the 'oeuvre' between a pristine plasticism – imparting a clinical quality where expression is a function of unpredictable asymmetry – and a sensuous evocation of landscape through an associative chromatic and textural naturalism. Where the well-known wood reliefs are concerned the nautical symbolism of boats, ropes and quayside paraphernalia demonstrates the Wiltshire-based Dannatt's long term allegiance to St Ives, an alliance acknowledged by a solo exhibition at Newlyn Orion, Penzance in 1983.

The sculptor Paul Mount's paintings also obliquely refer, through coloured geometric fragments, to the quayside. Devon-born Mount (b. 1922) studied painting at the Royal College, London during and after the war. Painting and sculpture developed in tandem thereafter, the large body of painting – academic portraits of family or of African women, impressionistic gardenscapes and French riverbanks near Paris followed by the clustered cubes of Mediterranean hilltop villages and harbours – trading in the same lyrical post-cubist language of interacting arcs, circles, rectangles and planes that define the multi-faceted aspects of the welded or cast metal sculpture. While not sculptural plans paintings like *Grand Bleu, Quayside* or *Night Shift* therefore bear striking similarity to the sparkling, reflective immediacy of the pristine stainless steel forms. Where *Regatta* is concerned, an abstract painting sharing with well-known publicly-sited sculptures like *Spirit of Bristol* (1968) a boyhood interest

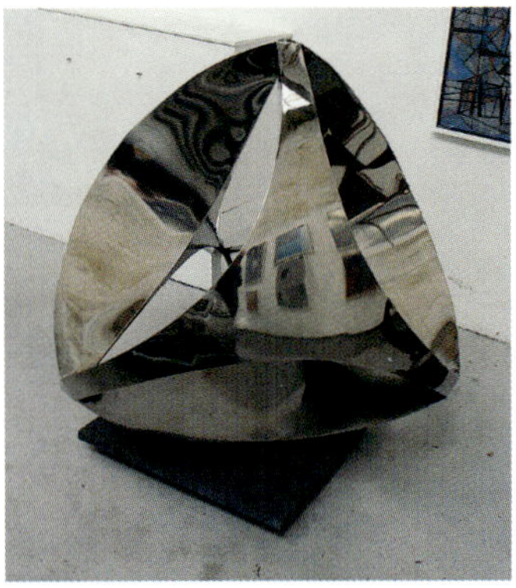

Paul Mount
Tetroid
stainless steel
courtesy:
Thompson Gallery, Marylebone

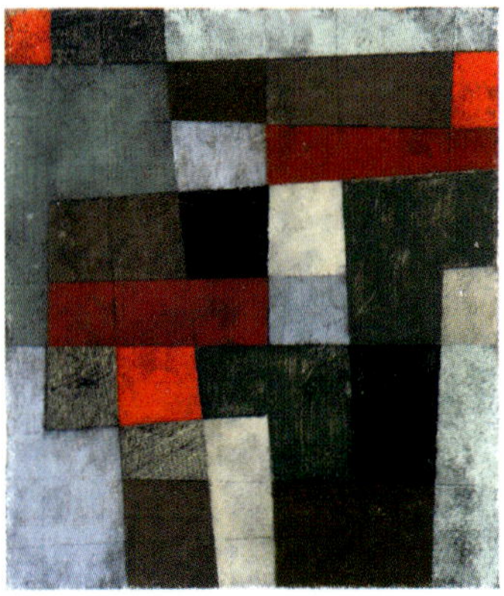

Michael Canney
On Black No.1 1991
Oil on board
courtesy:
Katharine House Gallery, Marlborough

in windjammers off the Devon coast, Mount engineers sail-like shapes in kinetic formal counterpoint.

Living in St Just since returning from West Africa in 1962 and using a Languedoc holiday home until 2004 Mount responds to environment. An admiration for French Romanesque architecture also has implicit, rather than overt, stylistic influence on the direct, asymmetric facades of the sculpture. Michael Canney also turned to the Mediterannean world inspired by what he termed 'the abstract qualities of the Italian architectural scene'. After retiring to Italy from Bristol in 1984, where he had taught at the art school under Paul Feiler since 1966, Canney developed his constructivist interests. The subsequent late 'oeuvre', encouraged by his friend Alan Reynolds and amounting to what he called 'structural or topological experiments' saw Canney creating endless permutations on the square, overlapped, cut or folded into coloured or plain white reliefs. White purism was countered by 'local' Tuscan colour - olive, orange or beige - in the *Capriccio* series or in *On Black No.1* (1991), a playful Klee-like composition made of wobbly coloured cubes made shortly before returning to England and a final seven year domicile in Devizes, Wiltshire.

The medium of the constructed relief extended the pictorial dimension into real space where concerns proper to sculpture took hold. The sculptors Roger Leigh (1925–97), Denis Mitchell (1912–93) and John Milne (1931–78), prominent among the half dozen assistants under Hepworth, used the medium in ways that conceived and executed form both in plan and elevation. Roger Leigh, trained in architecture and town planning in Liverpool, was an interdisciplinary polymath who indulged in wild, whimsical experiments, across media. These interests were sometimes synaesthesic in nature, Leigh exploring the relationship and meaning between alphabetical letters and visual images. Influenced as a schoolboy by the book: *The Art of Writing, Illuminating and Lettering* Leigh saw in his mind's eye broad topographic shapes as giant letter forms. These ideas informed the semi-utilitarian 'verbal' ceramic sculptures of the 1990's whose calligraphic shapes symbolised an idea, paid homage to a revered artist such as the architect Gaudi

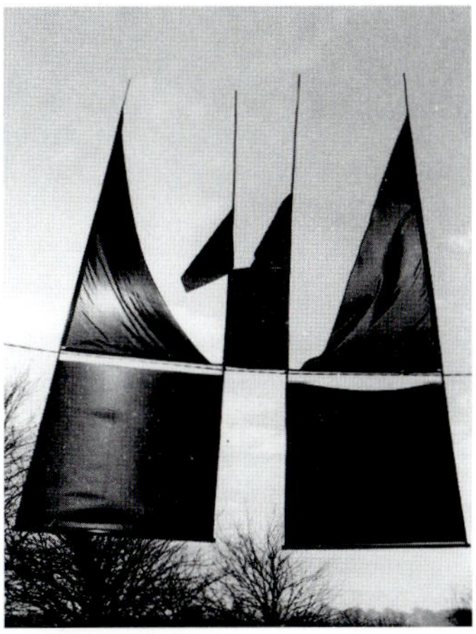

Roger Leigh
Dyptich Flight, 1969
1969
bamboo/nylon (destroyed)

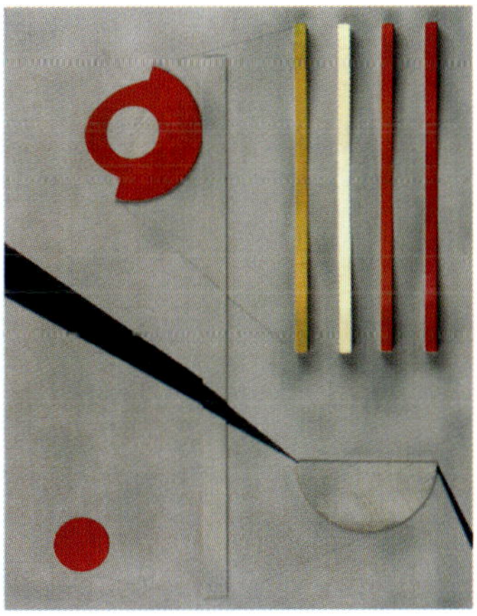

Nick Leigh
Splinter 2006
Painted wooden construction
courtesy:
Katharine House Gallery, Marlborough

or, where the floating nylon banners of the mid 1970's were concerned, the poetry of a friend John Fairfax.

These concrete poetry banners and kinetic nylon fabric structures, subject to the vicissitudes of climate as much as of light, represented Leigh at his most playful and dynamic. An extra-St Ives interest in the international sculpture scene embraced Chillida and Christo and, following their interest in environment, Leigh took to creating a temporary nylon sheet relief on the exterior walls of Exeter College of Art where he taught part time until retiring during the mid 1980s.(11) Moving from Cornwall to the Marlborough Downs, Wiltshire in 1966 where he acquired Sorbus – T.S. Tait's classic modern movement house – Leigh used Sorbus's grounds to mount *Sculpture in a Landscape* (1969), an anthology of eighteen major and lesser-known contemporaries among them Adams, Moore and Austin Wright from the former category and George Stephenson and Christopher Lane from the latter.(12) Its intergenerational diversity amounted to what Charles Spencer called in the accompanying catalogue 'a pistol-point marriage between technological abstraction and what Sir Kenneth Clark calls the Religion of Nature'. The prescience of Leigh's sensitivity to environment during a burgeoning age of outdoor sculpture events reflected his architecture background.

Nick Leigh (b. 1962), Roger's son, whose art making enterprise came late, used formative memories of major St Ives artists (he left Cornwall aged three), an art history training at Warwick and, latterly, an occupation as bespoke picture framer and gilder to make reliefs from 'found' wood off cuts and carpented section. Living in Roger's Carbis Bay holiday cottage during the winter of 1987–8 he re-acquainted himself with the art scene before travelling in America and finally settling to raise a family in Aldbourne, Wiltshire. Leigh's reliefs are 'architectonic', the interplay between flat design and extended form or between natural and artificial colour and texture providing rhythm between parts and the whole.

Unlike his friend Roger Leigh, Denis Mitchell retained the carved monolithic mode of the Trewyn Studio years. A versatile craftsman of the traditional, artisan kind Mitchell cut his teeth under Hepworth branching out as first an independent (1959–67), then full-time sculptor

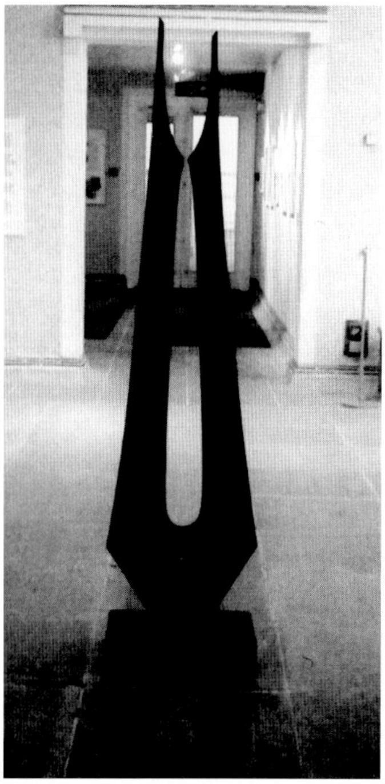

Denis Mitchell
Clowance
bronze
photograph: Peter Davies

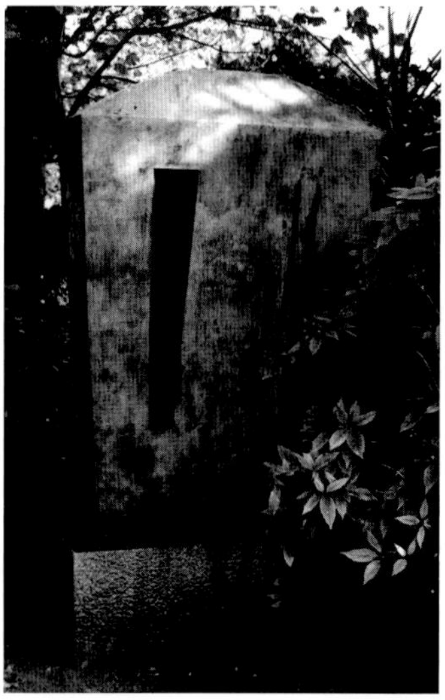

John Milne
Megalith II
bronze
photograph: Iain Rutherford

(1967 onwards). This was made possible by his Chelsea-based dealer Marjorie Parr with whom Mitchell enjoyed three solo exhibitions during the late 1960s and early 1970s. Three significant 'public' retrospectives, at the National Museum, Malta (1973), Plymouth City Art Gallery (1974) and Glynn Vivian Art Gallery in his hometown Swansea (1979) demonstrated post-Hepworth success. This was a function of patenting forms based on the tools of his trade (fishing, labouring and mining in the 1930s and sculpture making after 1950), on a collection of tribal masks and on what Tate St Ives curator Sara Hughes described as an 'interrelation of ideas in different media from the 1960s'.[13]

It was therefore sculptural use of applied media - bronze, aluminium, lino, slate, hard or soft wood and stone – that enabled Mitchell, an avowed non-intellectual, to bridge the gap between art and craft. The graphic source of old sketchbooks for many slim upright bronzes from the seminal John Wells-influenced *Turning Form* (1959) to the late sculptures *Treave*, inspired by a fish vertebrae found by his part-fisherman-part-sculptor assistant Tommy Rowe, and *Trewarveneth* (1992). The upright rhythms of these and the incised slate reliefs, wall-bound or free-standing, are testimony to a slender and elegant vision of formal economy and lithe movement. Last lifetime displays – locally at the Penwith, St Ives in 1992 and, in the metropolis, at Flowers East in 1993 – were followed a dozen years after his death by Tate St Ives' 'Ascending Forms' in which the sculptor's work accompanied a first posthumous exhibition of W. Barns-Graham.

Eccles-born and Salford-trained John Milne also employed Rowe to finish work for Marjorie Parr exhibitions. A fleeting Hepworth assistant only (1952) Milne retained lifelong reverence for the older sculptor and lived adjacent at Trewyn House[14] Like Mitchell Milne also liked relief-making and favoured flattened, rectilinear free-standing form embodying linear or elliptical cavities. Such qualities characterise *Megalith II* (1974), a large bronze representing the only publically-sited non-Hepworth sculpture in St Ives, installed in Trewyn Public Gardens in 1976 as a memorial to Hepworth. Sharing with late work allusion to ancient classical, archaic or Islamic architecture, *Megalith II* has a minimal design characteristic of *Duet,*

Cheops or *Obelisk* (1974). Mature expressions of contained power such late work chimed with late modern reductivism. The last few years witnessed an international exhibiting schedule and the publication of a monograph by J.P. Hodin in 1977.[15] His untimely death in 1978 was lamented in E.H. Ramsden's *Times* obituary which spoke of an artist 'at the height of his powers and in the midst of preparing a second exhibition for America'.[16]

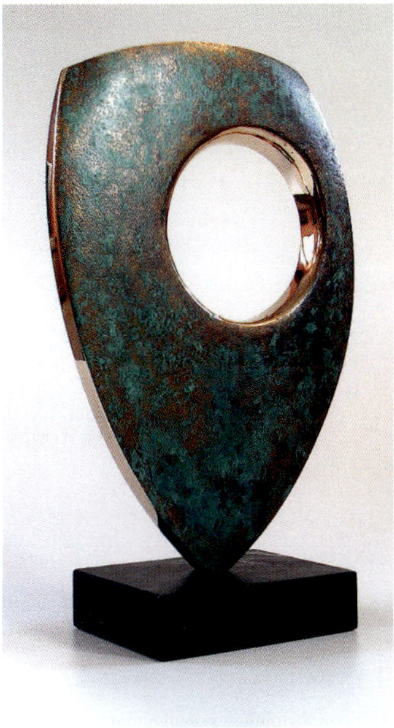

Chris Buck
Before the Rising Sun II
2006, bronze
courtesy: Belgrave Gallery

The monolithic bronze sculpture of Mitchell and Milne, which associates with ancient pagan monuments, is recalled by Chris Buck (b. 1956), a Slough-born and Redruth-trained sculptor who returned to Cornwall in 1982. Replacing his predecessors as an active Penwith Society member, Buck fashions abstract sand cast bronze forms that are subjected to a slow meticulous finish. The son of a toolmaker and a one time foundry worker, Buck follows Mitchell in elaborate post-foundry carving, grinding and filing processes. The slim, perfected objects that result are informed by industrial expertise; similar thrusting movement characterises the steel sculpture of Gordon Allen, another metalworker and toolmaker. Allen's domicile in Wiltshire and the Cotswolds and a twenty-year career with Vickers from 1953 was followed by a move to St Ives in 1997. Accquring a studio leased from First Great Western at St Erth station Allen constructed forms of lithe aerodynamic movement, the conceptual poetry of *Cloud Forms* in cement painted white and integrating engineering and artistic instincts.

Margaret Mellis (b. 1914), a Suffolk-based pioneering Cornish modernist (she lived in Carbis Bay during the

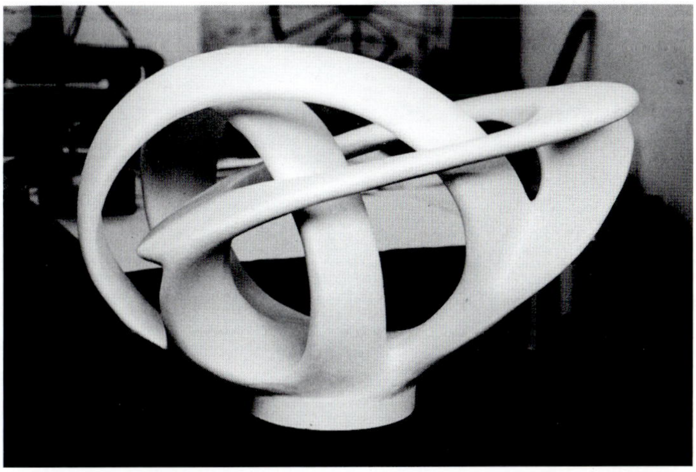

Gordon Allen
Cloud Form
painted cement

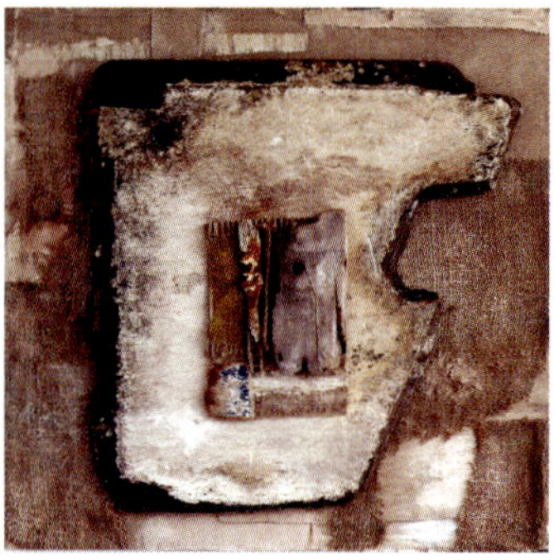

Bob Osborne
Sennen Cove 2002
collage
courtesy of the artist

war), is less 'classical' in mood preferring to construct from seaside flotsam. From the mid 1970s assembling driftwood reliefs pinned to the wall without frames, Mellis revisited the ship-in-a-bottle romanticism of the early Cornish years in a manner revealing the inspiration of Alfred Wallis who Mellis knew and whose work she avidly collected and salvaged from the deceased former mariner's flea-ridden cottage.

Wallis appears again in Mellis's post-1987 'envelope' series in which the 'given' shapes of envelopes are unfolded and used as background for still life paintings. Also informed by the coloured paper collages of her second husband Francis Davison, these works link cerebral constructivism with a more sensuous, random language using the natural effects of 'found' material. Treated retrospectively as a St Ives artist in East Anglian exile, Mellis enjoyed solo shows at the Pier Arts Centre, Orkney (1982) and at Austin Desmond, London (2001) the catalogue for which contained an endorsement from Damien Hirst. Bob Osborne (b. 1953), also linked to East Anglia where he studied literature under Malcolm Bradbury in the early 1970s, came to art late inspired by Mellis, whom he visited in 2000 in Southwold, and Sandra Blow in whose studio he assisted during 2001–2. Possessing through blood a gypsy instinct for discarded or recycled materials Osborne turned early box constructions of a literary Victorian nature on their head and composed in a more abstract, 'arte povera' manner expressing the intrinsic nature of the rough materials.

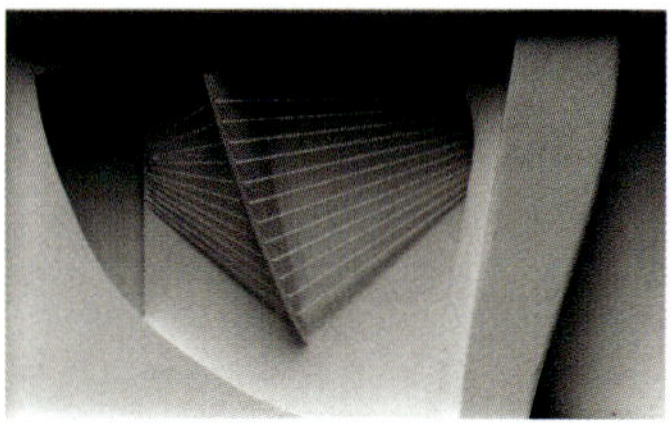

Morag Ballard
Out and Return 1992/93
mixed media, relief construction

This overlap between generations sees artists like Morag Ballard, the Bath and Chelsea-trained artist and relief maker, develop St Ivesian constructivism in a manner pertinent to a late and indeed post modern age. Architectural as well as natural features of Cornish and French landscape are reconstructed in terms of hard geometry. The iconography of dams, towers, walls and bridges were suggested in student work; a room-sized installation at Chelsea (a large plaster container full of enigmatic plaster pellets) embodied tension between enclosure and open space. Succeeding box constructions led to an all-important association with England & Co which went on, during the next fifteen years, to mount almost biannual solo shows.

Unlike many 'Box' artists at England & Co Ballard's intention was formal and classic, purist even, rather than

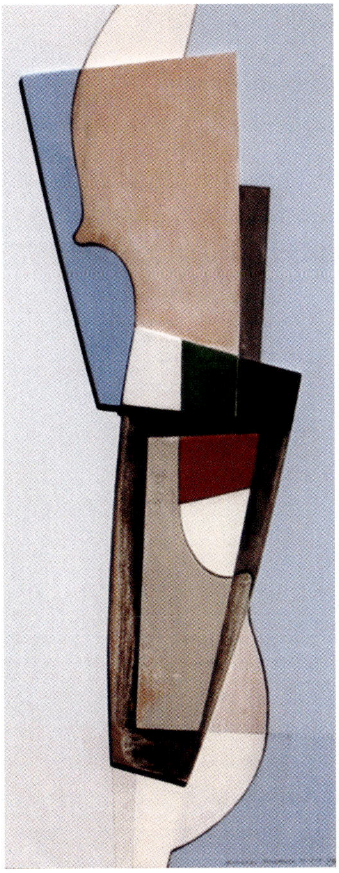

Patrick Haughton
Scherzo: Finistère
oil and wood relief
courtesy of the artist

ethnic or 'romantic'. *Out and Return* (1993), for example, recalled early Wells and Hepworth in its semi-sculptural mode of lifting and tilting flat or stringed planes into shallow space. By the millennium a more complex diagrammatic quality emerged in which broad expanses of white were punctuated by pristine, jewel-like colour. The illusion of the third dimension in these flat paintings was a function of cones, cylinders, cubes, spheres and other dimensional geometric forms. Through these Ballard was expanding her frame of reference not only stylistically in recalling Corbusier, Ozenfant and continental purism, but also thematically in suggesting subject-matter such as ancient walled cities like Carcassonne in the south of France.

Penryn-based Patrick Haughton also makes boxed constructions conceived as pictorial extension; mixing cerebral surface design with tactile collaging of 'found' materials like driftwood, rope, cork or pebbles he unifies natural and concrete, graphic and sculptural features within an abstract art of romantic vitality. A 'constructivist' vein discreetly accommodates elements that are like quotations from Schwitters, Rauschenberg or, nearer to home, late Lanyon. Plymouth-born and Bristol-trained Haughton, a former schoolteacher who retired to become a full time artist in 1995, uses Cornwall as a point of departure.

The linear and planar structure of Haughton's exhilarating compositions also hold references, if of an oblique, generalised kind, to Brittany – the other Cornwall – which the artist likes to visit. The tall *Scherzo: Finistère* (2006) or *Voyage to Scilly: St Marys* 'suggest aerial views as seen from a helicopter then reduced to their essential blocks and circles'[(17)] according to the Bristol critic Anna Britten. The transparent viridian, sky blue or stoney grey follow Haughton's ingenious, even original, use of inverted collage – 'found' objects cleverly slotted into window-like recessed space BEHIND the picture plane – to suggest and make tactile and concrete, as well as illusionistic, reference to nature. Such works characterised solo exhibitions with Michael Wright, Bristol, Plumbline, St Ives and Camden Fine Art, Gloucestershire and group shows at Thompsons, Marylebone or Edgarmodern, Bath.

Vanessa Gardiner was introduced to Cornish landscape by David Haughton during two Central School student

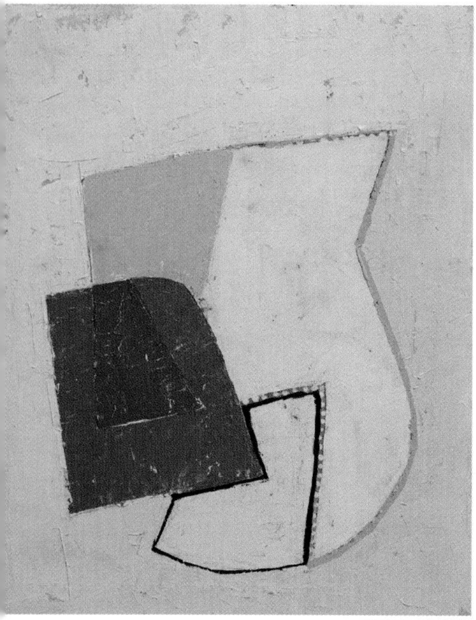

Jeremy Annear
Sand Debris II
oil on canvas
courtesy of the artist

trips to St Just in November 1980 and June 1981. Plein air drawings started a process of studio simplification in which broad topographic elements were re-constructed as scoured plywood compositions. Choosing to replace Haughton's St Just with the rugged coastline near Boscastle as the recurring frame of reference, Gardiner's mature work reduced broad coastal panoramas to still recognisable but schematised expressions of place. A restricted, recurring palette using turquoise, deep blue and beige characteristic of the sea between Boscastle and Port Isaac, by throwing the eye back on the simple architectonic strength of collaged composition, avoided what Elizabeth James termed 'the elegant vacancy of a too-easily re-worked St Ives style'. Dorset-based and exhibiting first with Duncan Campbell, London then Art First, Gardiner retained an aloof independence from the main throng of St Ives artists with whose work her own nonetheless shares fundamental qualities.

Exeter-trained Jeremy Annear (b. 1949) replaces Gardiner's reconstructed topography with still life as a suitably hermetic and contemplative vehicle for formal investigation in both analytical and synthetic modes. Jugs, vases and domestic bric-a-brac – extended to figural subjects – become receptacles for line conceived either as descriptive contour or freewheeling autographic trail and pale pastel-like colour or abraded texture. The critical relationship between line and colour wanders between the coherent and discordant; inadvertent patterns emerge and with them an expressive abstraction at limited remove from an originating motif. Despite its incisive clarity the painted line, sometimes broken into dotted pattern in homage to the admired aboriginal artists Annear encountered during a trip to Australia in 1993, contributes to the painterly repertoire.

Annear's feel for pattern is rococco in spirit, his fragmented post-cubist language of line and coloured plane possessing the brittle tension between the parts and the whole characteristic of Poliakoff, de Stael and other 1950s' 'French' painters. Interactive with other artists as a one-time committee member and even a director of a gallery at Dartington, Totnes Annear is a well-informed connoisseur and collector of art. Solo exhibitions at Messums, London in 1997 and 2000 and at New Millennium, St Ives in 2007 consolidated his standing.

Chapter Two

AFTER THE MIDDLE GENERATION

During the last quarter of the 20th century the St Ives art scene, bereft of its leading post-war artists, was dominated by the surviving, indeed thriving, figures of Terry Frost (1915–2003) and Patrick Heron (1920–1999). Beneficiaries rather than pioneers of the 'Hampstead by the sea' or 'gentle nest' phenomena that define the St Ives School's constructivist approach to landscape, Frost and Heron came into their own during the 1980s and 1990s, scooping up the renewed enthusiasm, historical reappraisal and commercial triumph enjoyed by all leading St Ives artists. Their contribution included the spawning of a new generation, among them offspring, former students or geographically removed metropolitan artists in thrall of the scale, painterly energy, colourism and creative daring of their late work.

Diverse artists of contrasting modernist lineage, Frost and Heron spent much of the post-1975 period in discrete, gentle rivalry. It is hard to find greater artistic and temperamental contrast within the ranks of the loose-knit and informal 'middle generation' grouping. While sharing a debt to the pivotal early influence of Ben Nicholson Frost and Heron subsequently drew on differing models, the former looking at European constructivism through the eyes of his early mentors Victor Pasmore and Adrian Heath, the latter graduating through the early influence of Braque and Matisse to enter into an intellectually dogmatic dialogue with Rothko, Newman, Francis and other key New York expressionists. Frost's preoccupation with first form and later colour as an emotional as well as structural vehicle may have chimed with Heron's 1962 dictum that 'colour is both the subject and the means; the form and the content; the image and the meaning in my painting today' but their respective styles contained as much in common as sandpaper and silk.

Notwithstanding shared participation in the important early exhibitions *Space in Colour* (1953) and *Metavisual, Tachiste, Abstract* (1957) at the Hanover and Redfern Galleries respectively, Frost and Heron were therefore fundamentally different kinds of artists and people. Frost's working class and ex-serviceman 'blokeism'; Heron's aesthete preciousness and social aloofness; Heron's art critic intellectualism, Frost's Basic Design shopfloor empiricism; Frost's later freewheeling exhibiting career based on a prolific, uneven output, Heron's commercially shrewd and expedient fidelity to Waddington pointed to differences of an ethical, as well as aesthetic, kind.

Heron's insistence on the absolute parameters of pictorial art-flatness and plastic, rather than illusionist, space-evoking colour-allowed a stylistically inclusive, even arbitary and eclectic, group to emerge under the 'Space in Colour' banner. In its catalogue Heron wrote that 'Painting is essentially an art of illusion . . . the illusion of forms in space . . . the secret of good painting lies in its adjustment of an inescapable dualism; on the one hand there is the illusion, indeed sensation, of depth; and on the other there is the physical reality of the flat picture surface'. Heron's analysis belonged to a lyrical 'belle peinture' however, rather than concretist vision. Frost's career during the 1950-55 period, by virtue of his assisting in Hepworth's sculpture studio and exhibiting in London under the aegis of Pasmore and Heath with the 'Nine Abstract Artists' group, trod in a more concrete and architectonic direction. Nevertheless Lawrence Alloway, author of the landmark book *Nine Abstract Artists* (1954), observed that Frost 'more than anyone else in this book,has been influenced by St.Ives.'(1)

As Heath later recalled Frost's association with the post-war 'constructionist' art of Pasmore, the Martins, Anthony Hill and himself 'deflected Frost's attention away from things perceived and concentrated it on the forms constructed'.(2) But Alloway felt that along with Scott and Hilton Frost belonged to a sub-group of 'painterly abstractionists who melt, bury or fracture platonic geometry'.(3) From then on Frost's art would waver between pure geometry and imagery of a more allusive and sensuous kind. Henceforth Frost would temper stringent compositional discipline and order – informed by the proportional systems and divisional principles described in the writings of Biederman, Hambidge, Ghyka and D'Arcy Thompson – with an emotive feeling for subject and materials. The spirit of open-ended experiment that attended his teaching career based on the Basic Design principals extolled by Pasmore, Hudson and Thubron led to the twists and turns of Frost's mature 'oeuvre'. While Frost was to fulfil Nicholson's early directive that the circles, squares, chevrons and other geometric fragments would serve an entire career and was later drawn to the reductive, minimalist power of Russian Suprematism he did so with a frankly maverick, playful and decorative verve that saw him backtracking or parodying previous forms in new arrangements. Much of his later work has a baroque frenzy and is, qualitatively speaking, hit or miss.

In order to be closer to London galleries and his teaching post in Reading – not to mention his native Leamington – Frost lived at Banbury from 1963 until a return to Cornwall in 1974. During that time Frost both tightened and simplified his formal language through use of large scale and a restricted number of pre-determined collage units-painted canvas cut-outs glued down to the main canvas support. The imagery of bikinis, buttocks, breasts suggested sexual content while the recurring analogies, endemic to the St Ives movement, between landscape and the figure reflected the hedonistic, fun-loving zeitgeist of the 1960s. By the next decade Frost delighted in signs, emblems and traffic symbols taken from the urban environment, for a time being inspired by commercial logos on lorries.

That changed after taking up an elevated residence above Newlyn with panoramic views across Mounts Bay. Revisiting the early iconography of St Ives harbour that had yielded his best-known picture *Walk Along the Quay* (1950), Frost reintroduced images, or rather unmistakable symbols of boats, rudders, taut rigging, sails, masts, tyres and other maritime objects or the reflection of sun and moon on the rippled water. Alloway's 1954 quip that in 'St Ives they combine non-figurative theory with the practice of abstraction because the landscape is so nice nobody can quite bring themselves to leave it out of their art' was borne out more than ever by Frost's later Newlyn-based work. Within this were *Newlyn Rhythms* (1981-8), a magnum opus comprising 20 conjoined canvases described by Chris Stephens as 'a polychromatic hurdy girdy'[4], *Black Sun-Newlyn* (1983) and *Floating Dawn* (2002).

Not long after returning to Cornwall Frost enjoyed an Arts Council tour (1976-7) initiated by the Serpentine Gallery, London. This confirmed Frost as a 'painter of controlled exuberance' who, the catalogue writer David Brown went on to observe, 'has explored the use of saturated colour.' The *Sunday Telegraph* reviewer Michael Shepherd spoke of 'straightforward expressions of joy . . . a painter's second childhood.' It took another painter, John Hubbard, to allude in the catalogue preface to Frost's 'combination of generosity towards others with a combative certainty of art's purposes'. Key early paintings were followed by the brighter colours of *Orange Moonship*, a picture that Adrian Heath later observed marked a point in which 'colour is no longer an element to reveal, conceal or disguise structure, it becomes the structure'.[5]

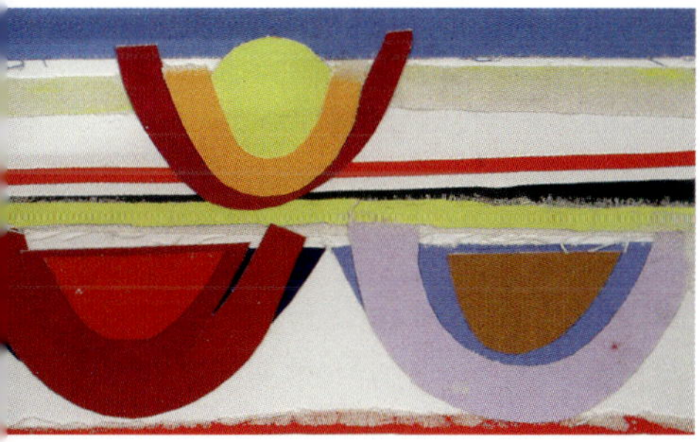

Terry Frost
Floating Dawn, 2002
acrylic and canvas collage
courtesy: Belgrave Gallery, St Ives

Heath's comments were from the informed and intimate insight into his friend and colleague's development which formed the catalogue essay for Frost's important survey 'Painting in the 1980s' at Reading University in November 1986. This represented a midpoint between the Serpentine tour and those late exhibitions, among them the Royal Academy's 'Terry Frost: Six Decades and Tate St Ives' display of Leeds period work in 2000 and 2003 respectively, that went hand in hand with the publication of a large monograph *Terry Frost* (1994) and two smaller books published by Tate Publishing and Belgrave Gallery, with appearance on the popular radio programme 'Desert Island Discs' and with a knighthood in 1998.

These achievements were late vindications of Frost's enterprise. During the hiatus of the 1975-85 period, however, Frost struggled commercially, falling back on his income from teaching and the odd sale through a slow market. A valedictory show with Waddington in 1978, followed by dismissal from this leading dealer, represented the nadir of lean commercial years. The turn around came after the Tate Millbank's 1985 St Ives exhibition after which Frost's market blossomed. Upset but not crestfallen by being released by Waddington Frost sold better on his own, selling through an ever wider network of galleries or dealers. This in turn encouraged the prolific late output in which printmaking, designs for ceramics, rugs, banners, Murano glass and even a tail fin for British Airways came to the fore. The naked commercial opportunism of Frost's late career laid bare an extroverted and egalitarian spirit of sharing. The strong colour and bold designs of the later Frost invested the minority interest of abstract art with a newfound populism. Chris Stephens' assessment that 'Frost's brash colours echoed aspects of popular culture, while, at the same time, his persistent commitment to painting distanced him from the mainstream avant garde'[(6)] revealed Frost as an artist for all seasons, acting both as standard bearer for a quintessential pictorial culture in the face of dumbed down YBA dadaism and, on the other hand, as an entertainer for the art masses in an age of ever increasing museum attendances.

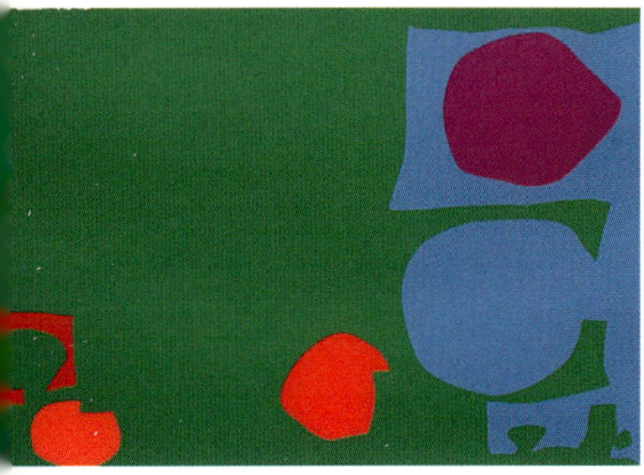

Patrick Heron
Untitled
silkscreen print
courtesy: Belgrave Gallery, St Ives

The Bloomsbury-like decorative extensions of Frost's imagery sent out mixed messages, Stephens' contention that 'Frost believed his brightly coloured abstract paintings were not simply decorative' but indeed spiritual contradicted first by *Apollo* magazine's view that 'the crude assurance of his visual assault is initially stimulating but leaves little of significance after the first momentary impact' and later by Nick Hackworth's 2003 *Evening Standard* review that complained of 'garishly decorative' and 'slightly rude'[(7)] colour and an easy formal virtuosity that Kandinsky warned would leave 'mere geometric decoration,like a necktie'.

After the early 1970s Patrick Heron's public reputation tilted from one based on art criticism to painting. The midway point of a fifty-year career – defined by the controversial 1974 *Guardian* articles *The British Influence on New York* attacking American art's alleged involvement in 'A Kind of Cultural Imperialism'[8] to quote the title of an earlier article in *Studio International* – saw Heron's powers as an objective commentator able to compete with Berger, Sylvester and Alloway diminish. But it also saw Heron's painting confidently emerge in pursuit of his much quoted 1962 maxim 'colour is now the only direction in which painting can travel'. Nevertheless, as much for his role as writer, critic, promoter, polemicist and, last but not least, political and cultural activist Heron was, from the mid 1970s, showered with various academic and other honours (he only turned down a knighthood in opposition to the Thatcher government).

A 1972 Whitechapel exhibition of early and recent canvases, for which Alan Bowness wrote the catalogue, confirmed the large scale preference that had first taken root after being, as he put it, 'elated by the size, energy, originality, economy and inventive daring' of the exhibits in the seminal Tate exhibition 'Modern Art in the United States' in January 1956. In 1973 Heron exhibited in Sydney, where his Power lecture 'The Shape of Colour' anticipated his 1978 William Doty Lecture 'The Colour of Colour' at Austen, Texas. It seemed that Heron's pronounced art of persuasion was now directed away from the formative modern French masters – Bonnard, Braque and Matisse – and from those contemporary British and American artists whose stylistic concerns he directly shared towards a polemical preoccupation with the dialectics of his own developing painting language.

A retrospective of work from 1966 to 1978 toured from Austen to other American venues and a series of Kelpra Edition screenprints *The Shapes of Colour* (1973–76) was published by his dealers Waddingtons whom he had joined in 1958 after a split with Rex Nankivell's Redfern Gallery. The medium of screenprint was an apt graphic expression for a painter of decorative and chromatic verve whose family background in textile designing and printing (his father Tom had been director of first Crysede then of Cresta Silks) made a clear imprint on Heron's sensibility. This link was evident in 1979 with the silk scarf Heron designed to celebrate the opening of the new galleries at Tate, Millbank and with the carpets designed for the Cavendish Hotel, London. A tapestry for the University of Galway followed in 1981 and three large banners for Chelsea and Westminster Hospital in 1992. Heron's role as public designer took on more robust guise when he designed the stained glass window for Evans and Salev's Tate St Ives (1993). The recent Honorary Fellow of RIBA went on to design *Big Painting Sculpture*, an outdoor installation at Stag Place, Victoria (1998).

Forays into applied art notwithstanding, it was as a painter in the grand tradition that Heron's reputation grew during the final twenty-five years. A Trustee of the Tate between 1980 and 87, he complemented his influence as painter critic with a committee role suited to his art political instincts. Heron's growing anti-Americanism proved no less compatible with fellow trustee sculptor Anthony Caro that it had been twenty years earlier with Clement Greenberg on the Liverpool John Moores selection panel. Heron's support for young British painters like Alan Gouk, who championed Heron's work in *Artscribe* magazine in the early 1980s (and enjoyed a Tate acquisition for his efforts), complemented what Alan Bowness had described in 1978 as a 'need to resist the American takeover of modernism'. The *Artscribe* editor James Faure Walker wrote an essay *Patrick Heron: the 1970s* for Heron's 1985 Barbican retrospective catalogue and Faure Walker's wife, Vivien Knight edited and wrote the Introduction for the first monograph *Patrick Heron* in 1988.

Other substantial publications followed; intermittent Waddington exhibition catalogues culminated in a major Phaidon monograph by Mel Gooding (1994). A posthumous catalogue by Andrew Wilson to accompany the 2001 Tate St Ives exhibition 'Early and Late Garden Paintings' and Michael McNay's monograph for the St Ives Artists series, gave timely critical endorsement during a period of escalating prices for Heron's work, a situation inadvertently facilitated by the tragic Momart storage fire in which several dozen major canvases were burnt.

The large interlocking colour compositions of the 1970s, flippantly dubbed by the artist the wobbly hard edge phase, achieved the 'creative emptiness' of American painting that had moved Heron in 1956. But European, and in particular local Penwith, factors came in to play again in pictures like *Big Cobalt Violet* (1972), the Tate's *Scarlet Emerald and Orange* (1976) or the mural sized *Long Cadmium with Cerulean in Violet (Boycott)* (1977). In an *Artscribe* review of the Barbican retrospective Peter Fuller explained that although 'English landscape was to play such a decisive role in Heron's life, and art, his intuitive love of colour drew his eyes towards paintings produced on the other side of the channel'.(9) Like the striped paintings of 1957-8, the 1970s hard edge canvases retained oblique, even residual, landscape associations, the hot saturated colour evoking Atlantic sunsets, the lop-sided discs the ubiquitous granite boulders strewn around his Zennor home 'Eagle's Nest'.

The technical construction of these large compositions was only gestural or spontaneous in a qualified sense, the spreading of oil pigment across large expanses relying on the miniature vibrancy of a Japanese watercolour brush that was subject to laborious, day-long alla prima sessions. Faure Walker's claim that 'the phases of the fifties do look transitional and incomplete in comparison with what was to follow,' led to the 'electric alertness' of the 1970's works. This effect was achieved through optically vibrating interactions of clear, unmixed and sharply delineated areas of adjacent colour. Another crucial factor, line, had moved from an overt to tacit element; in 1972 Bowness wrote that 'colour remains the dominant interest, but there is less insistence on it than in the past, and clearly now composition, form, even line are equally the concern . . . shapes are held suspended across the surface . . . Drawing assumes again that crucial role it played in Heron's very early work'. [(10)] The practice of drawing, both in terms of establishing a composition with an arm-wielded stick of charcoal (or more to the point Pentel pen) on crisp, bare canvas, of filling sketchbooks with deft on-the-spot landscape notations and, very late on, of drawing directly with colour using squeesed tubes of paint, became a primary feature of Heron's art during the final decade.

Despite writing in 1985 that 'Heron's criticism sprang out of very similar aesthetic beliefs to those which informed his painting' Fuller also questioned the exclusive status of colour alone declaring that 'Heron made decisions about both colour and composition on the basis of imagination and intuition'. Like Bowness, therefore, Fuller saw line and composition as almost equal partners with colour. Fuller observed in the work of the 1980s:

> *'a conspicuously greater freedom in his handling – a return to painterly gesture, rather than dependence on taut vibrancy . . . colours are often softer and no longer necessarily fully-saturated. The great expanses are broken up, and there is more than a whisper of a return to Bonnard whom he deserted for Matisse . . . references to natural forms and colours now seem undisguised and un-denied'.*[(11)]

These qualities are evident in canvases like *Scribbled Disc in Deep Ceruleum* (1983), *Afternoon Blue: July 1983, Big Purple Garden Painting* (1984) and *Red Garden Painting* (1985). Gouk's observation that Heron was 'overtaken once more by the rebellious prompting of arm and hand,'[(12)] was a call to expressive and gestural arms but missed the point that they were transitional works moving, as Andrew Wilson later explained, 'between the tight processes of the 1970s and the freer, more spontaneous approach he had described in 1957'.[(13)] By the mid 1980s, therefore, Heron had recovered from the disabling experience of his wife Delia's sudden and unexpected death in 1979 to recapture a momentum that developed the sublime achievements of the 1970s into an animated and looser mode.

A decisive moment in the late career was the four-month residency between November 1989 and February 1990 at the Art Gallery of New South Wales, Sydney Australia when he produced six large canvases in response to the spectacles of the Botanical Gardens and Sydney Harbour. These heralded the disembodied airiness and openness of compositions of the 1990s where line and colour operated either separately or in tandem. Broad areas of primed white canvases interacted with squiggles or amorphous colour patches. The rapid, part-painterly-part-graphic execution of the Sydney works recurred thereafter in works like *5 July;1992*, in a mural-sized mammoth *July-August 1994* and in the two final canvases from late January 1998 depicting Eagles Nest and its environs. These late paintings and the forty-three gouaches of the last months use titles which follow Picasso's recording of the dates the works were made, another sympton of an underlying existential mood that had driven Heron and his post-war generation.

Heron's Tate retrospective at Millbank in 1998 gave him pleasure (at a photo session on the first morning he described to me regret at its belated nature, a not untypical form of conceit given that other deserving contemporaries had been denied the honour). A.S. Byatt's was the last significant catalogue essay written on Heron during the artist's lifetime and reminds us of the difficulties of writing about formalist painting predicated by the optical criterion. As such it invokes Susan Sontag's arguments in *Against Interpretation* (1966) about leaving art to speak for its aesthetic self. Even without the polemics spun around it Heron's work can do that well enough within its own terms.

During the early 1970s two exhibitions consolidated Yorkshire-born Trevor Bell's reputation. A protegé of Patrick Heron, who in 1958 described him as 'the best non-figurative painter under thirty working in Britain,' Bell had established his name during those professionally formative and vital years in St Ives between 1955 and 1960. He followed Terry Frost and W. Barns-Graham in taking up a Gregory Fellowship in Leeds in 1960. The first major exhibition, in 1970, was a tour taking in Edinburgh, Belfast and Sheffield. The second was a 1973 Whitechapel retrospective in London. Not much else followed during that decade though the establishment of an American teaching career at that time was hugely significant. During the 1980s and beyond solo exhibitions in Florida and other parts of the United States represented not so much inverted 'cultural imperialism' as a cultural colonisation by a stray British painter.

The extended teaching at Florida State University in Tallahasse was followed, upon retirement, by a return in 1996 to Cornwall, thereby taking the circumstances, if not the style, of his painting career full circle. Inclusion in the Tate Gallery's 'St Ives 1939-64' exhibition in 1985 served as a reminder of his roots, and further British displays of the American-based artists's work during the first half of the 1990s - such as a solo show with his London dealer Gillian Jason in 1990, a group show with his one-time St Ives colleagues Brian Wall and Anthony Benjamin at Leigh-on-Sea, Essex in 1994 and inclusion in the 1995 Liverpool John Moores exhibition – anticipated the prodigal son's return to Britain.

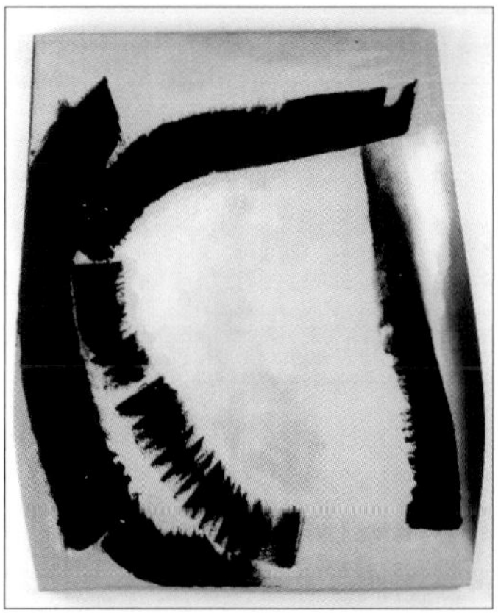

Trevor Bell
Wind Shift
oil
courtesy: Whitford Fine Art, London

The Americanisation of Bell's work during these years was registered in terms of scale and colour, which took on the vibrant, intense hues of the Florida coast, and the late modernist practice of emphasising the picture as object. Unlike Ellsworth Kelly, however, Bell's taking to shaping the canvas in wild curvilinear – rather than streamlined and geometric – ways suggested 'organic' as opposed to 'architectural' interests. This in turn reinforced the picture of an artist steeped in the British landscape tradition, Bell frequently donning his St Ives boots and exploring mountains and the sea on recurring expeditions. These included hiking in his native Yorkshire, in the Himalaya during the 1980s, along the Cornish south-west coast path and, during the early 1970s when teaching at Winchester School of Art, sailing in the Solent. In Chris Stephens' words Bell proved 'solidly rooted in the values of 1950s St Ives where artists sought to salvage the fantasy of utopian modernism for the post war world through a re-engagement with nature'.(14)

A confusion between British and American tendencies emerged however, Alex Kidson writing on Bell's 2000 exhibition 'Both Ends of the Stream' at North Light Gallery, Huddersfield that there 'must be doubts whether Bell has done the right thing in coming back to Britain at all'.(15) While Bell worked from a New York scale converted barn studio near Penzance and continued to show in Chicago and other parts of the U.S., his second Cornish period was acknowledged by the Tate St Ives exhibition in 'Beyond Materiality' (2004). A somewhat arbitrary selection of paintings between 1967 and 2004 the show comprised shaped canvases made in Britain before and after the Florida years. The one all-American picture – *Tall Seven* (1976) an ensemble of seven thin,vertical and standardised canvases using Denis Bowen-like vaporous trails of bright, fluorescent colour inspired by seeing an Apollo space launch at Canaveral in December 1972 – integrated American minimalism with a British taste for invention and sublime naturalism. These factors underpinned the brilliantly eclectic selection of artists Bell made to accompany 'Beyond Materiality' which included Stubbs, Turner, Clyfford Still, Anish Kapoor and Brian Wall.

Bell's later interest in the painting object, entering into concrete dialogue with a world of real things, is shared by the intensely-coloured and collaged abstracts of Anthony Frost (b. 1951) which remain, however, more impervious than Bell's to landscape associations. While both use gesture, colour and surface as primary structures in vital and tense relationship to the pictorial whole the younger painter's adherence to conventional four-sided, rather than randomly shaped, formats requires a compositional intricacy eliciting geometry, extraneous collage materials like sailcloth, rope, nylon thread, brass rings and wood section and a visually arresting palette limited to saturated primary, as opposed to naturalistic, colour.

While Anthony has successfully negotiated the problematic relationship to Terry Frost, a leading post-war abstract painter, to establish an independent reputation there are telling correspondences between the work of father and son. A link between construction and random expression or between geometry and informal gesture reflecting interchange between reason and emotion is endemic to both; so too is a loud chromatic punch, direct communication with a basic repertoire of repeated forms and a pragmatic though sensuous feeling for materials that, without compromising plastic integrity, make oblique and subtle reference to nautical culture and maritime environment in south-west Cornwall.

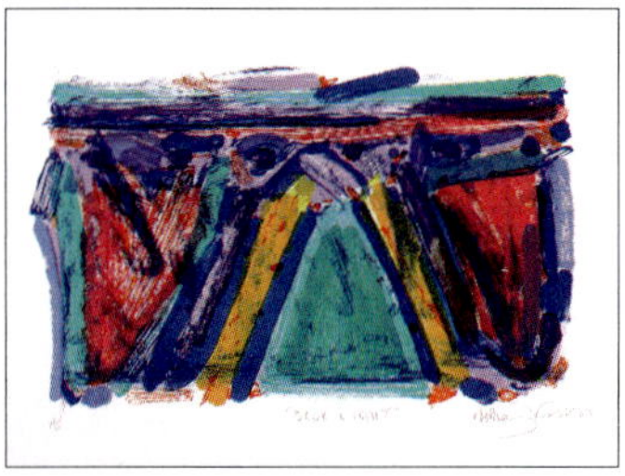

Anthony Frost
Blue Light 2007
lithograph

Studying at Cardiff in the early 1970s, Frost returned to set up as a painter in Cornwall in the mid 1970s at a time when Terry and Kathy abandoned a decade-long domicile in Banbury to re-establish a Cornish base at Gernickfield above Newlyn. A solo exhibition at Newlyn Orion in 1979 established a recurring relationship with the gallery during the next two decades, a 1986 one-man show 'On Colour' leading to 'Viva Blues' in 1995 which toured from Newlyn to the north. Newlyn director Emily Ash's observation in the catalogue that 'The triangle and diamond motifs are still prominent components within the overall structure'[16] chimed with family precedent, in particular with Ben

Nicholson's already noted decree to a young Terry Frost that the ovals, semi-circles and geometric fragments with quay-side associations would serve an entire career.

The crafted carpentry that draws attention to the painting as constructed object, as opposed to illusionist window on the world, ties Frost's work to the late modernist, even minimalist, work of Stella, Kelly, R. Smith or Buckley though the cogent gestures and deep colour recall Hoyland or Hodgkin as much as Terry. Anthony's foray into print-making using a combination of monotype, wood block and silkscreen, continues 'the fundamental importance of colour'[17] according to Sheila Oliner. The mechanical discipline of printmaking at Advanced Graphics in south-east London ironically proved liberating, Frost reducing 'superfluous stuff' as he put it in a quest for simpler, bolder statements. The Bert Irvin-like overprinting with several graphic media posited richly inked, as well as extravagantly coloured, surfaces that, according to Advanced Graphics director Louise Peck, made viewers 'question whether they are looking at a print or a painted work on paper'.

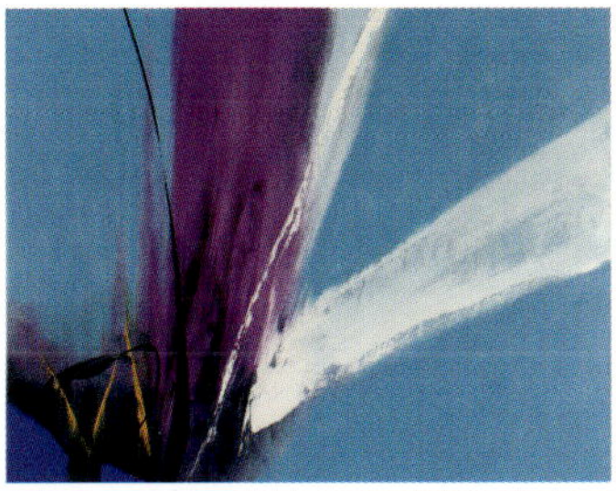

Neil Canning
Counterpart
oil on canvas
courtesy: New Millennium, St Ives

Neil Canning (b. 1960) also adapts abstract painting to print-making, entering like Frost into what the critic Mary Rose Beaumont terms 'a tug between wildness and control'.[18] While again sharing with Frost strident, saturated colour Canning is concerned, as Michael Bird has written, with 'the formulation of an abstract language for the experience of landscape'. If this pursuit links him more closely to the elusive 'genius loci' favoured by Lanyon, Canning retains a sweeping gestural paint handling that, while neither topographic nor purely abstract in nature, achieves both Frost's kind of compositional tautness and 'thrilling analogies to the flow and flux' of nature. Early exhibitions at Banbury Museum in 1981 and at other local galleries thereafter reflected Canning's Oxfordshire background in the same way that a Welsh domicile in the 1990s witnessed exhibitions with Martin Tinney, Cardiff and, after moving to St Ives in 1997, solo displays at the New Millennium Gallery.

The extended movement and unlimited energy beyond the picture plane suggested by Canning's sweeping painterly brush-work is absent from Henrietta Dubrey's art in which the gestural web and autographic tangle of dry or dribbled paint marks are centred as iconic, static design elements against broad expanses of uniform background colour. Any link to specific subject-matter is however at best elusive and arbitrary notwithstanding the orange of *One Extra*, the cover image of the 2005 solo exhibition catalogue at Belgrave St Ives, the ultramarine of *Cornish Nocturne* or the turquoise of *Lookout* positing dominant signature tunes with emotional and evocative resonance.

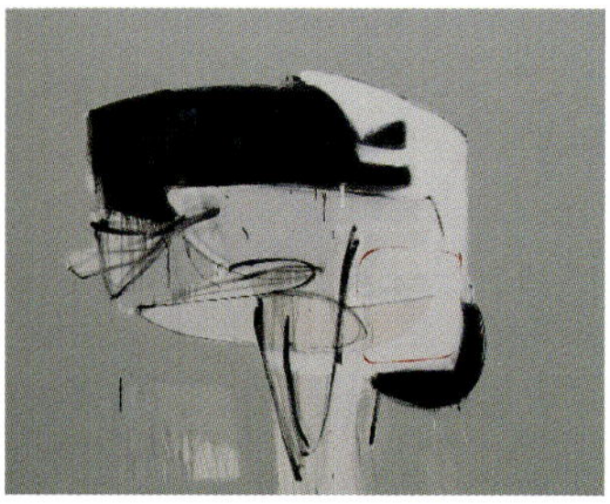

Henrietta Dubrey
Cry, 2005
oil on canvas
courtesy: Belgrave Gallery, St Ives

This vivid yet ambiguous imagery suggests the presentational strategy of advertising where a product is enhanced through highlight and isolation; Dubrey's art, despite its obvious links to the controlled abandon of post war tachist painting in Europe, to abstract expressionism in America and to 'middle generation' practice in St Ives, seems to be partly conditioned by the late or post modern lessons of 'pop,' 'post painterly abstraction' and conceptualism. Despite exploiting the fortuitous, fugitive properties of poured, dribbled or scribbled paint in which the accident or chance event plays an active role in image formation Dubrey's art is neat and 'clean', a temperamental product perhaps of someone – the daughter of a Sussex architect – working with a tinge of late modernist irony in a rich and well-trodden area. Studying at Wimbledon and the Royal Academy Schools between 1986 and 1992 Dubrey (b. 1966) followed Canning in exhibiting close to home, a mixed show at Charleston and at other Sussex galleries like the Star, Lewes in the 1990s followed upon her remove to Cornwall by solo or mixed displays at Rainyday, Penzance, Belgrave St Ives and Somerville, Plymouth.

Rachael Kantaris (b. 1967) also uses the coloured mark in direct and intuitive ways, the uncanny mix of chance and control in the painting extended to printmaking, mainly colour etching, an activity with which she established an early reputation. This blossomed after postgraduate printmaking studies at Brighton in the early 1990s, Kantaris spending four months in residence at a Berlin print studio (1993), assisting Trevor Price in the editioning of etchings in St Ives (1995), working alongside W. Barns-Graham on the large colour etchings of the *Scorpio* series (1997), editioning proofs for Heron, Frost and O'Casey at Stoneman Graphics near Penzance (1999 – 2002) and helping run Porthmeor Printmaker's Workshop which she helped set up in 1995.

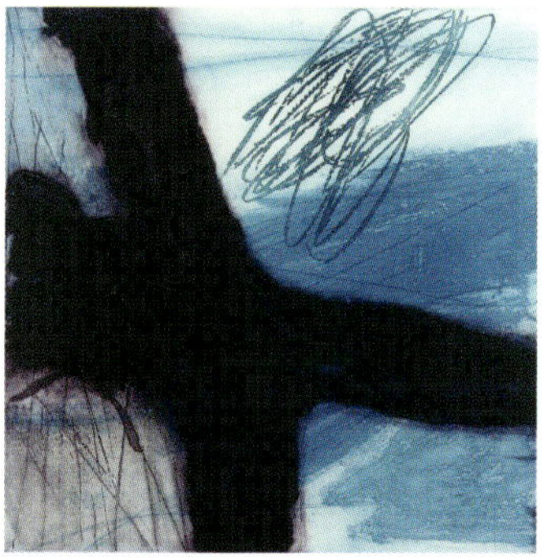

Rachael Kantaris
Plunge 2000
colour etching
courtesy:
Katharine House Galley, Marlborough

Kantaris's graphic expertise has, therefore, been used by her less technically adept seniors as well as adapted to teaching students and younger artists at Cornwall College and on other courses. This intergenerational continuity gives St Ives an ongoing relevance, providing a professional ambience of enduring vitality. Kantaris, who has expressed both the pleasure principle and work ethic in what she sees as the sculptural quality of 'altering the surface of the metal to create painterly marks on paper,'[19] reflects the unbridled gesturalism, accident and vibrant colour of her 'middle generation' elders. The complex struggle with inks, chemicals and metal plates nevertheless yields an end product deemed by the artist to have 'a freshness and glow not possible in a painting'. Texture is another key outcome, the scribbly, stained or corroded marks and structural patterns of etchings like *Plunge* (2000) or *Shoreline* (2003) reflecting the densely-worked physical surfaces of Tapies, Burri and, closer to home, Blow.

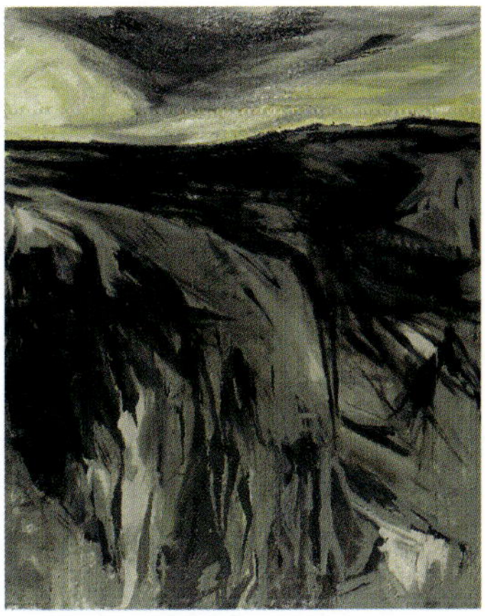

Sarah Poland
Disturbing A Sleeping Carn
2006, oil on canvas
courtesy: Belgrave Gallery, St Ives

Scottish-born and trained Sarah Poland (b. 1974) brings a tartan painterly brio to chromatically-reduced landscape abstractions inspired by the austere Penwith landscape encountered since moving from Scotland (she studied at Edinburgh School of Art during the mid 1990s) to Cornwall in 2000. Alighting on Dick Gilbert artistic territory, the landscape of Hayle Estuary and the dunes stretching to Godrevy, Poland made repeated studies of this sandy undulating topography. Later adopting the subject of the Penwith moors in brooding, dark light Poland owed something to Weschke and Wynter, two artists she consciously admired. These influences were evident in 'Tuath' (2006) her first solo exhibition, at Belgrave St Ives which was a culmination of mixed displays at Salthouse, St Ives and in Newlyn as a NSA member. The paint handling and acid yellow, black and grey palette of the 'Tuath' pictures 'bear the hallmark of Bob Crossley's painterly influence, Karl Weschke's exhaustively worked treatments of landscape in relation to the body and Bryan Wynter in its engagement with being and moving in landscape'[20] according to Richard Blackborow. But Poland's work also strikes a more contemporary chord sharing with Gareth Edwards, Mark Surridge, Marion Taylor and many other recent abstract painters a predilection for chromatic and tonal reduction and a use of cryptic subjects.

Implicit in such work is a re-complication of minimal reduction to accommodate not only spatial but naturalistic sensations. A critical self awareness is an almost obligatory feature during a post-modern age of restricted avant garde or progressive options. Gareth Edwards (b. 1960), for example, came to painting after studying art history at Goldsmiths in 1984 and teaching the subject first at Southend then at Liverpool Polytechnic during the mid 1990s. From this developed an awareness of style and its contemporary relevance, in his case a reduced tonal palette and a Sean Scully-influenced manner that integrated concrete surface design and soft spatial illusionism.

Other influences included Tapies and, closer to home, the young painter Simon Callery – whose forays into sculpture and installation encouraged Edwards's growing interest in the painting as concrete object – and Patrick Heron whom Edwards visited in Zennor. Edwards's art history background no doubt stood him in good stead at 'Eagle's Nest' and, while the younger painter's 'grisaille' was far removed from Heron's saturated and intense chroma, there was a common appropriation of the tension between flat surface and shallow space illusion. Edwards's bands of black, grey or cream held possibilities of ocean horizon or luminous sky; a maiden solo show with Hart Gallery, Islington in 1999, an event that hastened a move from London to Cornwall the following year, was indeed called 'Ocean'.

It was the quest for light, space and tranquility that hastened the move west with his wife Rachael, also a painter, and his young family. A new rawness characterised the first Cornish pictures fashioned at Acme studios in Porthleven. After moving studio from Porthleven to Falmouth and finally to Lamorna Edwards perfected further changes notably refining of residual landscape content in order to arrive at what he termed a 'relationship between structure and content'. Exhibitions of sculptural ceramics at Lemon Street, Truro in 2003 and of multi-panelled murals for 'Light, Speed, Sea, Spray' at the National Maritime Museum, Falmouth in 2004 witnessed a willingness to experiment in a more architectonic or object-based direction.

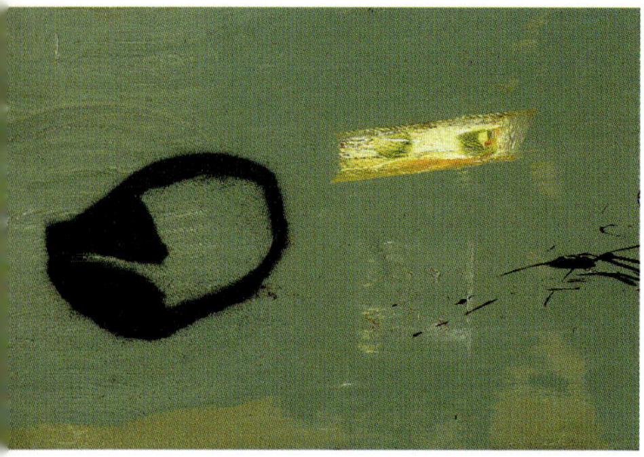

Mark Surridge
Script Sky Green
oil, acrylic & carborundum
on paper
courtesy of the artist

Mark Surridge (b. 1963) shares with Edwards and Marion Taylor dark, grey and beige colour, a repertoire of marks and paint gestures loaded with naturalist association and a psychological depth capable of relaying dream or memory. Long horizontal formats evoke landscape but it is a landscape without perspective, possessing what the painter Maurice Cockrill described in 2001 as 'the cropped, occluded look of fragments of topography only partially seen or tilted obliquely'.(21) The speed of Surridge's final paint application, belying impastoed accretion, speaks of the passing moment of fleeting impression of the kind gleaned through the window of a high speed Penzance to London train.

Since 2000 solo exhibitions at Beardsmore, London and New Millennium, St Ives, in bearing titles like 'Elemental Landscapes' (2001), 'Land Veils' (2003) or 'Air Voices' (2006) promote an air of mystery and reverie. The painter Liam Hanley described Surridge's painting as 'almost performances of landscape rather than a celebratory record'.(22) A Zen-like record of the moment of artistic creation, Surridge's rapid marks and ethereal colour cohere to form landscape-based pictures in psychic and plastic flux. The marks – broad brush sweeps, short paint stabs or flicked dribbles – have a calligraphic feel evidenced by the titles of the 'Air Voices' exhibition in St Ives; *Script Sky Blue* or *Land Script* invest the deft immediacy of the calligraphic mark with a lumpen monumentality, the gestures of oil paint bodied out with sand or the speckled metallic texture of carborundum. Catalogue essays by Cockrill and Hanley, painters with visionary romantic or lyric formalist tendencies respectively, suggested Surridge's claim as a painter's painter. This was despite, rather than because of, Surridge's use of what Cockrill described as 'the colour of inclemency' – the grey, mute colours of a drizzly day. The intonated greys, dingy limes, chocolates or light creams that constitute Surridge's palette provide a dominant emotional signature tune allowing paint mark and disembodied imagery to come to the fore.

Marion Taylor
Black is White, 2005
oil on canvas
courtesy of the artist

The Manchester-born painter Marion Taylor (b. 1948) shares these themes. Taylor's 'veils' of transparent blue grey, beige, cream or other reduced colour similarly contain barely disguised reference to often specific places such as Porthgwidden, St Ives, to which she moved in 1989 after studying at Cardiff in 1967 and raising a family in London during the intervening years. Belatedly completing her training at Falmouth College of Art in 1998 Taylor enjoyed solo exhibitions at New Millenium in 2002 and Lemon Street, Truro in 2005, events that accompanied regular teaching at the St Ives School of Painting to establish her as one of an emerging generation of post-'middle generation' painters.

The contemporary nature of Taylor's art sees an ethical accord between material and process viewed as alchemical agents in the transformation of subjective experience of the world into artistic imagery; influenced by Kiefer, Beuys and certain conceptualists (she participated in non-gallery events and environmental installations as part of the PALP project in 2001) Taylor associates image formation with the magic of alchemy. The use of graphite powder as a paint medium for instance, apart from positing the characteristic steely grey coloration of the visionary canvases of the 2005 solo Truro exhibition 'Idiom', elicited alchemy's understanding of transformation between one material and another.

The submerged glimpses of 'place' bear comparison with the otherwise different Peter Lanyon, an artist whose small scale glass or perspex constructions made to rehearse or articulate abstract notions of space for subsequent painting seem echoed in Taylor's PALP installations that may also be seen as informing the painting. Ryya Sanders's allusion to a 'tension between evoking some notion of 'spirituality' in juxtaposition with the harsh physical and cultural negotiations of existence'(23) is both true of Taylor's daily struggle and of a post-modern qualification of mid century idealism. The punning titles of Taylor's 'Idiom' canvases, among them *A Veil Drawn Over, On a Knife Edge* or *Watershed*, exemplify these tensions at nominal, face value.

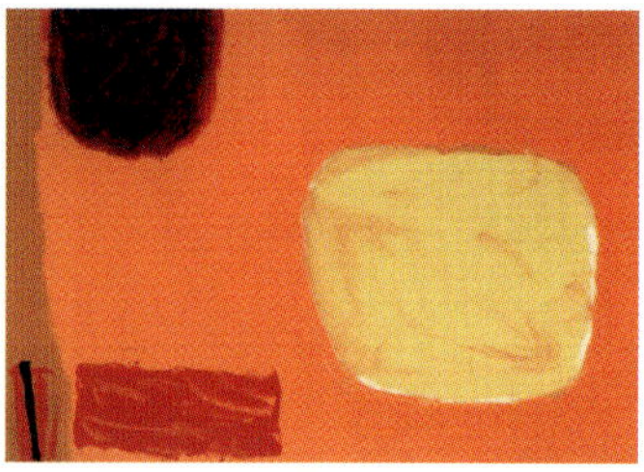

Sonya Walters
Segovia
monoprint
courtesy of the artist

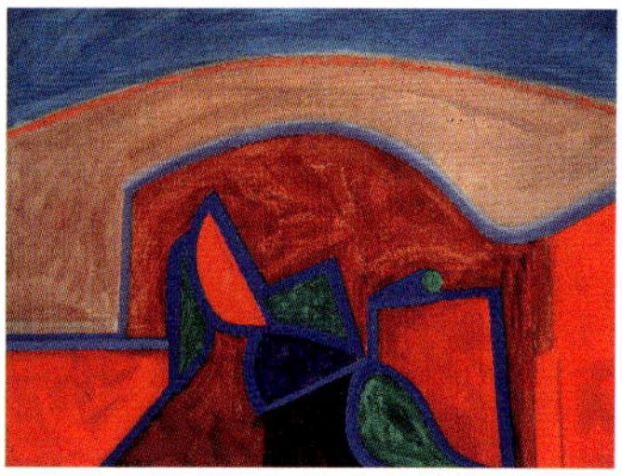

David Hampton
Porthmeor Beach and the Tate Gallery - St Ives
2006, oil
courtesy of the artist

Colourism re-emerges as a key aspect for artists working in closer accord with, or in homage to, Frost, Heron, Lanyon and other mid century expressionists. Sonya Walters, for example, composes directly with colour to produce soft-edged discs of orange, purple, yellow or blue against 'fields' of contrasting hue. These formats also follow Heron in being ideal for applied decor or extended pictoriality, in Walters' case a series of well-known banners for Trades Union or political useage. Also like Heron Walters was politically active in London during the years up to her move to Newlyn in 1989, contributing to the anti-racist struggle. Social engagement either in terms of teaching for ILEA or, after 1989, for CCC or of participating with Porthmeor Printmakers, has fuelled her career. Travel to exotic places and exposure to new cultures has also inspired work, not only in terms of colour – which remains characteristically intense, and bright – but also of symbol and abstract image. Another important feature in both paintings and prints is physical layering of painted or inked colour to create mystery, subtlety and interplay between surface and depth. The development of what she calls 'a free and painterly form of printmaking using the mono-printing process' has yielded a species of painted prints some of which were displayed with pots by Roelof Uys and Christine Gittins at the Printmakers Gallery, St Ives in September 2006.

Colour tied to the motifs of interior and landscape, simplified into silhouette, pattern and rhythm, highlight the paintings of David Hampton (b. 1926), a Royal College-trained artist who, after teaching design for 20 years at the London College of Fashion, painted full time and divided his time between two homes in Bath and St Ives. Hampton's penchant for colour, used both as a mimetic and abstract structural device, links him to revered French masters like Matisse and de Stael as well as Heron. Such influences reflect both his teaching years involved with the decorative and applied arts and a rich family heritage (his father and grandfather were professional artists) in which painting extended beyond the easel to embrace all aspects of everyday life.

Hampton's use of colour to bridge the gap between art and life holds true for the more gesturally assertive paintings of Matthew Lanyon (b. 1954), an artist deeply indebted to the work of his father Peter. Both in terms of scale, format, colour and mark Lanyon evokes an intimate connection with Cornwall, a connection that is biological as well as cultural and mediated, as in the work of Peter, through a use of classical or pagan myth. Lanyon talks of 'using landscape as a device to enclose myth,' a project that inevitably sees

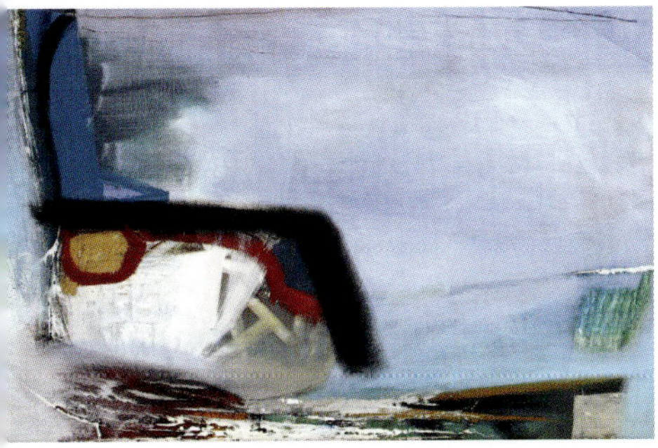

Matthew Lanyon
Wreck
oil on board

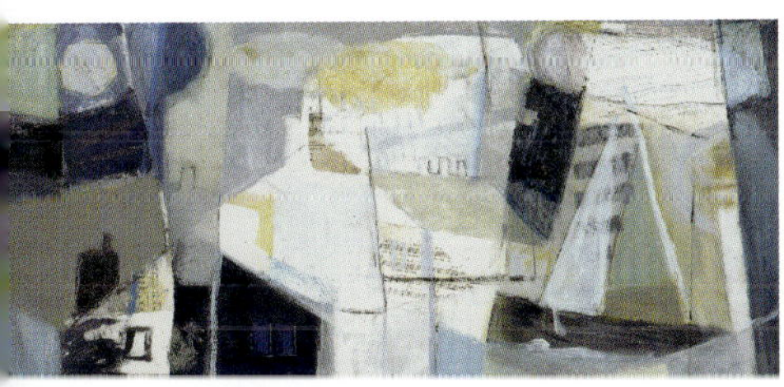

Liz Hough
Pat's Place
2002, oil on board
courtesy of the artist

Cornish landscape in relation to the sexual and spiritual presence of the human figure. Believing that 'painting is older than thought' Lanyon aims for the primal and primitive impulses lost to modern man. This emphasis on preverbal visual communication is however ironically accompanied by imagistic density and symbolic richness requiring extended deciphering. Des Hannigan's estimation that 'one great visual gulp'[(24)] needs to be followed by prolonged decoding puts Lanyon's work at far more than a 300-mile remove from the gestalt of metropolitan minimalist abstraction. A type of painting viewed by Hannigan as 'dense with heredity, influence and allusion' indeed travels beyond logical thought to strike at a very direct physical involvement with, and primitive experience of, landscape which is subsequently translated into the plastic language of paint.

Marilyn Middlemiss and Louise Fox, directors of the artist-led Salt Gallery in a peripheral run-down part of Hayle, studied under the gestural painter Graham Boyd at Hertfordshire College of Art, St Albans during the 1990s. Essex-born Stephen Prince also pursues an abstract approach that owes more to Roger Hilton than to his lodestar David Haughton under whose guidance as a Central School student in the 1970s, he visited and drew St Just on student expeditions. Subsequently a Central School technician Prince lost the creative spark until belatedly moving to St Just in 2006, a move that subsequently inspired abstractions of outdoor landscape experiences. These formed a solo display in 2007 at Great Atlantic Map Works, St Just. St Ives based Liz Hough also subjects a landscape vision to vigorous paint handling, that is close to abstraction.

A gloomier tonal palette, reflected in a solo exhibition 'Winter Bay Series' at Austin Desmond, London in 1996, accompanied the work of another Cornish-born painter taken with the direct immediacy of gestural mark. Stuart Knowles (b. 1948), who studied at the Slade, drove art removal vans, worked in a Hackney Space studio and married Elizabeth Knowles (one-time Tate curator and Newlyn Orion director), returned to Cornwall in 1986 and renovated a farm near Marazion. Inspired by Peter Lanyon, though in fact more influenced by Hitchens, Hodgkin and Cockrill, Knowles translates elusive memories or fleeting impressions of place in terms of a controlled spontaneity of paint handling. Matching the fluid unpredictability of the medium with tonal or climatic vicissitudes Knowles has an eye on the overall coherence of the picture plane to the extent that he has used elliptical formats to accommodate such subjects as stone circles or recurring curved bays along the coast.

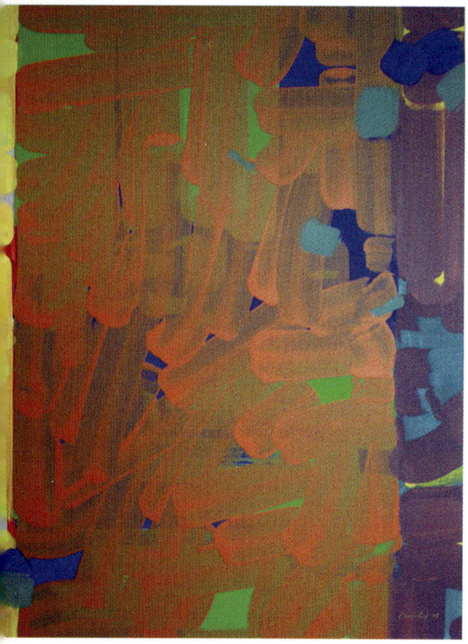

Bob Crossley
Diagonal Blues, 1978
acrylic on canvas
courtesy: Belgrave Gallery, St Ives

Bob Crossley (b. 1912) shares with much 'middle generation' abstraction use of gesture and strong colour. Distilling figure or landscape source material Crossley developed a latter day 'tachism' in which the image formed itself 'organically' and fortuitously from direct interaction of unmodulated and differentiated brush-marks, one stroke vying against its neighbour in a kaleidoscopic array of coloured pattern. Echoing perhaps 'middle period' Bryan Wynter Crossley's later works like *City Haze* (1981) or *Westward* (1983) have the energetic immediacy of calligraphy, the short to medium length brushstrokes uncannily evoking specific landscape experiences whether of a topographic, climatic or seasonal kind. Crossley's bright, rich and variegated colour emulates that of Heron, the Rochdale-born artist reintroducing from the mid 1980s residual subject-matter suggested by, or associated with, the chromatic and morphological configurations of his speedily executed abstract pictures. *Birds Migrating* (1984), *Sharks Feeding* (1986), *Atlantic Tornado* (1987) and *North Sea Oil Rig* use an abstract, gestural language to obliquely evoke subjects from the natural world.

Crossley, who moved to St Ives in 1959 having established an artistic reputation in Manchester during the 1950s, retained a certan independence from his Cornish contemporaries. However much his work chimes with that of Frost and Hilton during the early 1960s or with that of Wynter or Heron after Crossley depended on a family retail business rather than on art school teaching. Nevertheless he may be seen as a peripheral member of the 'middle generation' group whom he outlived, producing well into his 90s a brand of painting that both adhered to post-war St Ives abstraction and made new and idiosyncratic variations on, or parodies of, the individual labours of a remarkably long career. Three retrospectives at the Penwith Gallery, in 1979, 1987 and 1999 were followed by a homecoming retrospective at Rochdale Art Gallery in 2004 and a solo exhibition at Belgrave Gallery, St Ives in spring 2007. The unique longevity of Crossley's career forms a durable intergenerational strand linking post war and early 21st century painters for whom the most authentic mark of art's accord with the ongoing flow of life is the immediate and spontaneous language of gestural painting.

Chapter Three

LANDSCAPE PURE & SIMPLE

An allusion to more recent history since 1900 haunts the densely worked, impastoed paintings of Phil Whiting (b. 1948). Whiting departs both thematically and stylistically from the abraded, scoured and abstracted anthropomorphism of Mackenzie, Cann, Ray and Clegg, the Hull-born painter using loaded pigment in physical identification with an earth bearing the scars of man's agrarian, industrial or military intervention. Whiting's expressionism, while using desolate post-industrial wasteland as an emotive theme, links beyond Cornish subject-matter to embrace German, or German-inspired, art. Stylistic correspondence to Bomberg, Auerbach and Kiefer, as well as to north country painters Sheila Fell and Theodore Major, distances him further from pared-down Cornish modernism.

Retaining a very British link with the sea, Whiting studied at Newcastle, Portsmouth and Falmouth. While living in Norfolk between 1971 and 1984, where this socially-conscious artist briefly lived on a commune, Whiting met Leslie Marr, a Bomberg follower, who introduced him to his master's art. Later living in Hackney and teaching in a tough Islington school between 1984 and 89 Whiting hardened his social conscience in a way that would inform post-1989 work in Cornwall. This included large canvases focused on the topographic ravishes of the tin mining industry where what he termed 'the poetry of human endeavour' left indelible marks on the landscape. *Geevor Mine Winter no.1* (1989) is a dark, tactile work of compelling power. The stencilled lettering stamps in other canvases ethical meaning, words like 'Bounty,' 'Earths Sorrow' or 'Inheritance' adding to the emotional charge of the work. Like Hip Hop or political graffiti such lettering has an anarchistic air or protest.

These words also turn the painting into a manufactured commodity subject to marketing and a place in the consumer world. But the artist's concerns are not so much social and economic as political, Whiting affected by a grandfather's hazy memories of the trenches of the Great War. More recent atrocities like the Death Camps and the World Trade Centre attacks drove Whiting to visit eastern Europe and New York and make drawings of the sites. The potent mix of realism and romanticism owed something to Paul Nash whose brother John Whiting met briefly in Norfolk. A series of 'Places of Mourning in the Western World' encapsulated these tragic themes and a group of large compressed charcoal drawings on paper depicting barbed wire

Phil Whiting
Geevor Mine Winter no. 1
1989
oil

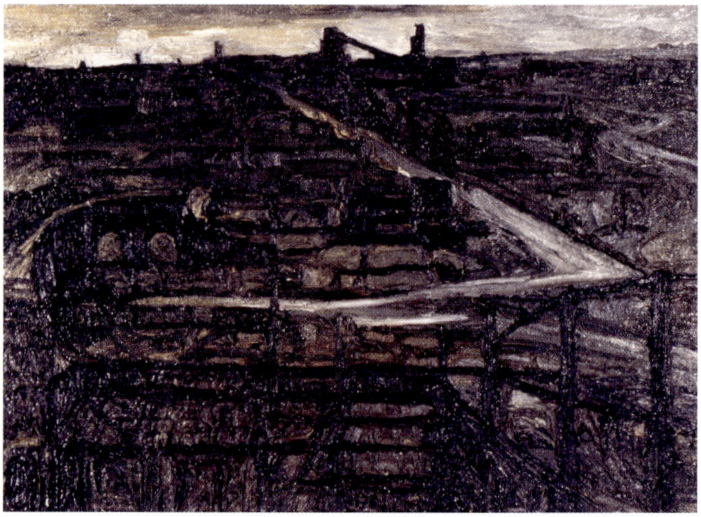

fences formed an exhibition about the recent holocaust in Bosnia at the European Parliament building, Brussels in 2006.

Whiting challenges high modernism's faith in a progressive future; this is accompanied by a new aesthetic relativism confirmed by Peter Fuller's assertion to Whiting, poignantly made the day before the critic's untimely death, that 'there are no guarantees when we make aesthetic judgements'.[1] Whiting's social landscape emulates key aspects of Lanyon's vision particularly its understanding of landscape as a social and industrial entity. A distinctive landscape idiom is therefore taken beyond painterly topography to highlight new moral, social and philosophical perspectives on a rapidly changing world.

Whiting's emotionally charged quagmire of paint is replaced, in Judy Buxton's landscapes with a painterly blizzard. Buxton (b. 1961) is more a painter of weather and light than topography, her elemental Turneresque paint handling capturing an atmospheric spirit of place. That place is near her base on the Lizard; Poltesco, Goonhilly or Carleon are visited, the artist setting up easel and following her former Falmouth tutor Ray Atkins in painting vigorously 'en plein air'. Large scale studio pictures ensue informed by the sensitive and spontaneous, yet also site specific, 'in situ' studies. Sydney-born Buxton came to Britain in 1983. Studying at Falmouth during the late 1980s and the Royal Academy Schools in the early 1990s Buxton married Jeremy Annear in 1993, moved to Cornwall and began an active exhibiting career at New Millennium, St Ives, Lynne Stover, Cambridge and Camden Gallery, Chipping Camden. Such a curriculum puts her in the mainstream of contempo-

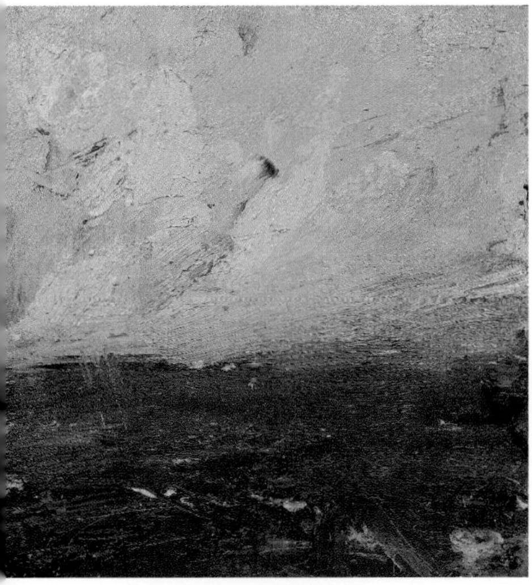

Judy Buxton
Cove Series: Steel & Serpentine I
oil on canvas
courtesy of the artist

rary Cornish painting though her inclusion in *The Guardian's* 'Living On the Edge' under the bracket 'Modern Turners' serves to underline the fact that beneath expressionist frenzy and improvisation lies a traditional old masterish base.

Buxton's light is limpid, the subtle modulations of grey or cream oscillating through black and blue to ochre. Monetesque surface texture adds to the impression of large looming skies with shafts of fugitive sunlight or gathering waves. Direct perception is filtered through memory and plastic process to create a telling picture of the elements in flux. Another Australian-born and Falmouth-trained landscape painter, Virginia Bounds (b. 1965) also translates the preferred location of the unspoilt Lizard peninsular into sweeping impastoed landscapes using similarly dense, naturalistic colour. Bounds' group displays with Belgrave, St Ives culminated in a first solo exhibition there 'Betwixt the Whiles' (2006). Richard Blackborow's description of an 'articulation of a human understanding of temporality with regard to the representation of landscape' suggests that Bounds, like Buxton, creates metaphor for an endlessly changing landscape in terms of patient working and reworking of paint surface through extended periods of time.

The plastic translation of landscape conceived as slow temporal evolution informs the paintings of Jeremy Le Grice (b. 1936), the Cornish-born and Eton-educated artist, which combine iconic form, rhythmic pattern, contre-jour tonality and frequently dark or black colour. Inherently autobiographical Le Grice's landscapes reflect a life spent within his native county alleviated by extended periods of absence at art schools like Guildford and the Slade, London during the 1950s, by transatlantic voyages at the end of the 1960s and by a twelve year domicile in the Cotswolds during the 1970s. This strong autobiographic thread – evident both in the early *The Artist's Mother* (1956), a tender Whistlerian theme that won him entry into the Slade, and in the desolate *Hull* (1956) a metamorphic coffin-like wreck with subliminally tragic references to the wartime death of his father at Dunkirk – continued throughout a career in which a keen sense of landscape perceived as a reclining human figure dominated.

Destined through circumstance to become an unlikely artist Le Grice married fellow Slade student Mary Stork in 1959, with whom he raised a family in St Just. This, and a six-month period painting in a Newlyn Gallery basement, encouraged a later spell under the revered Peter Lanyon at St Peters Loft, St Ives where the older painter's landscape empiricism encouraged ambitious panoramic compositions such as the diptych *Cape Cornwall* (1964). The artist recalled that Lanyon's death, following the passing of Camelot in America, 'caused my own buoyant mood to wane and evaporate'(2) at that time. Soon after, however, a solo exhibition at Plymouth City Art Gallery (opened by Bernard Leach) together with a second, abiding marriage and a life-changing transatlantic voyage encouraged Le Grice to advance beyond early portraits and still lifes to engage more intimately with landscape, using 'his eye idiosyncratically' (3) according to the critic William Packer.

The twelve-year Cotswold interlude impinged negatively on the output of work which increased again after a return to Cornwall. Using the hardly original but useful architectural device of the window view Le Grice authored the memorable *Sennen Window* (1987), *Chapel Carn Brea* (1990) and *Falmouth Bay* (1995), pictures of dramatic tonal and formal counterpoint. An atmospheric ability to create sensitive nuance from painterly application bi-passes the descriptive and illustrational aspects of conventional painting and anticipates Le Grice's flirtation with, and emulation of, the near-abstraction of late Pender and Miller. *At Moorings* (2004) and the azure monochrome *Early Start* (2005) create strong atmospheric effects from the sparest of means. These were displayed in Le Grice's 70th birthday retrospective 'At Seventy' at Truro during autumn 2006.

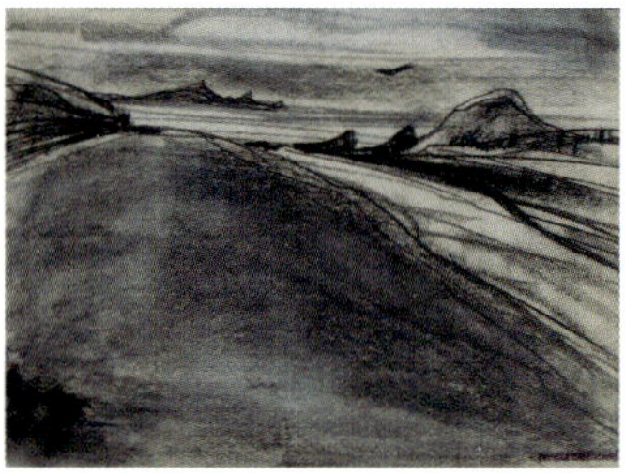

Margo Maeckelberghe
Porth, 1980
mixed media on paper
courtesy of the artist

Another Cornish-born landscape painter, the Corsham-trained Margo Maeckelberghe (b. 1931), also used paint in an expressionist accord with the explicitly rugged, wild and windswept north coast. Climatic vicissitudes, tidal ebb and flow or transitory light are captured by, and translated through, suitably energetic and gestural brushwork. The sometime Penwith Society chairman's penchant for dark mysterious blues highlighted – indeed relieved – by flashes of foamy white, rapeseed yellow or copper red accompany the vigorous and sweeping paint handling to posit a recognisable individual style. Perhaps these repetitions derive as much from cultural (her training under William Scott) as from natural sources (a site specific maritime environment). The otherwise very different Scott exerted an influence that could only be along the lines of schematic simplification and a recurring range of subjects that Lorraine Craig observed in 1974 'never remain static . . . the direction of her development is towards simplification, both of colour and content'.(4)

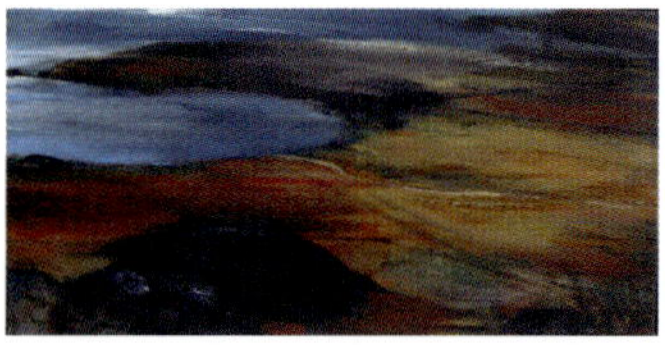

Margo Maeckelberghe
Dark Moor
1996-7, oil on canvas
courtesy of the artist

The generalised and 'apparent effortless' treatment of these paintings circumnavigate the analytical naturalism of late nineteenth century marine painting and indeed the darker, more detailed poetry of her early neo-romantic work. On the other hand the constant feeling for place

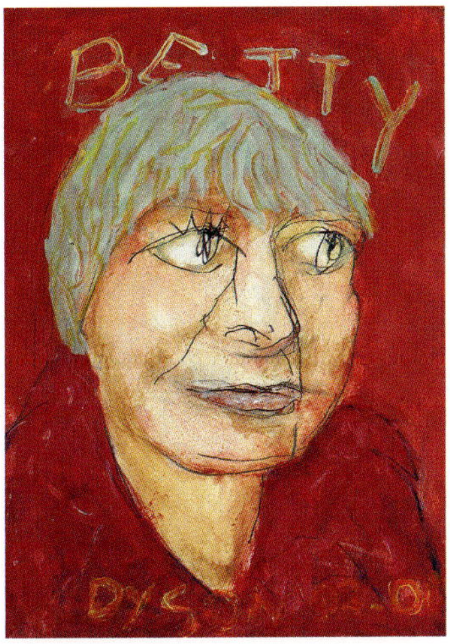

Julian Dyson
The Artists Wife Betty
Falmouth Art Gallery Collection

prevents any wholesale abstract development. The marine subject matter has courted diversity by moving beyond Cornwall, Maeckelberghe – the wife of a Belgian doctor – once making regular trips across the Channel to yield Ostend boat subjects (c. 1950). Later during that decade, while living in Gibraltar, Maeckelberghe produced Spanish landscapes. During the 1960s Greek and Tuscan subjects followed. Together with the 'Great Barrier Reef' series – the outcome of a trip to Hawaii and the Pacific during the 1980s – these exotic subjects add variety and a heightened, variegated palette. Maeckelberghe is an adventurer on the home front too, her enterprising if problematic acquisition of 'Carne Cottage' on Zennor Hill, her former tutor Bryan Wynter's drafty post-war home, leading to its renovation and use by the Belgrave Gallery's assistant and writer Richard Blackborow in 2007.

St Mawes-born Julian Dyson (1936–2003) shared with Maeckelberge a Cornish and medical background. A dentist by day Dyson still provided a sizeable and much-exhibited body of work, a 2001 solo exhibition at Falmouth Art Gallery capping a thirty-year exhibiting career that included notable one-man exhibitions at Southampton's John Hansard Gallery (1972), Salthouse St Ives (1988), Rainyday, Penzance (1992) and Oxford Gallery, Oxford (2000). Dyson's craggy landscapes, in which boulders, offshore rocks, quarries or cliffs feature strongly, contain subliminal tooth-like qualities; in the case of neo-primitive bird or animal compositions a painterly raggedness recalling late Hilton, Cobra or George Lambourn (1900–77), gives Dyson's work the stamp of an outsider.

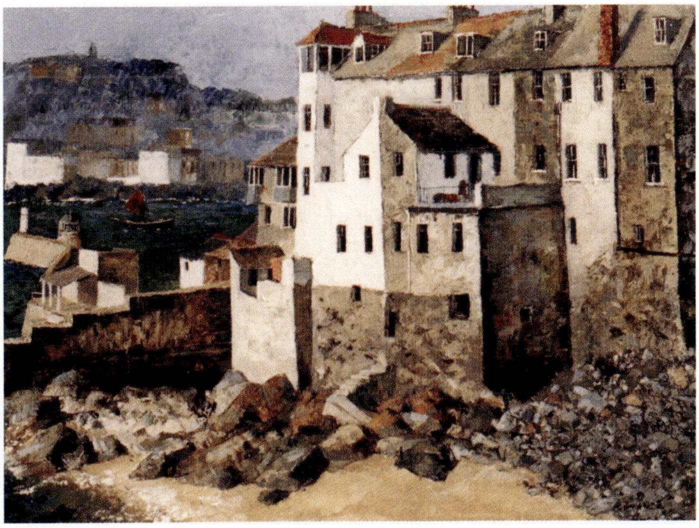

Jeremy King
Wheal Dream
oil
courtesy of the artist

Despite its virtuoso mastery of illustrated pastoral or architectural detail the paintings and prints of Northants-born Jeremy King (b. 1933) also touched a raw naive nerve. The deep blue choppy harbour waters with schooner in *Wheal Dream*, for example, is like a quotation from Christopher Wood and, through him, the revered Richard Eurich. Like Wood King is fond of Brittany to which he returns with sketchbook. Lancashire-trained, King relied on school teaching for a decade up until 1967 when, encouraged by frequent sales at Heals, Libertys and other outlets, he became a full time painter. Moving with Brenda King to Cornwall in 1975 King indulged his eye thereafter on Cornish ports or docks, seeking a degree of abstraction into planes of pure colour derived from large hulks or docked ships. And while landscape provided the principal motif an interest in crowd scenes such as the Henley Regatta elicited a Renoir-like mood of bourgeois leisure and reverie not on the Seine but on our own Thames.

Dick Gilbert (b. 1935) uses a looser handling for atmospheric renditions of the favoured motif of the Hayle Estuary curving away to Gwithian and Godrevy, a place where he was born and to which he returned after spells domiciled first in London (early 1980s) then Finland (1990s) practising and teaching the Alexander Technique. Trained briefly at the Regents Street Poly, Gilbert knew Lanyon, Hilton and others socially and loosely followed their gestural naturalism. His local exhibiting base, as a Penwith member, was complemented by metropolitan solo exhibitions at the New

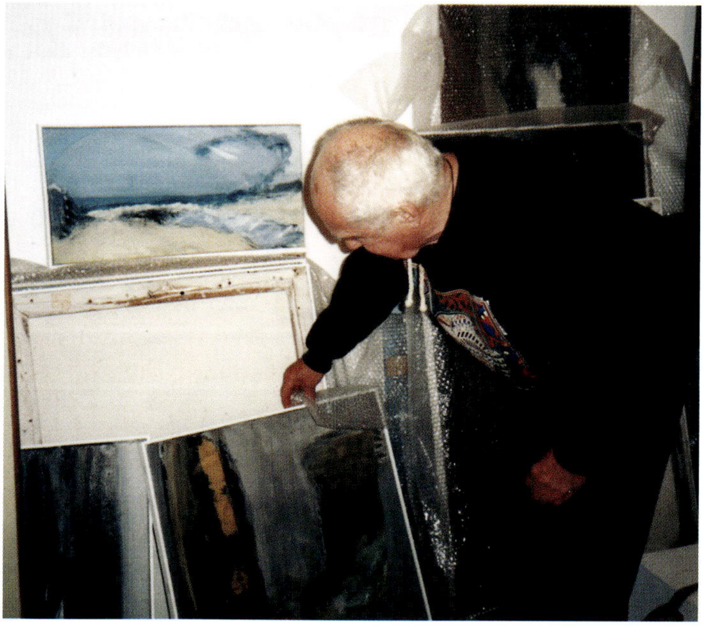

Dick Gilbert in his Gwithian Towans studio, c.2004
photograph: Peter Davies

Vision Centre and Rawlinsky Gallery. Based in Cornwall at a Gwithian Towans wood chalet Gilbert reverts to the wild and windy landscape beyond his door, a recurring subject in gouache, charcoal and oil.

In common with Gilbert and Maeckelberghe Daphne McClure (b. 1933) is another Cornish native whose artistic allegiance to her homeland has been partially broken up through extended periods of absence. Trained under the influential watercolourist Arthur Hambley at Redruth, McClure studied subsequently at Hornsey and the Central School, London where an introduction to Basic Design precepts was complemented by several years dying clothes for the Royal Opera House. This feeling for paint and colour as applied décor led not to mural or pictorial extension but rather to a poetic intimism in which landscape subject-matter threw up cogent pattern and eye-catching rhythm and interval.

Married like Maeckelberghe into medicine, McClure spent fifteen years in Oxford with her dentist husband before returning to Cornwall in the mid 1970s. Living in Porthleven for a decade after this return, where she ran an antiques shop, McClure pursued an interest in series paintings. These amounted to visitations to special places that haunted her imagination and depictions of Porthleven (1988), Hayle (1990), Levant (1994) and the stretch from Porthleven to Penzance (1997) led to thematic exhibitions at the Salthouse, St Ives, Newlyn, Wilson Stephens and Penwith Galleries respectively. The 1997 Penwith show was followed by an even broader travelogue in a 2006 exhibition 'Cornwall to Connecticut' at Badcocks, Newlyn, a display that resulted from her residency at the Albers Foundation, Connecticut in 2005. The artist recalled that 'being in a different environment from Cornwall pushed my work in a new direction'(5) and a series of tree compositions called into play varied patterns and branched silhouettes against dappled background colour.

Manchester born Linda Weir (b. 1949) uses the impasto of Whiting, Buxton, Bounds and others in a manner that embraces townscape – particularly that of St Ives harbour – topography and sumptuous still life. The weather, light and atmosphere of specific time and place is captured through a broad palette that, while remaining naturalistic, evokes the post-impressionism of John Park, another Lancastrian painter whose work focused – come rain or shine – on the endless visual poetry of St Ives harbour. Weir is a later northerner to walk the well-trodden path between the Irwell and Tamar, the warmth, vigour and strong colour of her painterly contribution belonging to the tradition of first Park then of fellow Mancunians Alan Lowndes and Fred Yates.

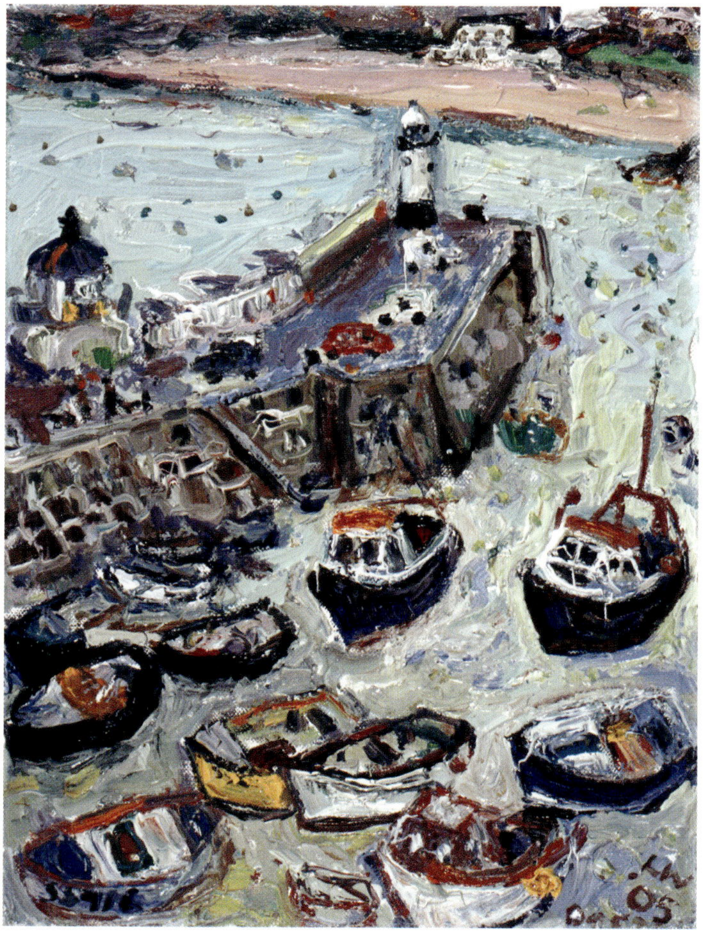

Linda Weir
Inside Boats, 2005
oil on canvas

Weir's panoramic views of St Ives harbour, from the vantage point of an Austrian poet friend, Evelyn Holloway's attic window, are more elevated versions of Park's or Yates's pedestrian subjects. Painted with what *The Guardian* critic Robert Clark described as 'a kaleidoscopic maze of luscious colour'[(6)] Weir's broadly-detailed townscapes reveal a love of a town to which she moved from Lincolnshire in 2000 having hitherto made annual painting trips to St Ives from her native Manchester. A founder member of first studios in Manchester (MASA) then the associated Castlefield Gallery during the early 1980s, Weir helped organise Heron and O'Malley exhibitions which hastened her resolve to later become a St Ives artist. *Big Blue St Ives with Frank's Flowers* (2006) typifies her St Ives 'oeurve' and has the autobiographical content of a homage to her recently deceased father Frank.

In his own entirely contrasting way Bob Bourne (b. 1931) shares with Weir pronounced colour and a degree of stylistic innocence. Exmouth-born Bourne, however, departs from Weir in eschewing topographic specificity - using instead 'representation as a means to convey his inner thoughts'[7] in the words of Mike Venning - and deploying flat planes of characteristically deep or pastel colour in place of Weir's breezy, expressionistic, churned impasto. The unmistakeable imprint of Cornwall does however obliquely characterise Bourne's landscapes or window views that are a psychic osmosis between memory, observation and invention. The palpable stillness reflects a contemplative spirit where narrative is sacrificed at the alter of simple compositional form and colour.

The imperative of stiff, naive drawing - inevitable in Bourne's handicapped case - flattened perspective and ambiguity between the domestic and external natural worlds calls colour into play as a key expressive element. Well-informed to the point of intellectuality, Bourne is an idiosyncratic artist with few illusions and can point to an active exhibiting career that makes him anything but a reclusive or forgotten artist. The widely travelled and self-taught Bourne, who moved to St Ives in 1960 after an education in Canada and Bermuda, spent the mid 1970s away from Cornwall in first Australia then southern France from where he returned to Newlyn in 1977. Since then Bourne, a Penwith and Newlyn Society member, has exhibited both locally at the Salthouse, St Ives and Rainyday Penzance - where he enjoyed a 70th birthday show in 2002 - and in London with Crane Kalman.

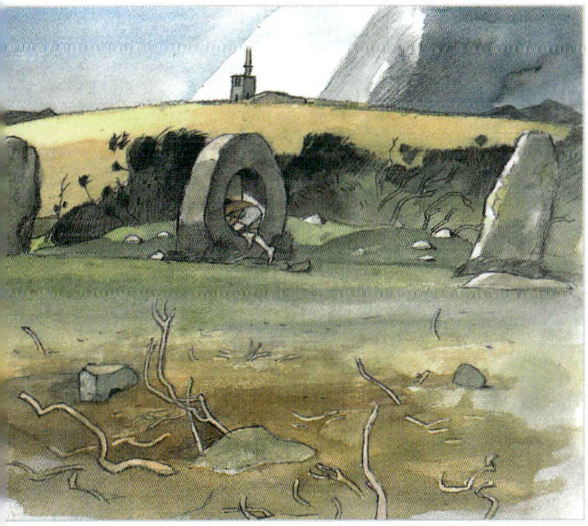

Ken Symonds
Men-an-Tol
from Around the Penwith

Ken Symonds (b. 1927) also moved to Cornwall in 1960, where he developed landscape and nude in tandem in terms of a conventional yet virtuoso use of oil, pastel or watercolour. A preference for elevated panoramic topographical views - of Cornish landmarks or of places further afield - amounted to portraits of specific places, an attribute paralled in standing or reclining nudes using particular named models in decoratively heightened interiors. An academic style integrating architectural precision with atmospheric naturalism is in marked contrast to the flat perspectives of Bourne. A Penwith member like Bourne, Symonds complements Cornish subjects with work from regular painting sorties to Brittany. Symonds allegiance to Cornish landscape was celebrated in *Around the Penwith* (1995), a book illustrating watercolours of the rocky Penwith coastline, and in the 1996 Penwith Gallery exhibition featuring forty-five portraits of notable local artists. Hayle-born and Falmouth and Brighton-trained Michael Praed (b. 1941) whose commercially expedient landscapes of similar rocky Penwith terrain led to his running a gallery for his own work in Marazion, enjoyed

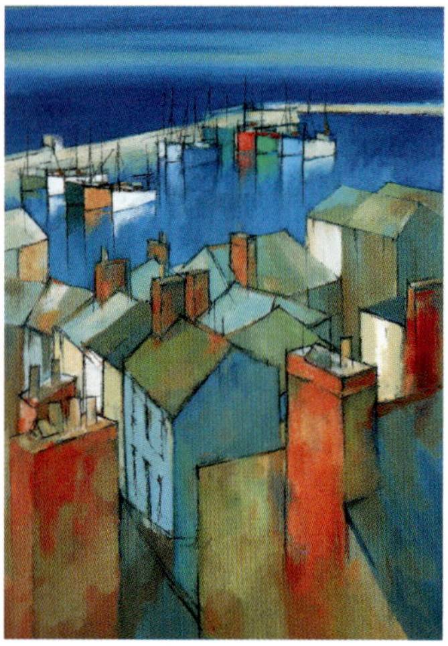

Michael Praed
Blue Light, Newlyn

a 2000 solo at the Penwith, St Ives. The consistency of commercial design in Praed's streamlined compositions of outcrop, tin mine, cliff, harbour or settlement have the intrinsic austerity of Penwith written with the empathetic handwriting of a native.

Like Bourne and Symonds Tony Giles (1925–94) also moved to Cornwall at the start of the 1960s establishing himself through a Penwith solo exhibition in 1962 (another followed in 1990) and two retrospectives at Newlyn Art Gallery in 1972 and 1983. Born into a Taunton working class railway family, Giles pursued a boyish interest in locomotives into adulthood, the iconography of viaducts, curving railway lines, embankments and bridges informing much of the mature painting. Giles also had a nose for key Cornish landmarks like derelict tin mines, ancient field pattern, china clay mounds, chapels and harbours which did not, however use figurative content. This provided unlikely kinship to those abstract St Ives artists (Barns-Graham and Wells visited him at his St Agnes home) in whose work architectural or topographical concerns took precedence over that of the figure.

This was also true of many representational painters like Anne Christopherson and Charmian Leonard whose landscapes in a photo-like or faux naif manner respectively precluded figure imagery. Instead Christopherson in her *Windswept Tree, St Ives* (1974) used truck, branch and leaf rather than the human form to dominate the foreground of an elevated St Ives view.

Twice-married Giles also avoided tourist Cornwall focusing on less obvious environments such as Charleston, St Agnes or places where something of Cornwall's industrial core remained. John Branfield summarised Giles as 'inspired by the way man has shaped the Cornish landscape'(8) and in this Giles, a connoisseur of mining architecture, again followed a central strand of Cornish landscape painting. Giles's *Levant* (1969), commemorating the fiftieth anniversary of the Levant mining disaster, won the 'Art in Industry' competition sponsorsed by English China Clays. These interests were informed by a job in the planning department of Cornwall County Council (during wartime service in the Far East he had been a cartographic draughtsman) and in Giles' later work there is indeed a dichotomy between the painterly and colourist paintings and the detailed ink line drawings of harbours.

Giles' interest in industrial obsolescence and mining architecture is translated in an accessibly literal style. For Burnley-born David Briggs (b. 1956), however, a Preston-born and Falmouth-trained painter who worked as an interior designer and maker of commercial figurines during the 1970s and 1980s before moving to St Ives in 1994, a more cryptic, pictographic abstraction expresses a vision of landscape replete with what Murray Milgate calls 'forgotten meanings and associations'.(9) The archeological symbols and frontal planes replace landscape topography with a densely-inscribed tableaux. Solo exhibitions at Towneley Hall, Burnley (1991) and Falmouth Art Gallery (2000) were followed by a 2001 show axiomatically titled 'Fragmented Landscapes' at Belgrave, St Ives.

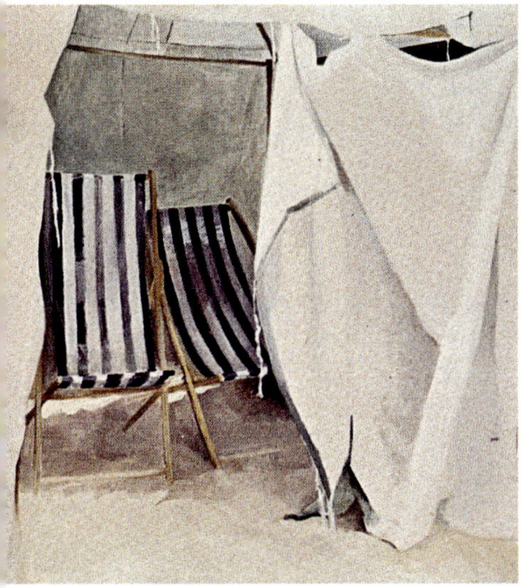

Bob Devereux
Two Chairs, 1980
oil on canvas

Kingston-trained Bob Devereux (b. 1940), the celebrated poet, painter, gallery proprietor and festival organiser, also used the subject of derelict mines and industrial architecture in small woodcuts and engravings sold from a Crafts Market stall he ran during the mid 1970's with his first wife, the still life aquatint printmaker Jenny. This enterprise was a prelude to the Salthouse Gallery; opened in 1979, expanded in 1983 and, against the odds, continued to the present, Devereux's gallery provided many notable contemporary solo exhibitions. Later it functioned more as a showroom for his second wife Pauline's sumptuous and energetic still life paintings and for his own lightly coloured and delicately handled abstractions based on landscape, on beach huts and deckchairs and on previous experience as deckchair attendant during the early 1970s. Later that decade Devereux was a virtuoso watercolourist first depicting landscapes in an accomplished academic capacity then using abstract gesture and atmospheric effects.

Simon Averill (b. 1961), a Brighton-born and trained painter who was given a Salthouse solo exhibition by Devereux in 1988 and who, in common with Devereux, was drawn to the south-west like a Home Counties moth to Atlantic light (as a student in Sussex he painted Cornish landscape in absentia). Further exhibitions, crucially in London with first Wilson Stephens then John Martin, confirmed that, although by now Marazion-based and sharing in what his dealer Martin described as "an aesthetic allegiance and a way of life.'(10) to Cornwall, Averill had eschewed local topography for what Martin again describes as 'an evocation of the landscape told through the poetry of objects and their relationship with the space that surround them'. The result were spare, semi-abstract compositions in which 'personal momentos of a landscape'(11) – feathers, flints, pods, blades of grass and so on – were given an iconic, patterned significance. Using the legacy of 'pop' art's interest in the direct and glamorised presentational strategies of advertising imagery and recalling the recurring shoe or hat compositions of Lisa Milroy or Laura Godfrey-Isaacs,

Averill both transcended conventional landscape and merged it with still life.

Pop art's interest in the ready-made or clichéd consumer object also makes an unlikely appearance in terms of the polychromatic ceramic sculptures of Francis Hewlett (b. 1930), a Bristol-born painter who studied at the Slade during the early 1950s. Transforming the Staffordshire Figurine into jokey Arman or Oldenburg-like objects from everyday life – suitcases, hands, books or domestic bric-a-brac – Hewlett brings his gift for pictorial verisimilitude and graphic exactitude into the world of 'real' things. Moving to Cornwall in 1957, where he was helped by Michael Canney, Jack Chalker and Michael Finn, Hewlett became Head of Painting at Falmouth under Michael Finn, contributing to the college's remarkable renaissance during the 1960's and beyond.

The masterful *Study for Hotel by the Water* (1979), depicting part of Falmouth's extended waterfront, is a virtuoso essay of almost photo real proportion. Using old sketchbooks Hewlett later worked up Sickertian drawings of the Theatre in Bristol and then of landmarks in Paris where he worked as a student. A return to pure landscape, his real forté, was hastened by a sabbatical year in Wales (1977) the products from which constituted a Welsh Arts Council tour that took in Newlyn Art Gallery. Retiring from Falmouth in 1981, Hewlett went on to enjoy solo exhibitions at Browse and Darby (1993) and a fifty year retrospective with catalogue by John Halkes, the former Newlyn director, at Falmouth Art Gallery in 2000.

Manchester-born Tom Cross (b. 1931) who studied at the Slade alongside Hewlett and took over from Finn as Principal at about the time of Hewlett's departure, also focused on landscape around Falmouth, in his case alighting on the weaving and undulating topography around Helford. Such

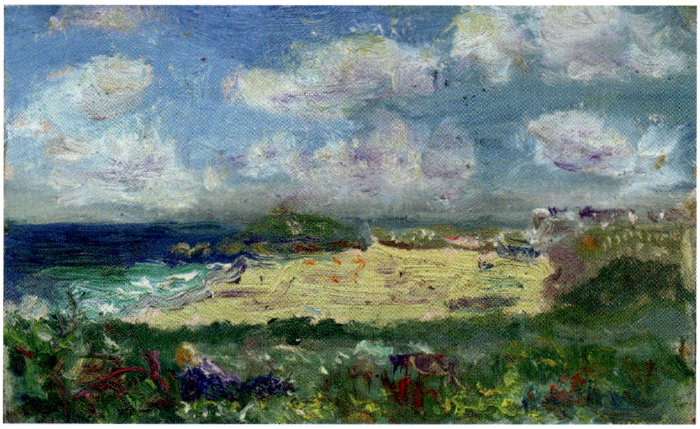

Michael Strang
Summer Afternoon, St Ives
1995
oil
courtesy of the artist

work formed the subject of a book *Helford: A River Landscape* (2004). Estuary studies are simplified into broad topographic silhouettes, the flat designs complemented by a limited yet intense and captivating palette of smokey blue, green and silver grey. The abstraction of surface design probably disguises, albeit to good artistic effect, Cross' technical inability to emulate Hewlett's virtuoso naturalism. Cross' painting does however compensate for the critical mediocrity of his writing which has yet thrown up a best-selling survey of St Ives art *Painting the Warmth of the Sun* (1984).

Michael Strang (b. 1942) a prolific, driven painter whose 'vehement pictures . . . proclaim zest and necessity to paint' [12] in the words of his former Camberwell tutor Anthony Eyton, also responds to place. Strang however paints impressionistically and in series, emulating Monet and the Impressionists in treating landscape motif - be it Tower Bridge or the Houses of Parliament in London, the rolling hills, rivers and bridges of south-east Wales or the sand and surf of St Ives – in various light conditions ranging from day to night, summer to winter. The Constable 'plein air' oil sketch clearly inspires Strang in the fifty panels of Porthmeor Beach that featured in Tate St Ives' 'Porthmeor Beach: A Century of Images' (1995). Among these *Summer Afternoon, St Ives* (1995), a deft essay in chromatic and tonal spontaneity, subsequently formed the cover of a book *Michael Strang at Tate St Ives* (2007).

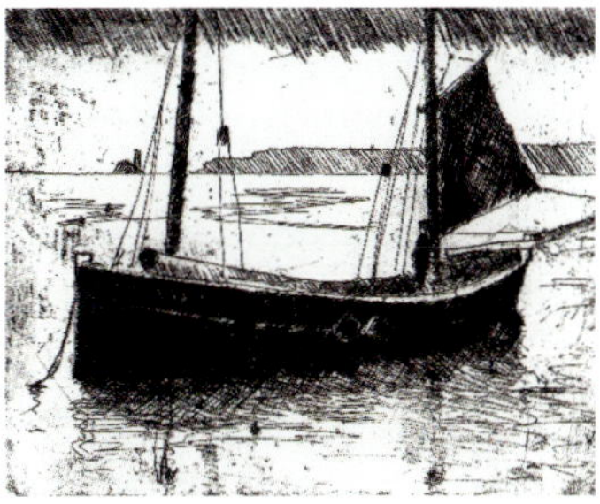

Eric Ward
Dolly Pentreath
etching
courtesy of the artist

The former St Ives harbourmaster Eric Ward (b. 1945) whose book *Eric Ward's St Ives* (2003) follows those on Cross and Strang addresses the tradition of the outdoor landscape oil sketch. Ward's impressionism evokes a wide range of subjects; so broad is this aspect that the Ward book is divided into iconographic sections embracing harbour, pub, interior and still life and marine landscape categories. A St Ives native with intimate professional knowledge of the harbour which he described as 'my playground as a boy in St Ives and workplace as a man',[13] Ward paints with graphic and tonal mastery. The latter recalls Sickert and the contemporary Clive McCartney with both of whom Ward shares an association with the dimly-lit interiors of Clubland. This takes the work beyond the salt and surf of Cornwall and into the smoke of favoured London haunts like Soho's bohemian 'The French House' and the Chelsea Arts Club. Similarly Ward travels with palette up the mainly south Cornish coast taking in subjects like St Michael's Mount, Portscatho, Charleston, Fowey, Salcombe and, through professional links with RNLI, Poole in Dorset.

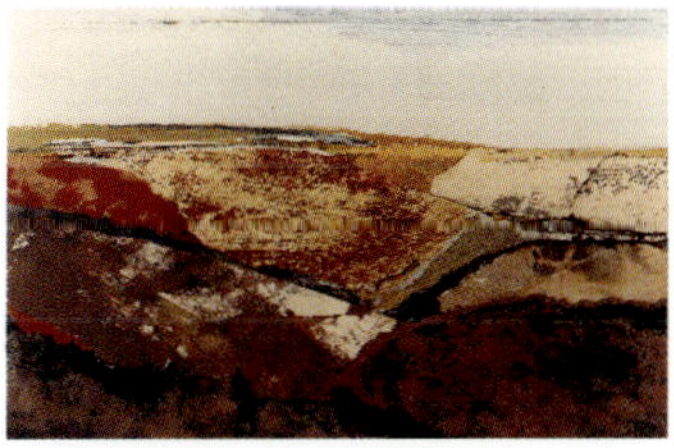

Vincent Wilson
Above Dartmeet
oil and collage
courtesy of the artist

Mold-born Vincent Wilson (b. 1933), a Liverpool-trained painter and collagist who moved in 1962 to Saltash and taught both in local schools and Plymouth College of Art evening classes, tackled local landscape with the raw-nerved emotionalism and empathetic spirit of Welshman turned adopted Cornishman. Where Wilson's torn paper topographic accretions are concerned – alighting on the rocky wild moorland and coastline of Bodmin and west Penwith – a desire to walk a middle path between what he termed the 'remoteness' of St Ives abstraction and a conventional descriptive naturalism yielded a body of work in which fidelity to 'genius loci,' plastic experiment and imaginative speculation cohered.

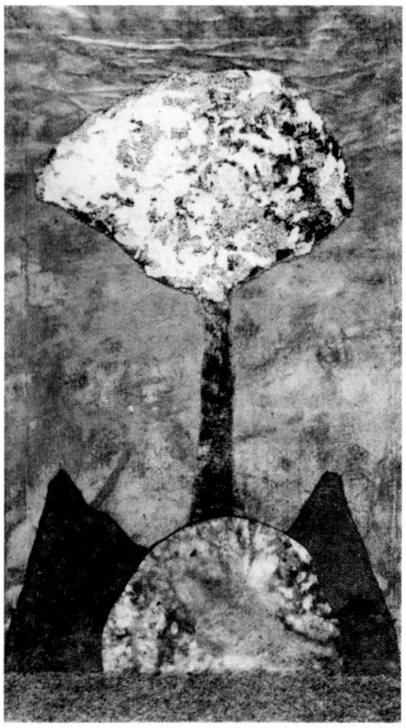

Alan Wood
Tremedda Fields 1972
oil and collage

A key aspect of achieving these effects was the use of accident, the fortuitous combination of collaged paper and randomly-applied rust, green, ochre or grey paint capturing the light, atmosphere and weathered texture of preferred landscape settings. These effects, adapted to striking effect in his 'painterly' and haphazard aquatints, stood out in the 1987 exhibition 'Cornwall in the Eighties' at Pallant House, Chichester, Larry Berryman writing of the way Wilson's 'pulled paint textures and torn edges knit together . . . into one sensation of landscape space'.(14) *Above Dartmeet* (1986) exemplified this textural accord between paint and paper. Introduced to etching by Anthony Currell and Roy Walker at Plymouth Wilson made aquatints that, courtesy of robust deployment of step-out varnish and aquatint, added to an expressive landscape vision fashioned by National Service experience of Expressionist art in German museums. Based at an opposite end of Cornwall Wilson nonetheless maintained close involvement with first Newlyn (an NSA member from 1970) and then Penwith Society (1988 on) where he enjoyed a 1992 retrospective reviewed by Toni Carver.(15) A slightly later Liverpool student, Alan Wood, also made texturally explicit use of collage and painterly process to identify with wild terrain, particularly near Zennor. Widnes-born Wood lived in Cornwall during the 1960s. Before leaving teaching in Cardiff for a teaching post in Vancouver, Canada, Wood produced evocative Lanyon-influenced images of the ancient, rustic fields, his *Tremedda Fields* (1972) having a simple but gripping strength.

Kent-born and Gloucester and Reading-trained Paul Armitage (b. 1953) also uses the rugged Penwith landscape as psychic and plastic tableaux. This is achieved both through tilting topographic perspective to the picture plane and by shaping his supports into irregular off-square formats which draw attention to painting as architectonic object rather than as window on the world. These devices, encouraged by assisting in Sandra Blow's studio after belatedly moving to Cornwall in 2001, were perhaps informed by an early Geography degree at Nottingham where his interest in landscape as a geological and archaeological cross-section no doubt took hold. Winning a Boise Travel Award in 1989 and teaching in Basingstoke during the 1990's St Buryan-based Armitage exhibited at Badcocks, Newlyn and Rainy-day, Penzance where a 2004 show was shared with the Truro-born and Falmouth and Wimbledon-trained still life and landscape painter Lucie Bray (b. 1974) whose atmospheric landscapes of sky and sea use chance in a way consistent with her view of painting as akin to 'thinking without words'.(16)

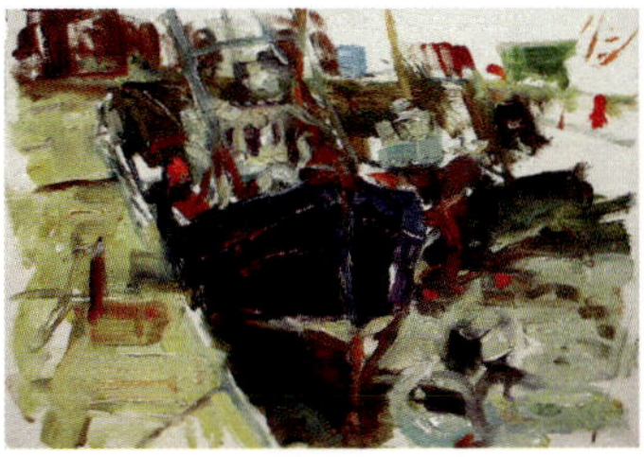

Liam Spencer
Mevagissey Harbour
oil
Andrew Stewart collection

Burnley-born Liam Spencer (b. 1964) whose training at Manchester School of Art predisposed him to taking on urban townscape and the mantle of Lowry, walked the well-trodden path between the north and south-west. A member of the Manchester Studios group Spencer made painting excursions with Linda Weir and other MASA members to Mevagissey, St Austell, the Roseland peninsular as well as St Ives. His focus on Mancunian canals, back-streets and industrial architecture was reinvented in terms of the working Cornish quayside, his *Mevagissey Harbour* using the moored vessel as an icon of looming formal shape and colour. Incorporating drawing as a cogent factor in the Auerbach-influenced painting Spencer enjoyed a solo exhibition at Manchester City Art Gallery in 2006.

The group excursions enjoyed by Spencer's Mancunian colleagues recurred with *Sharing A View*, a roving five-man group comprising Tim Cousins, Denis Bowen, Iain Ruther-

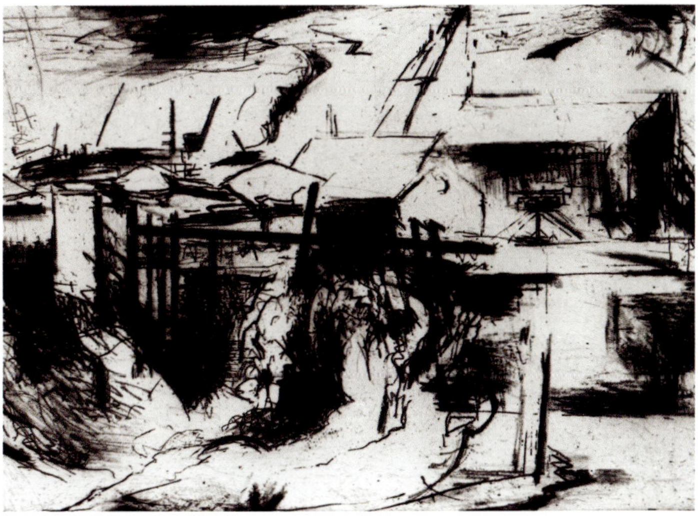

Jane Joseph
Harbour and Fence
etching

ford, myself and a guest, who conducted a plein air workshop in St Ives in 1999 as part of a ten-year cycle of annual visits to diverse locations across England. Jane Joseph's etching *Harbour and Fence* also resulted from an educational workshop, the west London-based printmaker and draughtsman following Bryan Ingham in producing convincing intaglio impressions of the industrial area of Falmouth waterfront. Printmaking and the use of drawn gesture as landscape 'architecture' also informed the abstracted paintings and prints of Slade-trained Anthea Richards (b. 1940), a former chief examiner for art who moved to St Ives in 2000 and worked part-time at Tate St Ives. A love of literature informed the 'poetic' idea behind landscapes, many of which were invented rather than literal, and portraits based as much on photographs as on life sitters.

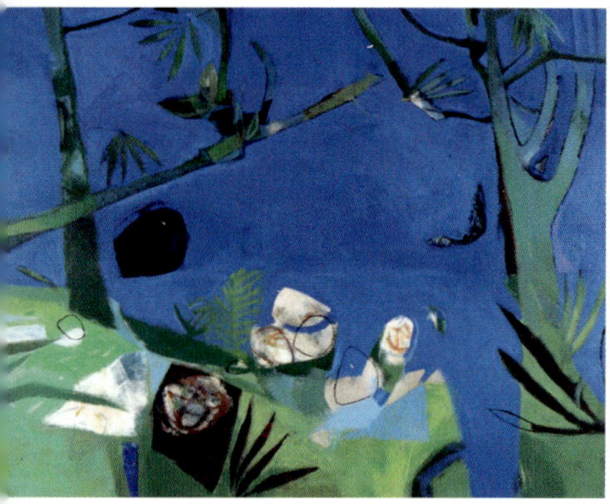

Simon Pooley
Lamorna Wood
acrylic on canvas
courtesy: Stour Gallery, Warwickshire

Cheshire-born Simon Pooley (b. 1955), who moved to Cornwall in 1992 after practicing as an architect in London and Sheffield during the 1980s, paints landscape neither topographically nor with an architectonic precision. Instead Pooley reconstructs landscape compositions in the studio using 'plein air' drawings as memory jolts. Distributed across flattened William Scott-like surfaces in soft pastel or more strident hues are landscape, architectural or even figurative elements standing like visual or rescued and obsessive memories. Inspired by the tango and exotic dance in general Pooley also produces animated figure compositions where the admired qualities of 'poise,balance, tautness and agility' is replicated through a graphic suppleness. Solo exhibitions at Great Atlantic Works, St Just and Badcocks,Newlyn were accompanied by biannual solos at Stour Gallery, Warwickshire.

Colin Orchard (b. 1935), formerly a compositor with *The Times* newspaper then a graphic designer, came to St Ives in 1983 where he developed an impressionistic style of painting based on landscape and interior subjects. Inspired by Bernard Dunstan and through him the legacy of Vuillard and Sickert, Orchard became a painter of deft atmospheric naturalism.

Chapter Four

THE FIGURE

The iconic subject of the human figure, central to the anecdotal naturalism of the late nineteenth century Newlyn School, seldom informed modern St Ives art in either its pre-war impressionist or post-war abstract guises. The inter-war impressionists did not follow Newlyn realist strictures preferring to depict the play of light or the vicissitudes of seasonal weather on the vast maritime environment. The neo-romantic, constructivist and abstract expressionist styles of post-war St Ives art used natural and landscape themes as a point of departure only; a formal, quasi-scientific analysis of the hidden blueprints of natural growth and landscape evolution led to geometric or diagrammatic styles that incorporated the poetics of colour, rhythm and movement. Landscape was so fundamental to the art of Nicholson, Barns-Graham, Frost, Wells, Heron, Wynter and Lanyon that even in representational drawings they preferred landscape or architectural themes to that of the figure. There remained, however, more than subliminal references to the figure in Hilton, Lanyon and Weschke.

The symbolic power of the figure also emerged strongly in the work of emigré artists who, reflecting their social and cultural displacement in Cornwall, introduced an emotive mid-European humanism. Like Francis Bacon, to whose work he owes a palpable debt, Karl Weschke proved a seasoned independent, even outsider. Moving to Cornwall from London in 1955 this former German POW established a central role for himself in Cornish art for the next fifty years, a situation acknowledged by a string of Tate acquisitions in the 1990s and a valedictory retrospective at Tate St Ives in 2004. The culmination of rare Weschke solo exhibitions – notably at the Whitechapel, London in 1974 and a Kettles Yard tour in 1980-1 – the Tate show fulfilled the Kettles Yard curator Jeremy Lewison's call in 1980 that the artist he so assiduously championed 'deserves greater recognition'.

Weschke's figures have an inscrutable air set within bare interiors or austere landscapes. His harrowing personal history – partly raised in a German state orphanage he later joined Hitler's Youth Movement and served as a Luftwaffe Commando before being captured by Canadians in Holland and serving as a POW in England – was reflected in the expressionist scale and stark monumental figuration of his mature work. He found his feet fast, the politician Tom Driberg taking him to see major post war exhibitions in London, marrying the daughter of a British army officer and briefly studying

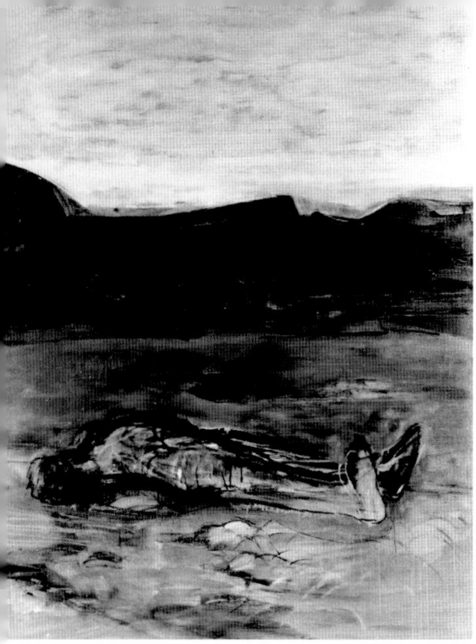

Karl Weschke
Body on a Beach
oil on canvas
courtesy: Tate Gallery

sculpture at St Martins, London. By the end of the 1950s settled in south-west Cornwall, Weschke had effectively established himself as an artist of vision and vigour who John Berger in the *New Statesman* judged was 'worth going to see'.

In contrast to Bacon, whom he befriended during the London painter's St Ives sojourn in the winter of 1959-60, Weschke habitually posited the figure in landscape, rather than interior, settings. But like Bacon a feeling of violence was conveyed in terms of washed-up corpses, as in the Tate's typical *Body on a Beach* or in implied rape scenes like *Four Women and a Dog.* Bacon's homoerotic world was also absent as the thrice married Weschke revelled in strong heterosexual scenarios. An erotic energy also transformed the humdrum domestic subjects of *Lizz in repose* (1980) or the upright *Girl in the Bath* (1978) while an affectionate, slightly humorous note accompanies *The Fire Eater,* a popular image used on the cover of the Tate St Ives catalogue with essay by the art critic Frank Whitford.

In contrast to expressionist art dominated by strong colour, thick paint and formal distortion, Weschke's painting used thin, dilute washes and dark, dingy but highly tuned and subtle tonal colour. A return to landscape featured in later works inspired by the discovery of Egypt in 1990, 'phallic' images of tall erect palms against uniform blue skies, Nile riverbanks, ancient columns and other arcane architectural subjects featuring in a 1994 exhibition at the Redfern Gallery, London, the year he received an honorary doctorate from Plymouth University. During the professionally expansive early 1990s Weschke moved from a Porthmeor studio to a new purpose-built working space at his exposed home at Cape Cornwall. A book by Lewison *Portrait of a Painter* appeared in 1998.

A friend of Weschke, the Slade-trained Sheila Oliner (b. 1934) also alternated between elemental landscape and simple but powerful figures. Aligned with Lyall Watson's Woodstock Gallery, London where she enjoyed three solo exhibitions between 1966 and 1974, Oliner acquired a Zennor cottage in 1970 into which she moved permanently in 1985. Locally active, Oliner was a founding member in 1990 of Porthmeor Printmakers, a STAG fundraiser for Tate St Ives and exhibiting Penwith Society member. Oliner's printmaking expertise saw collaboration with first Philip Sutton in London then Karl Weschke in St Ives – for both of whom she helped make etching proofs – and a spate of interviews with, or technically informed articles on, Bryan Ingham, Terry Frost, Anthony Frost and W. Barns-Graham for *Printmaking Today.*

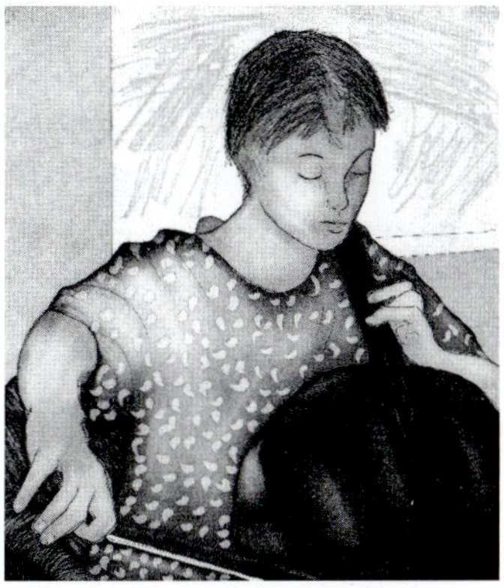

Sheila Oliner
Naomi with Cello
etching
courtesy of the artist

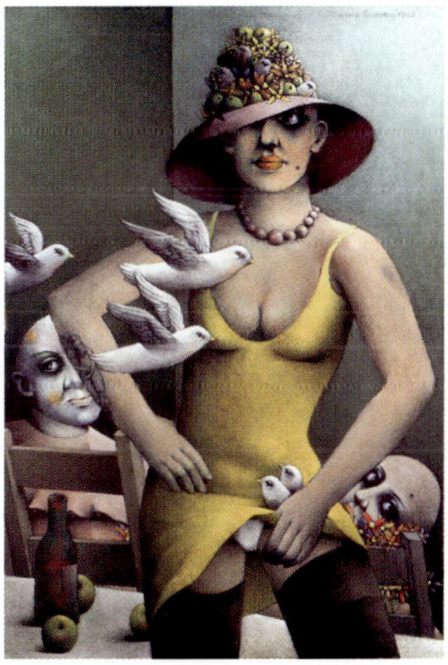

Maurice Sumray
Doves
oil on canvas
photograph: Toni Carver

The critic Edward Lucie-Smith detected 'a powerful draughtsman of the figure'[(1)] at Oliner's 1967 Woodstock exhibition. Conroy Maddox too noticed 'austerely simplified nudes, spread, cut-out like giving an inherent expressiveness without loss of the vigor of their naturalistic origin'.[(2)] Oliner, who enjoyed two Penwith solos – one of the figure in 1998 another of landscapes in 2002 – derives imagery from drawing directly in front of known and specific models such as Naomi Frears in the etching *Naomi with Cello* or 'en plein air' within the Penwith landscape. Oliner's Penwith studio, formerly used by two committed fellow figurative painters John Emanuel and Maurice Sumray, further establishes her figurative credentials. Sumray paid tribute to Oliner's 2002 Penwith exhibition writing of a 'sense of decoration and . . . absolute mastery of her craft'.[(3)]

A sense of decoration and mastery of craft also characterised Sumray's peopled interiors and crowds of bald or scantily-clad women in wild piggyback or carnival arrangements. Moving from his native London to St Ives in 1968 at the request of his wife Sumray brought a bit of bohemian Soho with him. His oddball compositions indeed seemed out of place though gave his work a stamp of individuality, albeit one recalling Vorticism, William Roberts and Wyndham Lewis. The latter described Sumray, the son of an East End Jewish tailor, one of the 'best artists in England'[(4)] in a 1950 *Listener* article, a sentiment no doubt inspired by Sumray's unwavering commitment to the figurative cause.

A near twenty year hiatus in Sumray's career during the 1950s and 1960s when he ran a hand printed cotton and wallpaper printing business in London – gave this intellectual cockney with a bluff, lovable exterior financial independence with which to encounter the Cornish art scene on his own terms. It also marked a divide between the melancholic early figures such as *The Old Jew* (1948) or *The Hunchback* (1950) and the chromatic and thematic lightness of the post-1971 crowd compositions. *Lovers* (1971) announced the end of Sumray's exile from painting, the amorous pair looking back with the pathos of early Picasso. Common to both early and late styles is probing draughtsmanship anchoring the figures within an otherwise enigmatic, dreamlike setting.

John Emanuel's figures by contrast possess an earthy gravitas functioning in an ambiguous and reclining accord with landscape. Like landscape Emanuel's figures have a solid tactility and textural explicitness that is the outcome of layered accretions of collaged or applied material. His abiding preoccupation with the female body, mother earth,

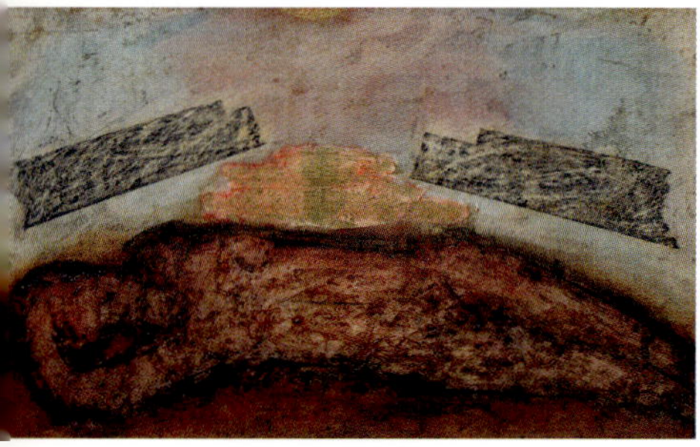

John Emanuel
Reclining Figure with Two Headlands
2007, mixed media on canvas
courtesy: Belgrave Gallery, St Ives

therefore relates to Lanyon's interpretation of the figure in terms of landscape while positing archaic, sculptural attributes that the critic Anne Tuckwell detected in 1984 distanced his work 'from the rather cliched St Ives school of figure into landscape'.[5] Like Hilton, surely an influence, Emanuel uses the figure, compressed into caryatid-like arrangements, to structure the composition. The large, weighty, impastoed nudes belong more to the northern expressionist – he hails from north west – or emigré tradition than to the slender, nimble classicism of St Ives abstraction. There are hints too both of Modigliani and of Henry Moore. Russian icons, decorated ecclesiastic sculpture and stained glass are also recalled in poetic and tactile uses of colour such as spiritual gold leaf and knifed slicks of vermilion or ultramarine. Like Oliner Emanuel enjoyed two Penwith retrospectives, in 1979 and 2005, exhibitions that accompanied successful commercial forays with Wills Lane, St Ives, Montpelier Studio, London and later Stour Gallery, Warwickshire.

Angela Barron's reclining figures also merge with landscape or lie above it as stricken metaphors of violence and dispossession. Whereas Weschke's gloomy symbolism stems from 1930s Germany, Barron's more hopeful vision is based on global travel with her husband Brian, the seasoned television foreign correspondent who reported on trouble spots. Studying art in Australia and America, Barron later entered the London Film School. Working for twenty years as an advertising designer and film maker, she first visited St Ives in 1973 to make a film on Hepworth, Heron and other leading St Ives artists for the Gulbenkian Foundation. Developing her painting since moving into a Piazza flat above Porthmeor, Barron alternates between residual figurative images and abstracts. A large Weschke painting in the Barron collection serves as a reminder of an influence on Barron's work.

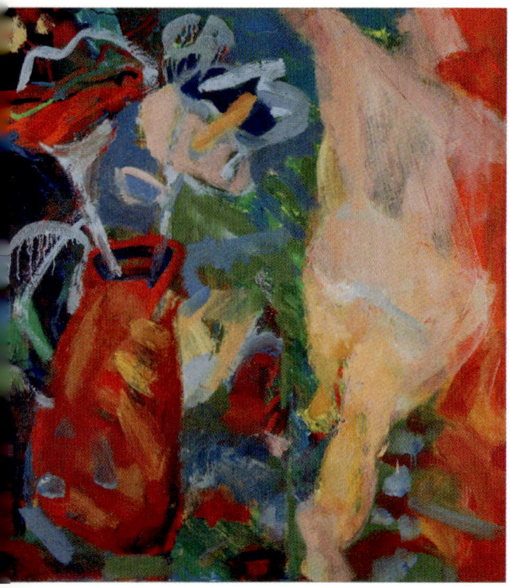

Angela Barron
Mythologies Series: Taurus
2007, oil on canvas
courtesy: Brian Barron

Mary Stork's deft, rapidly executed pastel drawings of the figure contain a sculptor's heightened feeling for the body as a solid object in space. Trained at the Slade, Stork (1938–2007) put the disciplines of the life room to expressive effect both through calligraphic immediacy with broad sweeps of ink, charcoal or pastel and a rich, varied range of colour. Once married to the painter Jeremy Le Grice, with whom she had three children, Stork later concentrated on her exhibiting career. From the mid 1980s onwards her vigorously coloured drawings, widely displayed both at David Messum's West End gallery and at many provincial outlets, met with critical and commercial recognition. Rose Hilton (b. 1932) expands Stork's context, capturing the

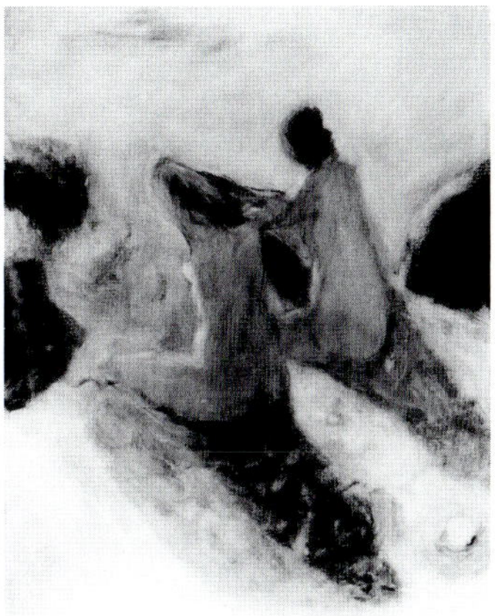

Rose Hilton
The Polandese Pool
oil
courtesy: David Messum, London

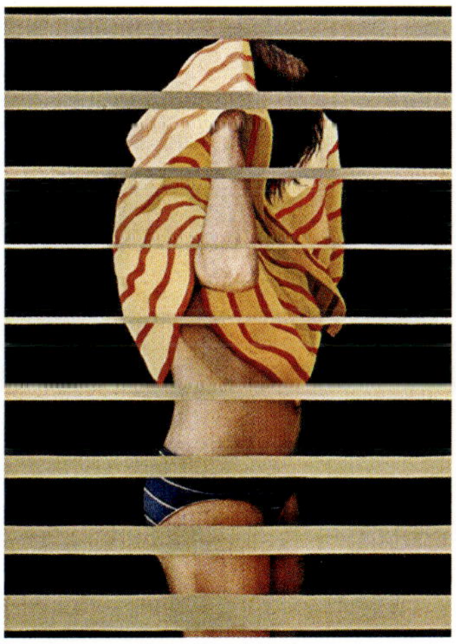

Robert Floyd
Outside In 1981
gouache on paper

figure in moments of reverie and domestic intimacy. Both repressed and liberated by marriage to Roger Hilton, Rose developed without distraction after his death. Roger's knowledge of, and alignment to, modern avant garde French art was translated in Rose's work, not in terms of his involvement with concrete or lyrical abstraction but through the colourism of Matisse, Dufy and Bonnard.

A cogent mix of observation and improvisation transforms interiors into poetic spaces whose point of departure is the close study of female models in the studio or, in the case of *The Polandese Pool* in the open air. Like Weschke Hilton developed her home at Botallack near St Just into a live-in studio. The commitment to the human figure, established at the Royal College in the early 1950s and later reinforced at the Central School in London under Cecil Collins provides discipline, focus and continuity. The loose and relaxed paint handling of Hilton is absent from the almost photo-realism of Robert Floyd (b. 1951), a Wolverhampton-trained figurative painter who left behind a hippy-like disaffection for urban life in the 1970s and moved to St Ives in 1976. Working from a Porthmeor studio Floyd created popular images of bikini-clad or wetsuited figures informed by idyllic high summer beach life, a subject to which he had become attached after surfing expeditions to Australia and the Mediterranean. Floyd, who enjoyed a successful solo exhibition at Wills Lane Gallery in 1981, seemed for a few short years to shake St Ives painting out of its late modernist vacuum and introduce a contemporary look. Moving on in the 1990s to a very different anthropomorphic interest in horse heads adapted from the Parthenon in Rome, Floyd divorced, left St Ives to teach in Cornish schools and all but disappeared from the St Ives art scene.

Portraiture featuring well-known faces from the art community inevitably attracts attention for social rather than aesthetic reasons. The retired G.P. Roger Slack's photographs of prominent artists at private views create a vivid record of St Ives artists in celebratory mood during the 1970s and beyond. There was a bone fide portrait painter, Leonard Fuller, whose St Ives School of Painting became a sanctuary for beginners and seasoned artists alike. Memorable portraits of his wife, the painter Marjorie Mostyn, and Sven Berlin adorned the walls of the school. The Welsh-born Jon Henton, a regular visitor to the school near the end of Fuller's career, went on to teach life drawing at evening classes in Minehead and organised talks at the Brewhouse, Taunton featuring Frost and Davie in 1980. Inspired by Modigliani's nudes of the kind displayed in the Royal Academy's 2006 exhibition 'Modigliani and his Models',

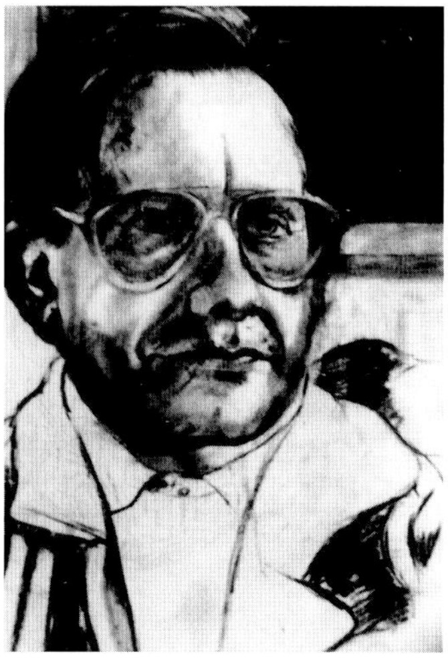

Bill Bolger
Portrait of Bob Devereux
charcoal

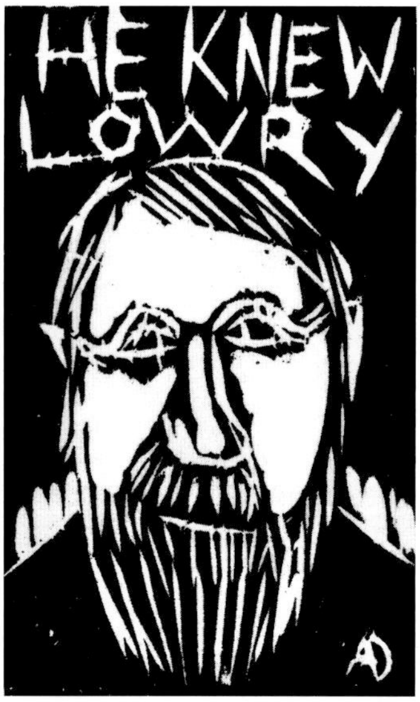

Alan Dixon
Portrait of Bob Crossley
woodcut

Henton produced powerful reclining figure compositions. Retiring from Taunton to St Ives in 1999 and expecting something of Modigliani's bohemian Montparnasse in fin-de-siecle St Ives, Henton was disappointed missing the earlier cohesive art colony before the property developers moved in. Nothing changed on the walls of the Sloop Inn, however, Hyman Segal's charcoal drawings of local fishermen enhancing the old world charm of the well-known pub. Ken Symonds' pastel portraits of fellow artists like John Wells, Liverpool-born and RCA-trained William Bolger's (b. 1940) charcoal study of Bob Devereux or the Eastbourne-based poet, art collector and relief printer Alan Dixon's humorous woodcut of Bob Crossley contributed to this vein.

A more experimental take on the conventional subject of the human face is evident in the 2004 'Face Value' project of Henry John, the great grandson of Augustus and heir to the John family house 'The Fishloft' in Mousehole. The young Ruskin-trained artist zoomed in on physiognomic fragments of friends, the historically celebrated or the anonymous. Using the transparent subtlety of water-colour which also freed up his graphic versatility John emulated the confident virtuosity of Augustus while appropriating the conceptual image-making process typified by the abbreviated styles of Hockney or Proctor in England or Close and Katz in America. Subjecting the faces studies to computer-enhanced reproduction jet ink prints subsequently doctored with further water-colour touches John marketed these part reproduction-part original prints through a novel 'name your price' mail order strategy. A successful solo exhibition at Badcocks Gallery, Newlyn in 2004 launched his career in Cornwall, a career underwritten by family heritage and a natural and deceptively sophisticated flair for the landscape or portrait sketch.

Sharing with the Johns a recurring interest in the figure, Ray Atkins's heavily worked paintings derive from the rigors of the Slade life room, where he studied during the early 1960s, and the expressionism of Bomberg and Auerbach. A retrospective in 1996 at RWA, Bristol was followed by a 40-year retrospective 'Painting of the Figure from London, Reading and Cornwall' at Royal Cornwall Museum, Truro in 1999. The critic William Feaver noted in the Truro catalogue that for Atkins figure and landscape represented 'two takes on the same practice,' both demanding direct scrutiny and physical engagement with materials. Atkins's language grafted expressionist impasto and colour onto an austere fiftyish realism, the artist describing 'a sort of new realism based on feeling rather than intellect, based on action, on the involvement with process'.

Atkins' career-long commitment to working from direct observation made him seem 'an absurd maverick'(6) during the 1960s when 'passé' life drawing and outmoded figurative art in general did not chime within a zeitgeist of experiment and iconoclastic novelty. Studying alongside the kindred expressionist and Welsh landscape painter Peter Prendergast at Reading during the late 1960s Atkins lightened his palette from the dark early masterpiece *Quentin Crisp* (1958). In 1974 he moved to Cornwall, teaching life drawing at Falmouth from which experience the energetic, multi-limbed and gesticulating figures of the 'movement and dance' series of paintings emerged. The popularity of the *Late Picasso* exhibition at Tate, Millbank in 1988, celebrating Picasso's final flush of erotic figures (early 1970s), coupled with the expressionist revival of the 1980s, brought work of Atkins's kind back into the spotlight.

Atkins's painterly transformation of the life room figure into large presences that directly link with landscape strikes a pantheistic chord of continuity between man and nature. In their quieter ways the expressive, painterly and anecdotal paintings of Yankel Feather, Gill Watkiss, Bob Bourne, Simeon Stafford and Fred Yates also intimately connect the figure to urban or rural environment. While Atkins' labours with trowels of paint in physical accord with directly observed posed models or 'plein air' landscapes, Feather, Watkiss and the aforementioned indulge their inner eye, that compound of memory, imagination and fancy. The result is a pronounced strain of social narrative.

Feather shares with his Mancunian counterparts Fred Yates and Simeon Stafford early allegiance to Lowry whose influence was transformed into the lyricism of Vlaminck, Dufy, Utrillo or Soutine. The latter inspired the Bristol-based expressionist and friend of Alan Lowndes Barrington Tabb. Natural facility is a mixed blessing for Feather whose work exudes an easy virtuosity and eclecticism. Feather's peopled street scenes – Lowryesque evocations of the impoverished Liverpool of his youth – Cornish beaches and Brighton subjects do, however, have a personal charm and reflect the artist's much-travelled biography. Moving to Cornwall in 1977 from Liverpool, where he ran a club, the Basement, during the Mersey-beat boom and latterly dealt in antiques, Feather gravitated to fellow figurative artists like Hilton, Stork, Oliner and Bourne and lived near them in the St Just area. Rose Hilton was always supportive visiting all Feather's exhibitions. In place of the Liverpool Academy, in whose midst he exhibited works at the Walker Art Gallery, Feather found artistic outlet at the Newlyn Society of Artists. Group displays as a member throughout

Yankel Feather
Twenty-one Celluloid Dolls
2006, oil

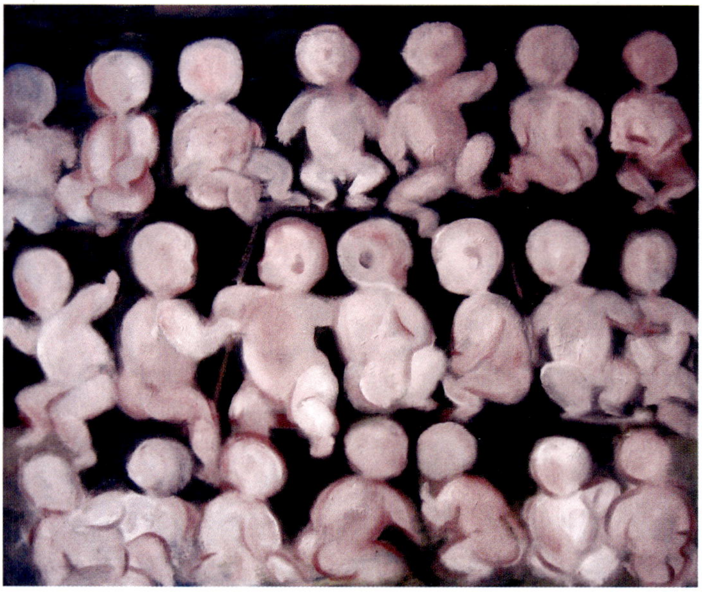

the 1980s were augmented by solo exhibitions at local galleries like Salthouse (1981) and New Millennium (1996) in St Ives and at G.X., London. Five solos at G.X. between 2002-6, some of which were opened by his erstwhile Liverpool acquaintances Cilla Black and Beryl Bainbridge, proved commercially and artistically successful.

Feather's figure and still life subjects, also essays in colour and painterly immediacy, attest to an imaginative iconographic versatility. The recurring male nude recalls Keith Vaughan though in *Twenty One Celluloid Dolls* Feather's wit registers a novel, indeed conceptual, approach to the figure using the secondary source of mannequins. A short abstract interlude while briefly living in Dulwich, south London in the late 1990s was not so much a 'me too' exercise as a nod and wink to Terry Frost, his lifelong friend whom he first met in 1947. Restless and mercurial, Feather moved from Dulwich to a 'London by the sea', acquiring a converted warehouse studio near Hove seafront. The sea was indeed never far from Feather's life which is reflected in moody Boudin-like beach scenes, in melancholic depictions of decommissioned boats on the Sussex beach front and in bustling harbour scenes derived from Liverpool docks or Newlyn harbour. The inherent celebratory mood is registered through Renoir-like brushstrokes and speedy Dufyesque calligraphy though the influence of Bomberg and of mid European expressionist forbears is equally relevant. A gripping autobiography 'Passion, Paint and People' highlights a socially-engaged career.

Sharing with Feather and Yates the influence of Lowry whose tonal palette he enlivened with injections of bright and vivid colour, Simeon Stafford (b. 1956) melds images of Cornish beaches and quaysides with the viaducts and red brick terraced housing of his native north-west. Stafford, who studied at Hyde College in 1973 and moved in 1996 to Cornwall, proved the latest in a long line of Mancunians to paint the kind of escapist holiday pictures once deemed by *The Guardian* newspaper to have marginalised the local documentary or social realist strain epitomised by Lowry and his industrial landscape followers at the Manchester Academy. Stafford cleverly merges the two. Out of this chaotic fantasy emerges an authentic vision from a distinctive and idiosyncratic artist who wears early and later lives on his sleeve.

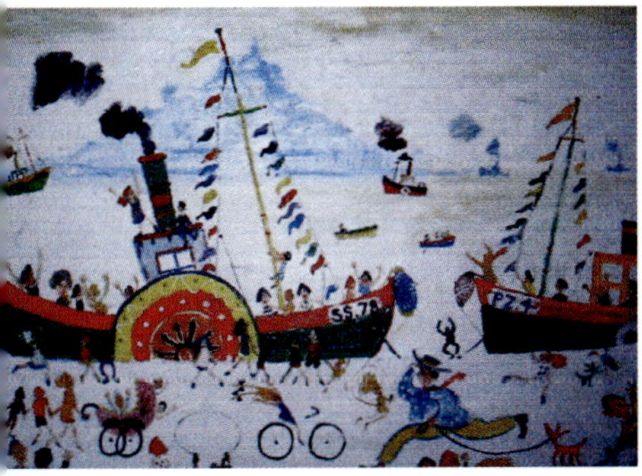

Simeon Stafford
SS78, Mount's Bay
oil on board
courtesy of the artist

There is no doubting the expressive vigour, strong colour and imaginative warmth of Stafford's crowded beach scenes. Substituting Lowry's yellowing lead white with purer titanium and replacing the older man's ubiquitous cats and plodding mill workers with donkeys and animated holiday makers Stafford creates new renditions of *Britain at Play* – to use the catchphrase of his 2005 solo exhibition with his London gallery Oliver Contemporary – which posits an optimistic, anodyne mood. Like Lowry, however, Stafford strikes a quirky vision of humanity observed with a distanced and satirical, though affectionate, eye. The popular – perhaps too popular since it poses the question of a mass plebian appeal – quality of Stafford's work ensures commercial success and its acquisition by both the Queen and Prime Minister.

The influence of France impinges as a third iconographic factor (after Manchester and Cornwall) on the colourful, exuberant, impastoed 'oeuvre' of Fred Yates (b. 1922). Born one of twins into an Ardwick family Yates – a rugged, handsome man though strangely a lifelong batchelor – served in the Grenadier Guards during the war before living for five years 'like a foreigner in sophisticated Bournemouth' as he later described it. A restless and peripatetic artist Yates spent further periods teaching in Brighton and in Fowey during the early 1970s before 'joining' the west Penwith art community. Leaving his Marazion base in the late 1990s for a second French domicile – via a short Somerset interlude – Yates lived and painted in first central and then southern France. A series of Monetesque gardens, wooded landscapes or village scenes issued from his exceptionally prolific hand.

Describing himself as a 'happy Lowry' Yates paints humanity head-on, setting up easel in public spaces and

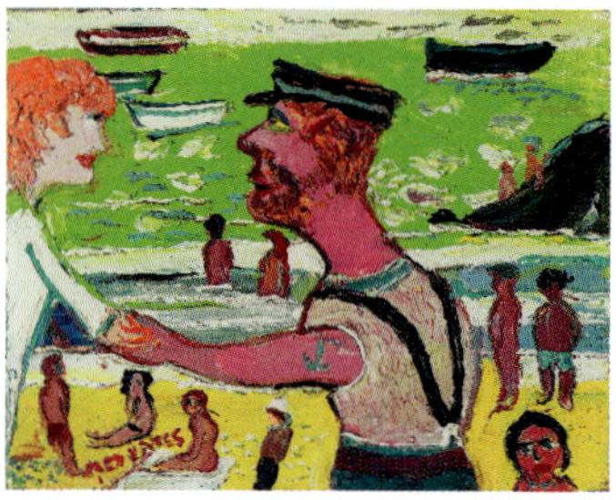

Fred Yates
The Sailor Returns
oil on canvas
courtesy: John Martin, London

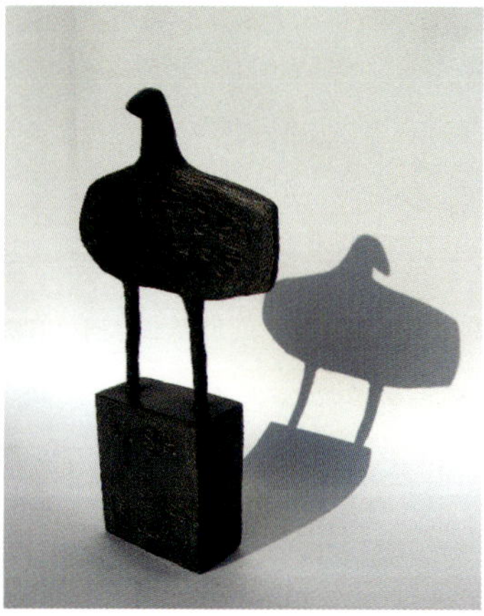

Christopher Marvell
Small Penwith Bird
2007, bronze
courtesy: Belgrave Gallery

rendering everyday life. A theatrical realism based on both recreational and workaday sources lends itself to the special event; pantomimes, carnivals, parades and social or civic gatherings bring out Yates's relish for ritual, celebration and decoration. The commercial boom in Yates pictures culminated in near sell-out shows with John Martin, his West End dealer, who mounted a successful 80th birthday exhibition in 2002.

London-born Gill Watkiss (b. 1938) also uses landscape for what she told Tom Cross was 'a backdrop for portraits of those fashioned by its elemental charácter'.(7) The looming presence of Lowry on Yates and Stafford is however absent, Watkiss' soulful, bright and breezy depictions of workaday Cornish life tinged instead with Carel Weight's sense of drama and mundane poetry. Married to the Royal Academy-trained painter photographer Reg Watkiss, which whom she had five daughters, Watkiss focused on the congenial subject of mothers in the park, cocooned from Weight's metropolitan menace, children playing or, in the lithograph *North Coast Walkers* (1999) on family excursions. Moving to Cornwall in 1959 they lived first in Zennor then at St Just before moving to Newlyn in 1975. These locations fashioned micro-cultural physiognomic changes, the artist discreetly making thumbnail sketches of people in public places. After Newlyn these were worked up into studio pictures at her large home near Penlee House, Penzance.

Watkiss' people friendly vision is echoed in the nostalgic, enigmatic and quasi surreal, rather than faux naif, vetrianoesque figure compositions of Alan Kingsbury. Kingsbury uses the glossy verisimilitude of high society Edwardian painting (Lavery, Orpen et al), his anachronistic scenes with the paraphernalia of the antique shop conjuring an era that, by virtue of disappearing from living memory, enters the contemporary fray with a splash of post modern irony.

Ethnic and primitive, as opposed to naive, impulses characterise sculptures of the animal or human figure by Breon O'Casey (b. 1928) and Christopher Marvell (b. 1964), the woodcuts of Peter Fox (b. 1952) or the intensely worked iconic heads of Michael Rees (b. 1962). Newcastle-trained Marvell's blunt anonymity creates universal metaphor relating to the existential tautness of post-war sculpture. Darkly patinated human, bird or animal forms, by virtue of being, in Richard Blackborow's words, 'sparing in detail but fulsome in association'(8) create strong silhouette and monumentality. In the particularised imagery of *Boatman*, *Traghetti*, or *Falling Man*, cogent pieces displayed in *Boats Birds Boys and Beasts* at Belgrave St Ives in 2006, trapped narrative creates symbols of vulnerability, the pot-marked, eroded or abraded bronze surfaces relaying an individualised textural 'skin' different in kind to the robotic totalitarianism of Antony Gormley's lumpen 'jellybabies'.

Breon O'Casey's sculpture may be seen in the interdisciplinary context of a versatile artisanal output. Son of the celebrated Irish playwright Sean, O'Casey grew up in London and at Dartington Hall during the war where an interest in the fine and applied arts took root. A painter, weaver, printmaker, jewellery maker and latterly sculptor, O'Casey created formal and thematic osmosis between for example painting and weaving or jewellery and sculpture. However, the correspondences are not merely technical and plastic, overriding anthropomorphic and primitive concerns running through the entire 'oeuvre'. 'My main influences,' he wrote in 2000 'have been Picasso, Matisse and Braque, and the French school generally, with jewellery Calder, with sculpture perhaps what's called ethnic sculpture'.(9) Whereas O'Casey's painting, in a dark, rich or sombre palette, relates to the generic primitive and archetypal influences (symbolism and abstract patterning) that informed or inspired all modern art – be it in Paris, New York or St Ives – the sculpture is as much a product of the logic of materials manipulated with discerning wit or inventiveness as of accord between structure and symbol.

O'Casey's three dimensional iconography, in contrast to the generally abstract nature of the paintings, uses bird, fish or animal subjects. These sculptures divide into trinket-like silver configurations in which linear wit and spatial economy emulate the decorative lightness of jewellery, and solid bronzes which demonstrate the value of what he described as a 'tough apprenticeship' in Barbara Hepworth's studio at the turn of the 1960s. The Irish critic Brian Fallon, author of one of several books on the artist(10), characterised the legacy of that formative experience as establishing a 'care and patience for materials, the spare, often unconventionally elegant forms, the fine but not overfine finish, and an

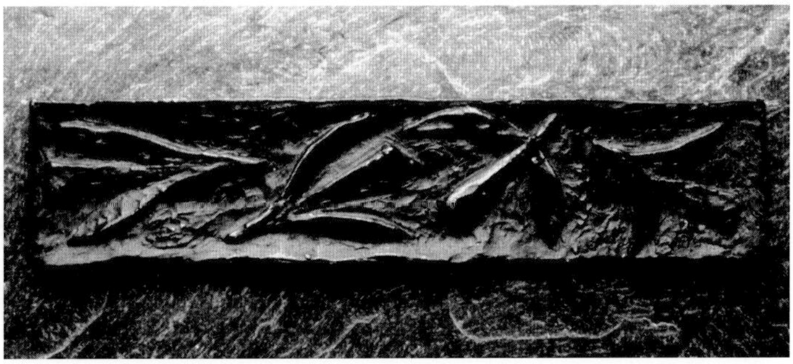

Breon O'Casey
Bird Relief
bronze

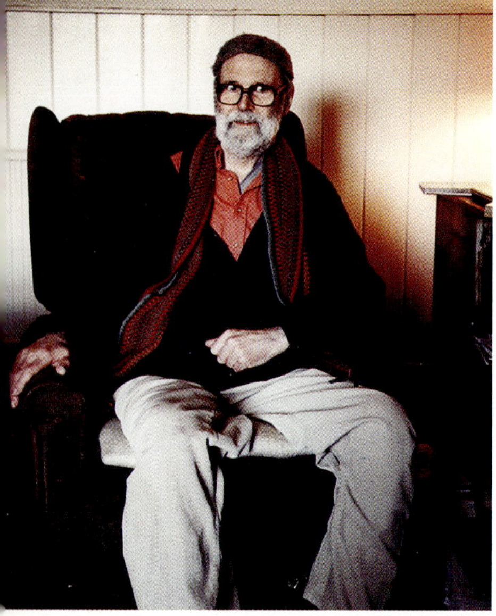

Breon O'Casey in Paul
April 2007
photograph: Peter Davies

organic unfussy quality'.[11] With the conclusion of O'Casey's financially expedient jewellery career, announced at a 1996 Oxford exhibition aptly called 'The Last Jewellery Show' this versatile artist focused on painting and sculpture as two distinct abstract and figurative disciplines which did, however, overlap in terms of the bronze-cast pictoriality of *Bird Relief*.

Within the semi-sculptural languages of the woodcut, engraved shallow space slate relief and box assemblage Peter Fox pursues O'Casey's interest in 'primitive' symbols and abstract patterns as well as in animal imagery. Northampton-born and Falmouth-trained Fox, who lived briefly in St Ives during the late 1980s before taking on Jeremy Annear's former cottage on the St Leven estate near Marazion, studied native Inuit printmakers and tended, as he explained, 'to identify with non-western artists and the art of ancient cultures'.[12] Stark animal imagery possessed direct symbolic, rather than narrative or illustrational, significance. Fox's ecological concerns, predicated on a heightened sensitivity for man's increasingly problematic relation to both the animal kingdom and to the planet in general, led to recurring animal imagery relayed via the appropriately direct, physical and indeed neo-primitive medium of the relief print. Unusual in its opting for the relief print as a main vehicle of communication, Fox's work seems, in John Lane's estimate 'to grow from some substratum of myth and rough magic quite outside the currents of his time'.[13]

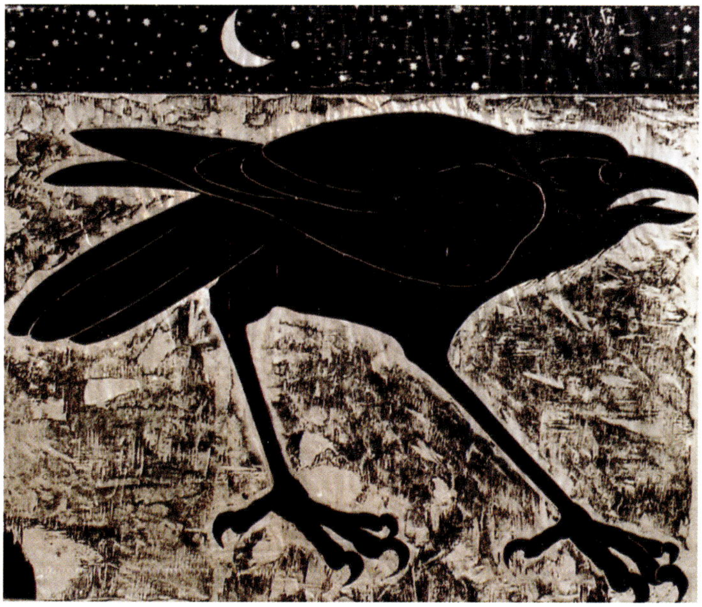

Peter Fox
Marburan the Raven
woodcut

The anonymous, somnambulant and solitary figures of Watford-born and Ipswich-trained Michael Rees (b. 1962) also seem to emanate from myth and magic, their abraded, pockmarked faces 'carved' from densely textured and intensely-worked paint surfaces. Like Fox Rees identifies with the ethnic self determination of the Cornish counter culture. Dropping out of art school at an early stage in order to avoid a system felt to turn 'students into employable designers'(14) and to give full creative focus to painting Rees was inspired by Bacon and Dubuffet, both of whom circumvented the academic. While inspired by visits to Kettles Yard, Cambridge and to 'St Ives 1939–64' at the Tate Gallery in 1985 – experiences that were catalysts for a 1987 move with his wife to Ludgvan, Penzance – Rees retained a fierce independence and a determined distance from the primitive cult centred on Wallis, Mary Jewels, Patrick Hayman and others.

Rees' gritty recipe of paint, wax and grog posit textures that ironically give the emerging figures a dense monumentality and physical presence while providing a mysterious, anonymous and even ethereal aura. Without any specific landscape reference Rees' pictures nonetheless echo what the artist describes as 'the colour in nature of Cornwall'(15), the rusts, creams, beiges, lead blacks and metallic greens evoking weathered and eroded topography. The timeless ancestral presence in Cornwall chimes with Rees' early religious education, the artist again eschewing institutional convention for a wilder, imaginative mystic sense that yields iconic and ritualistic worship figures.

The early neo-primitive figures of Louise McClary, which have a Ken Kiff-like air of whimsy and make-believe, are relinquished in the Penzance-born and trained artist's recent paintings. These continue a surreal vein, the botanic and biomorphic coming to the fore. The home grown McClary (b. 1958), who became Head decorator for Troika in the late 1970s before working from a Porthmeor studio during the first half of the 1990s, later became inspired by the translucent light and flora and geology of the Scilly Isles as well as by gardens on the mainland. The aptly-named solo exhibition 'Echoes' at Waterhouse and Dodd in 2006 represented a belated West End arrival for a hitherto seasoned westcountry exhibitor at venues in St Ives, Newlyn, Plymouth and, during the Porthmeor studio years, Beaux Arts, Bath.

The direct inscrutability of Rees' solitary figures is emulated in the melancholic art of the Redruth-based Norweigan painter Kristin Vestgard (b. 1976) who studied in Oslo before attending Falmouth College of Art during the late 1990s. A sell-out degree show in 2000 anticipated equally successful shows with Badcocks in Newlyn. Vestgard's invariably female figures seem to carry a feminist tag though a nordic introspection attending muted, grey, mist-like backdrops speaks of a quirky and poetic, rather than explicitly social, sensibility. In the case of 'to all my grandmothers' depicting a group of women ambiguously 'crowned' with reindeer antlers (possibly fixed to walls behind their heads), allusion to her native Scandinavia in terms of arctic animals is evident. Nature is indeed seldom far away, the floral headdress of the Marie Laurencen-like *Little Hunter* or still life objects holding leaf twigs using the ephemera of the outdoors for domestic decoration.

Another artist who favours her own gender is Barbara Karn (b. 1949). Wiltshire-born and trained in Cheltenham Karn moved to Cornwall in 1992, worked for Tate St Ives, became a Newlyn Society of Artists member and set up studio in Perranuthnoe. Unusually, Karn relinquished rather than embraced landscape in Cornwall, concentrating instead on coloured drawings of the nude figure either produced in front of a studio model or worked up from imagination. Using distortion to emphasise what she terms 'an attitude or character' Karn's reference is not of anatomic description so much as 'one of human possibility' and in this the nudity of the subject is a prerequisite for capturing what is seen as 'a person in their original state, allowing vulnerability and a sense of the private person to enter the story'.

Nudity or near nudity is also at the heart of Lisa Wright's depiction of children – her children – who are candidly captured playing on the beach, wading in the sea or sitting, standing and lying with carefree abandon. Despite their large scale and impastoed surface Wright's canvases are essentially painterly drawings; the iconography of the world of childhood is relayed not through the infantile styles of Yates, Stafford or others, but through a sophisticated plastic osmosis between drawing and painting recalling the contrasting examples of Sickert, Dufy or Patrick Caulfield. This 'organic' relationship between drawing and painting using pale or acid colour represents a healthy accord between structure and sensuous paint surface.

Wright's training under first Arthur Neal at Maidstone in the mid-1980s then Norman Blamey at the Royal Academy Schools during the early 1990s bucked late modernist trends by placing figure drawing at the centre of her professional practice. Yet Wright (b. 1965) is a child of her times and becomes something of a post modern magpie in commenting on, or making a parody of, eclectic style. Though not an abstract painter the legacy of 'pop' (she drew commercial storeyboards for a London film company between colleges), minimalism, post painterly abstraction, New Image painting and conceptualism variously inform the shape and look of distinctive compositions. These feature single or paired figures within large, vacuous or schematised spaces.

A prolific exhibition career since her 1993 graduation vindicates a winning combination of thematic timelessness and transient or trendy contemporary style. Almost annual inclusion in the Summer Exhibition at Burlington House confirms her Royal Academy background, complemented by biannual exhibitions with Beardsmore, London and Lemon Street, Truro. William Packer and Virginia Button, her two main critical apologists, celebrate how she avoids the loaded subject of children becoming 'mawkish' or 'saccharine'(16) while maintaining a vital tension and ambiguity between abstract form and figurative content. The Hunting Prize Award in 2003 announced the arrival of an officially recognised figurative painter able to take that traditional genre and integrate it into the pluralism of a new era.

Wright's paraphrasing the 'life' figure in terms of the universal child therefore retains the vital link between drawing and painting or between objective scrutiny and subjective interpretation. Kathy McNally, Steve Dove and, latterly, Ges Wilson and David Beer excel at life drawing to the extent that the figure sketch stands as a full artistic statement. A Principal of the St Ives School of Painting

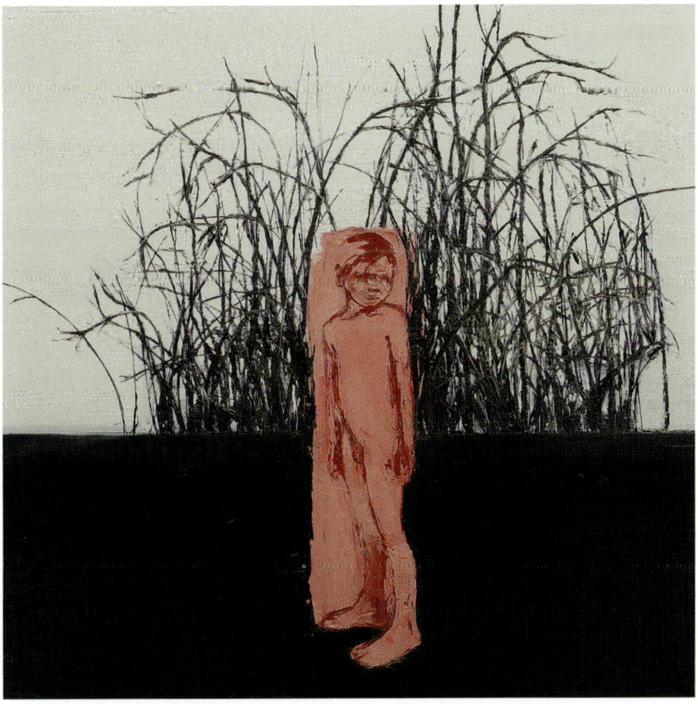

Lisa Wright
Twilight Shadows
oil on canvas
courtesy of the artist

(2000 – 2004) the Exeter and Falmouth-trained painter Ges Wilson joined the Art Space Co-op Gallery in 2007. Wilson's drawings of the figure are not however finished statements so much as part of a process she describes as 'allowing an intuitive response to the unexpected.' Beer, owner of the Penhaven Gallery, St Ives positions the nude figure against a uniformly coloured background, his neat and tidy style reflecting the methodology of a former headmaster.

The open-ended process of drawing is an undisguised component of the work of Leicestershire-born Naomi Frears (b. 1963) whose phantom-like heads or figures emerge from scraped back fresco-like backgrounds. The terracotta, beige or faded brown palette complements the iconic human content articulated through drawn line. This Sunderland-trained artist who studied sculpture before establishing herself as a St Ives painter during the 1990s painted in a manner informed by earlier sculpture and printmaking studies (she became a member of Porthmeor Printmakers).

A feeling for the figure in exotic, non-European settings characterised the Moroccan canvases of Jane Furness, latterly a Bristol-based painter who made annual trips to North Africa. Occupying Jill Garnier's former studio in Newlyn during the later 1980s Furness looked after an aged mother in Penzance. A large forty-year retrospective of paintings and drawings at Penlee House in 1989 impressed Frank Ruhrmund who wrote that the ninety works 'display as astonishing maturity and grasp of essentials.' [17]

Chapter Five

STILL LIFE

Landscape is rightly seen as the defining factor in the ever popular art of St Ives. The powerful and compelling coastline of Cornwall in general and West Penwith in particular inspired varying artistic responses at the centre of which was a softening of abstract and constructivist styles to accommodate references to the natural world. Portraiture and still life, among other traditional genres, were not as apparent. Still life, however, often accompanied landscape in terms of the window view with jug, bowl of flowers or windowsill trinket. A reminder perhaps of how St Ives art carried a self conscious feeling for craft and for making things in both an arts and crafts and cottage industry context.

Still life painting, therefore, formed a distinct strand, epitomised in the work of Christopher Wood, Winifred and Ben Nicholson and their talented daughter Kate and Bryan Pearce. So influential was the soulful fusion of the domestic and outside worlds that, as well as reverberating within the ongoing tradition of St Ives, this quintessential manner with its post cubist or faux naif affectation inspired artists well beyond Cornwall. The hugely popular art of the three Marys – Fedden, Newcomb and Potter – consciously drew on this tradition as did the work of younger practitioners Sarah Bowman and Elaine Pamphilon.

Colin Johnson (b. 1942) subjects still life to a sweeping and summarising graphic outline giving force, energy and unifying structure to pictures that might othewise dissolve into a confusion of detail. In terms of its arching curves, arabesques and formalised arrangements, Johnson's art recalls the simplified designs of Art Deco and stylised pre-war Railway posters. And like much art of the 1930s a timeless calm emerges. The Royal Academy exhibition 'Matisse and his Textiles' (2005) revealed patterned cloths as an important decorative device in the French master's painting. Closer to home Patrick Heron's saturated colour field painting reflected his family's involvement with textiles. Manchester's thriving 19th century textile industry also had an enduring artistic effect, particularly at the municipal college of art where Johnson studied in the late 1950s under Harry Rutherford and Terry McGlynn. Although he resisted pressure to study textile design full time his introduction to the subject had its effect the artist later recalling that 'forty years on that short period shows in my work'.(1) A full time painter since 1960, Johnson began regular visits to St Ives soon after. These culminated in his settling there in 1986, a domicile interrupted only by a period in Teignmouth between 1991 and 1997, Johnson attracted to the working port which he had often passed by train on frequent artistic tours of the British Isles.

Music also inspired, Johnson incorporating musical instruments into his still life iconography and also organising and reviewing jazz events in St Ives. An indomitable energy and flair for organising festivals and cultural events impinged on his artistic output which is nevertheless prolific. Johnson's wide cultural interests are apparent in *Window Still Life with Bill Marshall Pot* (1993), ironically a work produced in Teignmouth rather than St Ives, which presents a sweeping rooftop panorama of St Ives from his attic studio in Bedford Road. The centre-piece of a large retrospective *Paint and Found Pieces* at the Crypt Gallery, St Ives in May 2005, *Window Still Life* is a magnum opus in Johnson's frequently underestimated work.

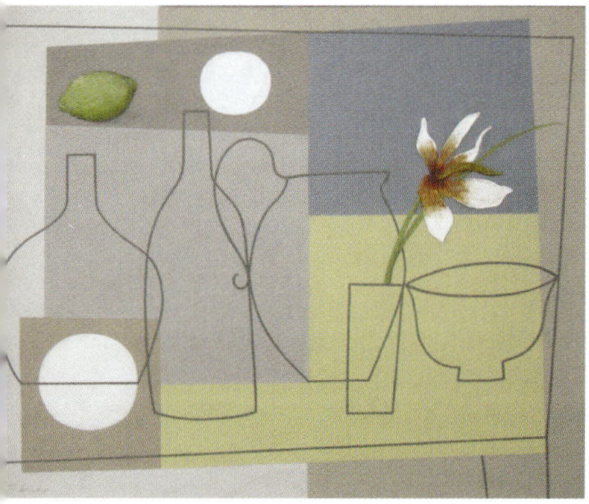

Geoffrey Robinson
Sour Lemon
courtesy of the artist

Music also drives the still life painting of Geoffrey Robinson (b. 1945) a Bournemouth-trained painter who later worked as a freelance commercial designer and songwriter/performer. Robinson returned to fine art through 'doodling' with collage and making homemade films on artists; one on Gillian Ayres in 1988 led to a week-long liaison with Ayres in Bude, an experience that gave him confidence. Michael Gaca exhibited his work in the mid 1990s at Beatrice Royal Gallery, Eastleigh then later at Belgrave Gallery, St Ives. Further successes with Bettles, Ringwood, Lena Boyle, Cadogan Contemporary, London, and Grapevine, Norwich, together with a two-man show with John Emanuel at Stour Gallery, Warwickshire in 2007 proved the validity of a project that successfully reinterpreted the legacy of Scott, Nicholson, Fedden and other modernist still life practitioners in terms of a stylistically inclusive post modern eclecticism. Robinson therefore uses modernist strategies that impart a thirty-ish stylisation; a dichotomy in the work between geometric reliefs ordered along intuitive, rather than systematic or concrete, lines and richly textured 'rococo' still life imagery gradually coalesce into a distinct, even idiosyncratic, composite style. Interweaving between abstract, decorative or mimetic styles, Robinson's art becomes an arthistorical hybrid that borrows from cubism, constructivism and pop. It has an abstract and architectonic basis, however, the artist explaining how he is 'doing something akin to arranging found objects within a rectangle . . . I never work my abstract composition back from a found collection of objects'.(2)

This constructive purpose perhaps reflects the graphic designer's visual wit and need for immediate communication. And while the still life objects are presented in the direct and appealing manner of advertising they inhabit what is in many ways an abstract environment in which the flattened perspectives of cubism, uniform colour of abstract 1960s 'colour field' painting and geometrical composition of constructivism hold sway. The artist describes how the governing motif of the tabletop 'carries the main impact colour of the painting'[3] positing the signature tune against which textural detail or linear counterpoint is introduced. The pristine hard edged clarity of Robinson's still lifes, where a modernist invention inadvertently recalls the high focus verisimilitude of Dutch 17th century still life painting, is replaced by a hazy faux naif reverie in the pictures of Emma McClure (b. 1962). A London-based Cornish painter who studied at Falmouth, Winchester and Chelsea Schools of Art during the 1980s, McClure also tilts still life arrangements toward the picture plane, creating within this dislocated shallow pictorial space a discrete alliance between abstract pattern and poetic allusion. Both her interior and parkland scenes are suffused with a soft, grey light, very London in mood. Here the parkland drunk or tramp is excluded for an ideal world of birds, dogs and football players. Launched by recurring solo exhibitions first with Vanessa Devereux and later with Cadogan Contemporary, McClure's paintings possess wit, charm and affection for anecdotal incidents of everyday life.

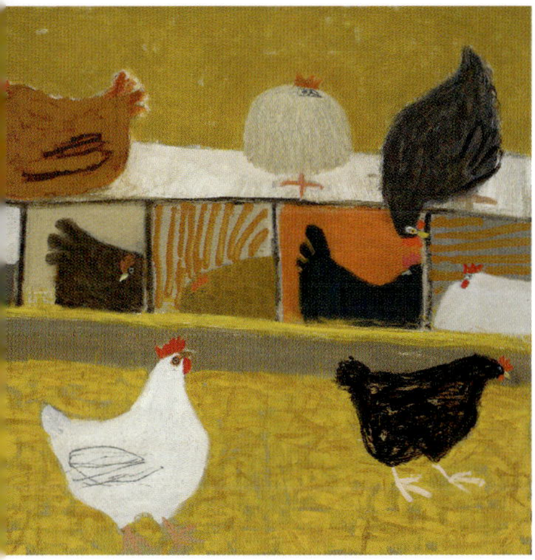

Emma McClure
No Vacancies
oil on board
courtesy: Thompsons', Marylebone

Jessica Cooper (b. 1967) relies on the raw and unadulterated power of the pure mark on crisp expanses of untouched canvas. The subjects – trees, flowers, bowls of fruit or furniture – are repositories of line and colour. The feeling of space and emptiness elicited by these light and airy compositions perhaps reflect her growing up on west Penwith's exposed north coast where, as she put it, the feeling of unlimited space and isolation 'set in my vision from an early age'.[4] This vision indeed has a primal immediacy, the brushmarks feeling their way around iconic objects with a child like wonder and unapologetically awkward grace. Like McClure Cooper finished art studies in London – in her case at Goldsmiths College – after an agreeable year at Falmouth. Goldsmiths pushed her to the limits, forcing a complete re-evaluation. The pared down images that followed perhaps bear the Goldsmiths stamp, Michael Craig-Martin's linear and conceptual approach recalled in Cooper's still lifes. The student work, however, grappled with dense collage out of which emerged rudimentary figurative imagery – a subject to which she instinctively not to say therapeutically returns in moments of artistic uncertainty – inspired by the late work of Roger Hilton,

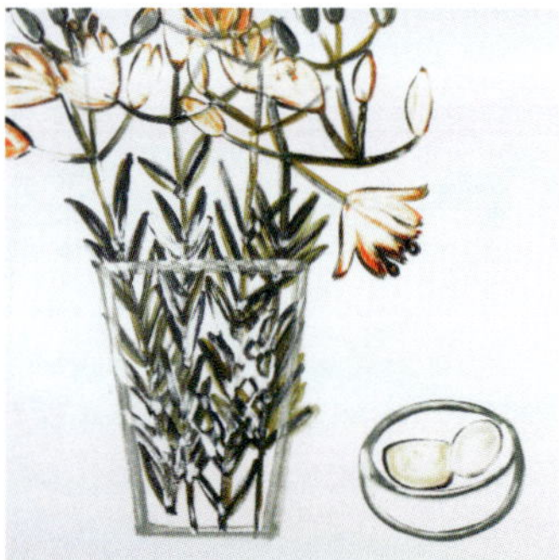

Jessica Cooper
Ooh La La
acrylic & pencil on canvas
courtesy: Stour Gallery

a legendary figure in modern Cornish art whom she had known about since very early childhood.

After travels in Spain Cooper returned to Cornwall at the end of the 1980s. Accompanying life transforming events in her private life, such as marriage, motherhood and later, sadly, the death of her father, Cooper's career developed apace throughout the 1990s. She only painted full time after 1997, however, when growing commercial success, particularly at Thompsons Gallery, London where she enjoyed bi-annual shows, relieved her of freelance teaching at Tate St Ives or Newlyn Art Gallery. The distinction between line and colour, either merged or operating in tandem, assumes expressive potency in the reductive environment of Cooper's art. Nowhere is this in greater evidence than in a plant and tree series, created during a workshop at the Eden Project, which formed a theme show at Badcocks Gallery, Newlyn. A trip to Italy also proved productive, yielding a series based on chandeliers and a notable canvas *Peggy Guggenheim's Table*, another sparse composition that, despite its controversial slightness, won an award at the R.W.A.'s 'Open Painting' exhibition in 2005 in Bristol, the city in which she was born.

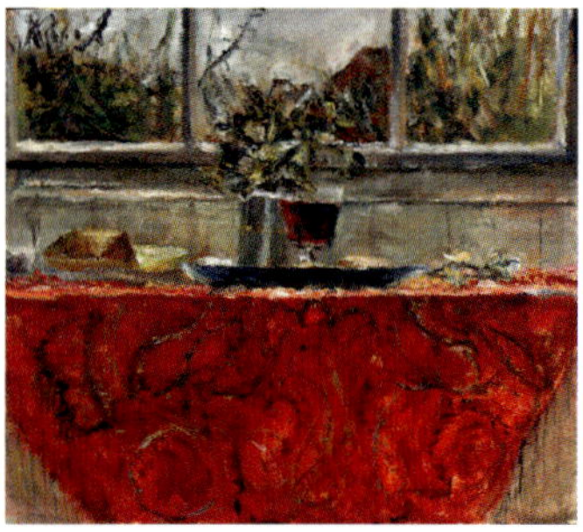

Alice Mumford
The Redcloth and Red Wine, Polgrean
oil on canvas
courtesy of the artist

Alice Mumford (b. 1965) also exhibited still life and interior paintings, albeit of an entirely different kind, at Badcocks. Mumford's more conventional impressionism of cluttered tabletop, light-filled interior corner and windowsill, built up carefully with a controlled churned painterliness, also resonates with autobiographic or metaphysical significance. Mumford describes interiors like *The Red Cloth and Red Wine, Polgrean* as 'an analogy for our inner and outer worlds'. Within that interior the familiar and reassuring decorative objects or functional utensils of everyday life provide subject-matter that allows the artist to 'connect the simple act of looking and my inner world'(5).

This intimism is therefore accompanied by an introspective streak that lends psychological depth. The everyday objects thereby 'symbolise the presence of human beings'(6) according to Richard Demarco. Art historically aware since student days at Camberwell, Mumford follows what the painter Michael Strang has termed a 'Camberwellian sense of perfect tonality'(7) and in so doing links the revered Chardin with Euston Road. Taken up and promoted by the Hampstead dealer Julian Lax, Mumford enjoyed commercial success. Lax's first Mumford show, a sell out, was aptly titled 'Intimate Interiors and Favourite Objects'. This featured alongside pictures of china cats, teapots, flower vases and other comforting objects compositions such as the biographic and anecdotal *The Arts Club Cat, Penzance* (2002) or *The Kitchen Table Polgruen.* Mumford's interiors have faded, even grubby, Newlyn School charm and rusticity eschewing the suave high society naturalism of Nicholson senior or Lavery. After Lax's untimely death in 2004 Mumford went on to exhibit with Badcocks, Newlyn and Belgrave Gallery, London.

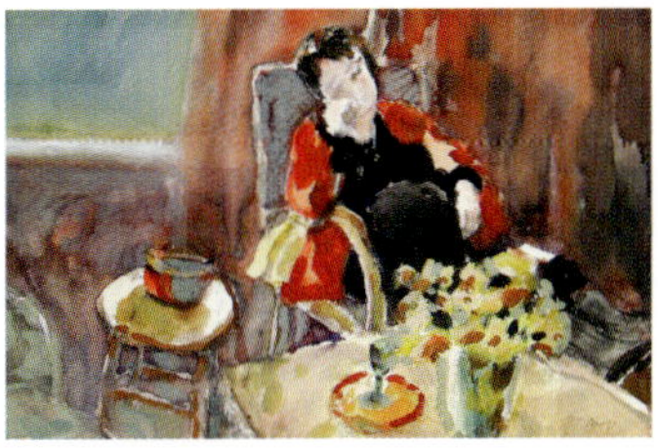

Janet Treloar
My Daughter Alice
watercolour

Mumford's mother Janet Treloar (b. 1940), a watercolourist of robustly executed landscapes and architectural subjects, was an important facilitator. Studying first at Penzance then later at Heatherleys, London, Treloar used a natural gift for watercolour to create work in thematic series; well-travelled (she lived in Norway for eight years) her sense of Europeanness led to the exhibition 'The Romanesque Arch: A Visual Language for Europe' at Piers Feetham Gallery, London in 2005. Celebrating what she describes as the essential 'simplicity born out of elegance' that characterises the ubiquitous Romanesque style, Treloar invests the same emotional resonance in depictions of arches, apses and vaulted interiors that Mumford uses in her assembled domestic objects. Treloar also displays landscape intimacy, particularly in response to her native Cornwall. An interior with pregnant Mumford describes cultural and biological continuity and a domestic Bloomsbury-like intimacy.

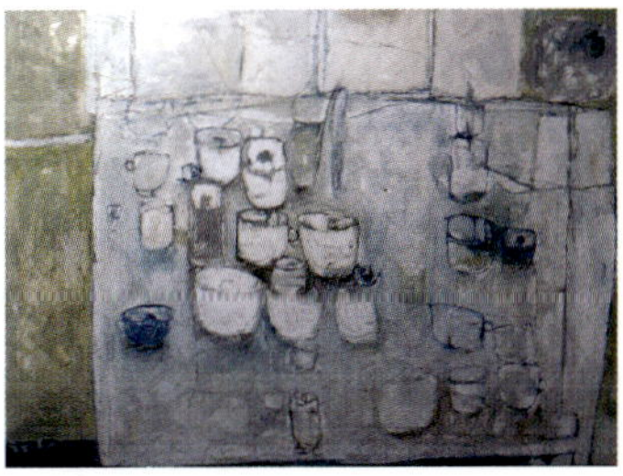

Ffiona Lewis
Top Table, Blue & White
2002, mixed media
courtesy: Redfern Gallery

The humble culinary object is transformed into significant form in the luminous and bleached, yet impastoed, still life painting of Ffiona Lewis (b. 1964), who trained as an architect, and Elspeth Spottiswood, an older Scottish-born and Camberwell-trained painter. Both are influenced by Scott's uncanny mix of austerity and sensuality. Lewis's 'formal awareness of how things sit together after they've been interfered with'[8] produces apt correspondence between the subject of dining table clutter and the random, fortuitous or chance effects of broad and sensual paint handling. Lewis came to prominence through solo Redfern Gallery exhibitions from 1999 having 'graduated' to Cork Street via the westcountry conduit of the talent spotting dealer Gordon Hepworth. In the Scott-like jumble of *Top Table, Blue and White* (2002) Lewis trades in subtle colour intonation (ochre and blue) within a dominant chalky white surface. Spottiswood, who received informal tuition from Kokoschka, lived near Looe where landscape and still life were reduced to minimal elements. The muted, creamy impasto was a striking feature of her Rainyday Gallery exhibition in Penzance in March 2006.

The interface between interior, still life and landscape dominates Rachel Nicholson's art in a manner that immedi-

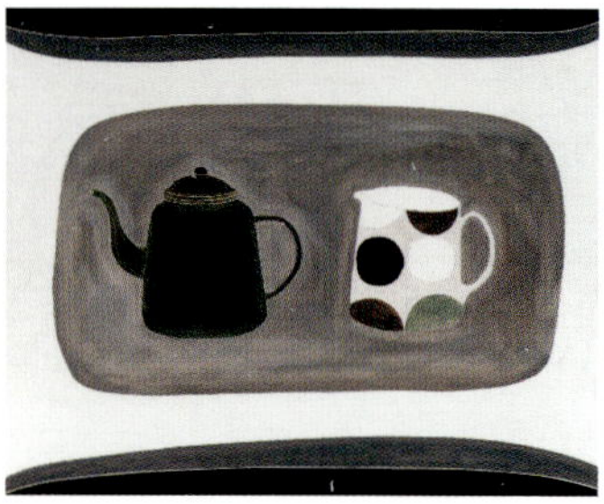

Rachel Nicholson
Green Teapot with Julia's Mug
2005/06, Oil on board
courtesy: Caroline Wiseman, London

ately links it to that of family precedent. What Jill Paton Walsh described in 1997 as a site specific 'marriage of still life and landscape'[9] serves to perpetuate the Nicholson family's role in defining this essential strand of modern Cornish art. Rachel's style, in which flattened perspectives present a 'faux naif' vision and the pale blue, grey and beige palette an English reserve, is at once personal and endemic to family tradition. The delineated coffee pots, cups, jugs and forks seem pinched foreground props for more significant landscape views beyond the window. These objects have, according to Walsh, been 'rendered abstract by their mysterious scatter in relation to each other'. In the iconographic scheme of things the objects depicted – designed, Lucie Rie-like domestic ware – have a humble St Ives simplicity different to the gleaming grandiloquence of the silverware or cut glass of her paternal grandfather William. Her interest in the place of St Ives is a recurring feature of townscapes that, as in the mid century work of Ben, trade in the 'gently skewed perspectives'[10] of the Cornish port's unmistakable skyline. The subject is both personal and one that serves as arthistorical metaphor, the town synonymous with key developments in post-war British art.

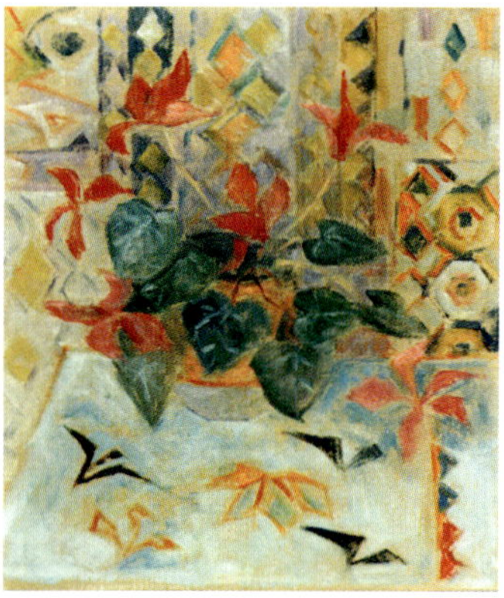

June Miles
Red Cyclamen
oil
courtesy of the artist

June Miles' (b. 1924) thinly painted canvases, which divide into still life, landscape and portrait themes, are essays in what Ronald Gaskell calls 'the primacy of the picture plane'[11] since Cézanne. Like Cézanne Miles uses still life objects and the cube-like prospect of West Penwith or French villages to form a situation in which 'an almost sculptural feeling for solidity and space comes into play'. Miles is a painter of tranquil subtlety who, after marriage to Paul Feiler with whom she had three children, married a sculptor. Something of Paul Mount's sculptural sensibility rubs off when Miles creates cogent patterns from spatial interval. Indeed Gaskell wrote that 'pattern, rather than space, is the organising principle, so that the picture has something like the intricacy of an Indian carpet'. Trained at the Slade under Schwabe, where she frequented the life room, Miles draws with paint and constructs with colour. Tentative and understated in an elegant English way, Miles's marks and coloured daubs also burst into bright, vivid colour, a process suggested by the 'given' chromatic intensity of floral or textile fabric subjects. The enclosed spaces inhabited by recurring flower jugs, plant pots or fruit bowls create an independent tapestry of abstract, decorative intensity. In *Red Cyclamen* the complementary greens and reds of leaf and petal loose their iconic foreground status and merge with this background.

The Royal College trained Brenda King, while sharing with Nicholson, Miles and others partiality for pattern, introduces an even greater decorative richness reflecting mid 1950s textile studies and a later job designing fabrics for Libertys, London. Often miniature in scale, King's detailed still lifes are the product of invention, interpretation and rearrangement. Flower vases, fruit bowls, mementos and bric-a-brac co-exist with patterned tablecloths – perhaps ones made by her own hand – wallpapers or framed window views whose source in nature or art remain tantalisingly ambiguous. Domiciled in Port Isaac (1975–82), Falmouth (1982–5), St Ives (1985–2005) and finally Penzance King makes oblique, distanced references to environment. A modest yet successful exhibitor, King displays work in local galleries as well as at the Royal Academy, London.

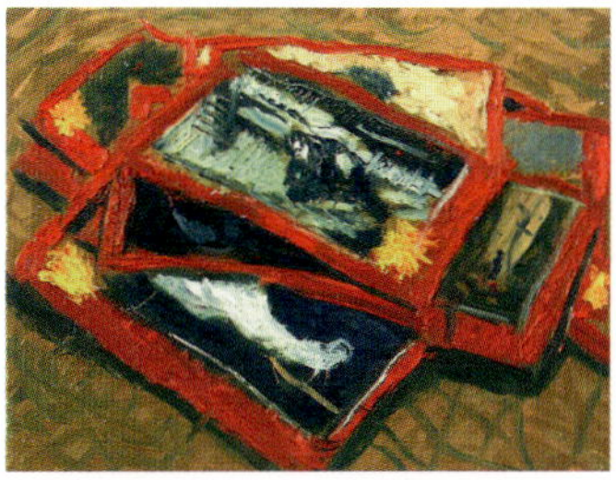

Michael Broughton
Star Wars Cards Pile
2007, oil on board
courtesy: Belgrave Gallery, St Ives

Pat Algar (b. 1939) also favours intimate domestic settings with a window view but models paint in a freer impressionistic way to reach focus and definition. Trained at the Royal Academy Schools under the portrait painter Peter Greenham in the early 1960s, Algar follows mentors like Sickert and Bonnard – taking realism from the former and striking colour from the latter – to produce a compelling mix of control and exuberance. After a move from St Ives to Marazion, Algar introduced imagery of sloping gardens with views of the Mount beyond.

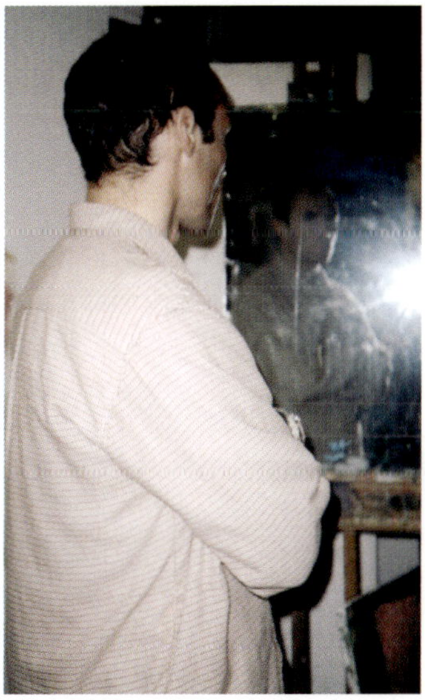

Michael Broughton in his Falmouth Studio, 2006
Photograph: Peter Davies

The Falmouth-trained Michael Broughton (b. 1977) uses an element of still life painting – the interior with window, table and furniture – as a metaphor of introspective privacy where what he calls 'compressed memories' abound. These empty, anonymous, souless rooms compensate for a lack of charm, ornament or habitation with a painterly tactility that gets to grip with the problem of physical reality and space. Broughton's banal themes attain iconic status through surface, amplified scale and the conceptual elevation of the mundane and familiar, the results being like hybrids of 1950s British 'kitchen sink' and 1970's American 'New Image' painting. Variously influenced at Falmouth by the limpid or loudly coloured impastoed landscapes of Richard Cook and Ray Atkins, or the interiors of Mary Mabbut, Broughton developed impasto as part of paint's plastic and allusive double life. The limpid light of gloomy, empty interiors, some institutional others domestic, express a psychological matrix, the imagery processed more through memory and the sieve of consciousness than through direct observation. The existential concerns of both post war realism and abstraction is adopted as Broughton, born into an age of post modern malaise and late hippie angst, seeks to interprete the world in terms of the self. A Falmouth student thesis on Leon Kossoff, with whom he corresponded, set the course for his painterly interpretations of experience.

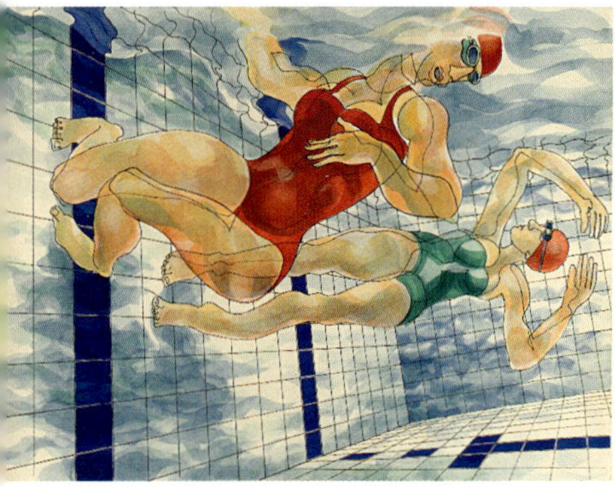

Roy Walker
Swimmers
1978, watercolour
courtesy: Vince Walker

Roy Walker (1936–2001) and Bryan Ingham (1936–97) used still life as a vehicle for post-cubist formal analysis and investigation. Walker used the medium of watercolour or etching to do this yielding a prolific series of fruit bowl subjects, a little known aspect of his large 'oeuvre'. Trained at Gravesend, Regents Street Poly and the Central School in the 1950s Walker did National Service in the RAF before working first in automobile factories and finally, after moving in early 1966 to St Ives, for a local metal fabrication firm. These experiences inevitably informed abstracted and flattened-out compositions of automobile or mechanical forms. Despite their softer nature the still lifes continue the use of flat, schematised design and rhythmic silhouette.

The still life or auto etchings were displayed at a 1974 Marlborough Graphics exhibition in London – arguably his most significant lifetime display – which the critic Pat Gilmour described as revealing 'a certain linear effortless'. (12) Also in evidence were texturing skills. The mechanical process of printmaking suited a temperament which sought integral effects proper to the medium that could also express feelings related to the subject at hand. The steel plate used in preference to the more usual zinc or copper allowed the emergence of what he called 'infinite blacks,' those velvety and saturated inks that absorbed light and highlighted through stark tonal contrast the middle and high tones of adjacent areas. The use of steel made Walker 'most certainly a master' according to Gilmour and had a personal ring relating to his industrial jobs while anticipating the more

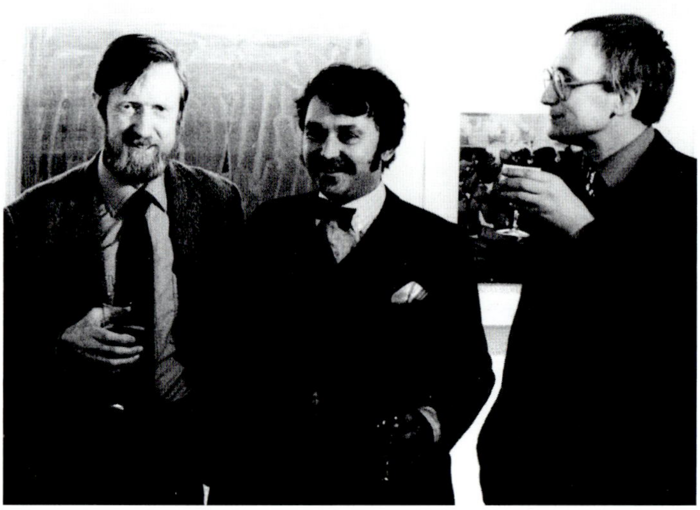

Bryan Ingham (centre)
with Bob Crossley and
Patrick Hughes at the Penwith
Galleries (1970s)

experimental metal reliefs and environmental sculpture produced during the 1980s and early 1990s,

Yorkshire-born Bryan Ingham also excelled at etching a medium used to explore, in styles indebted to the three main phases of cubism, still life. Ingham's attraction to still life as an apt arena for formal investigation relies on the iconographic neutrality and unassuming ambience of familiar functional objects. In concert with Cornish tradition the jugs, mugs and bottles create counterpoint against a landscape backdrop, often that of the Lizard peninsular where he lived and worked after moving to Cornwall from London in 1972. In London he studied first at St Martins and then at the RCA during the early 1960s. The level of formal analysis, where heightened appreciation of the three dimensional identity of objects posited in hermetic, domestic space suggest sculptural possibilities led, Ingham into relief carving. What Mel Gooding terms a 'predisposition to the sculptural'(13) in Ingham's work is borne out by the artist's description of his habit of 'carving and quarrying' the etching plates. Through this self confessed 'combination of bravura, chance and experience'(14) Ingham created breadth of linear and depth of textural effects that impart 'rococo' richness and decorative density.

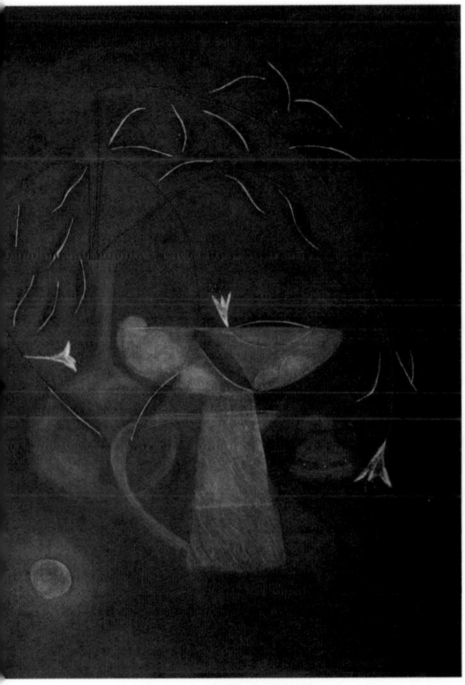

Jane O'Malley
Still Life at Dusk – Bahamas
2006
oil on board
courtesy: Stour Gallery

A brittle precision co-exists with rich, deep or saturated colour in the stylised still lifes of Jane Harris O'Malley (b. 1944), a Canadian-born painter who lived in St Ives after marrying Tony O'Malley in 1973. Between 1973 and 1990, when the couple moved to Eire, O'Malley exhibited locally, the pictures exuding a sharp, clean cut sophistication in keeping with the strong, clear light and defined profiles of the environment. The colour, however, is informed by annual visits to the Caribbean, where she had relatives, that alleviated Cornish winters. There was also interaction, even collaboration, between members of a husband and wife team who shared a large beachside Porthmeor studio and used common stylistic devices like razor incisions that created tactile surface pattern and linear striation.

The recurring interface between exterior and domestic worlds in Cornish still life provides an arena for graphic punning and playful exuberance in the paintings and related screenprints featuring rainbows by Patrick Hughes (b. 1939). At the instigation of Terry Frost Hughes moved in 1974 from London and lived in Cornwall until 1979 where he formed a showbiz-like double act with his then partner the writer Molly Parkin. The mix of 'pop', urban and commercial elements in Hughes' work – extended even into performance where his partnership with Parkin was concerned – was not at odds with St Ives' eclectic post modern phase which, in any case, struck a chord with a latent erstwhile strain of conceptual and surreal wit in the later work of Lanyon, Wynter and Hilton.

Hughes' work, moreover, drew obliquely on Cornish references, images of a Rediffusion-like sun propped against grey and blue walls in *My Sun's Holiday* (1980), a D'Arcangeloesque roadway in *Deja Vu* (1976) suggesting the long westbound car journey to Cornwall or the piercing entry of light through his Porthmeor studio windows in *Rainbow Coming In* (1975) conjuring what he termed an almost obligatory 'poetic response to country'.[15] In similar fashion Hughes responded to his early 1980's domicile at the Chelsea Hotel, New York in terms of architectural and skyscraper imagery. With a distinctly surreal 'take' on the nature of artifice and reality Hughes – who lived next door to the arch surrealist Conroy Maddox in Belsize Park during the 1990s – transforms fugitive, elusive phenomena like rainbows and passing light into objects of palpable solidity which, in the words of Brian Smith author of *Behind the Rainbow* (1983), 'contradict reality by showing a transitory phenomenon as a substantial object, capable of being wrapped, carried, given as gifts'[16]. *Sunshine* (1974) and *Darkness Falls* (1976) achieves this invasion of day or night into interior recesses delineated with the precision of Jeffrey Edwards, Patrick Caulfield or Michael Craig-Martin.

The rainbows of the 1970s captured the popular imagination while retaining private or autobiographical resonance, the still life *Angela's Flowers* (1977) substituting flowers for a bunch of rainbows in homage to his London dealer since 1970, Angela Flowers. Hughes' sophisticated trompe l'œil distortions and Magrittean perspectival parodies underline the subjective nature of vision in a manner effortlessly

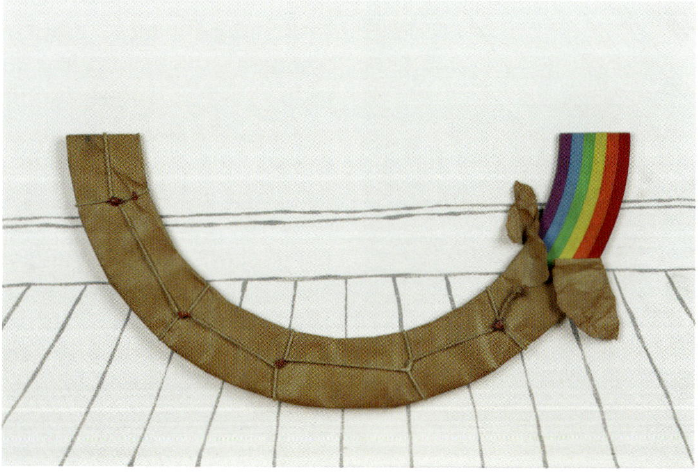

Patrick Hughes
Perfect Present, 1983
oil and collage
courtesy:
Katharine House Gallery, Marlborough

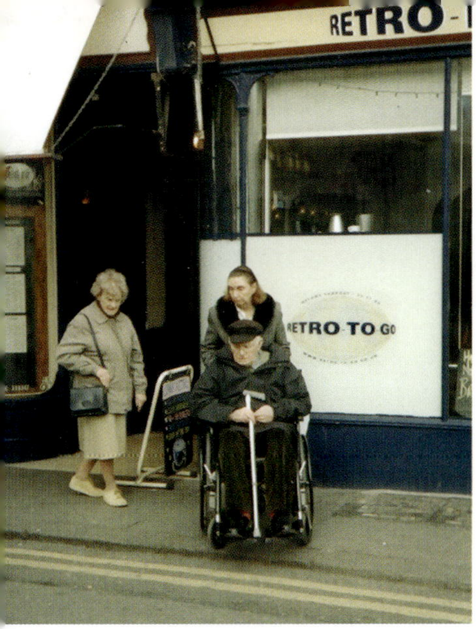

Bryan Pearce in York Street, Bath before his retrospective at the Victoria Art Gallery, April 2004.
photograph: Peter Davies

achieved in the very different context of Bryan Pearce's innocent and idiosyncratic art. While sharing with Hughes a gestalt of direct and immediate perception relayed through basic delineation and flat, striking colour the unselfconscious work of Pearce contains none of Hughes' artiness and urban dandyism. Pearce is a slave to circumstance, the external 'given' of a lifelong environment – his native St Ives – complemented by a skewed vision and impaired technique that is the result of his suffering since childhood from the rare cerebral disease phenylketonuria. With a frank fatalism Peter Lanyon wrote early on that 'it is necessary to accept these works as the labour of a man who has to communicate this way because there is no other'.

Pearce, who studied under the paternal guidance of the portrait painter Leonard Fuller at the St Ives School of Painting (1953–57) evolved his unwitting style – characterised in the mature work by an emblematic flatness of pattern and an unmodulated, bright palette uncannily evoking the clean, unpolluted environment of St Ives – from unbelievably stiff but appealingly simple early still life watercolours. The key to what Alan Bowness described as a later 'great sureness of touch and sensitivity to colour' was the discipline and rigour of a regular nine-to-five studio routine. The early success of Penwith Society displays, a 1959 solo exhibition at Newlyn Art Gallery and entry into the 1961 John Moores biannual in Liverpool vindicated the belief and support of his mother Mary and painters Shearer Armstrong and Misome Peile. Together with Ruth Jones, Marion Whybrow and Janet Axten, later authors of books on Pearce,[17] these women formed a strong maternal support system around a vulnerable artist's slow but inexorable rise to commercial success and prominence.

The popularity of Pearce's unaffected and colourful landscape or still life paintings was reflected in successful exhibitions at the New Art Centre, London during the late 1960s and early 1970s. These culminated in a 1975 MOMA, Oxford retrospective and later important solos at Royal Cornwall Museum, Truro in 2000 and Victoria Art Gallery, Bath in 2004. After a 1967 move into the new beachfront Piazza flats Pearce crafted still lifes against Porthmeor window views yielding pictures that contribute to a Cornish tradition of composite still life/landscape.

The art historical significance of still life as a vehicle for experiment and innovation is not lost on Chris Insoll (b. 1956), an erudite Chelsea-trained painter who, since settling in Portscatho during the early 1980s, has martialled his verstile talents into painting, dealing, writing, forming an art society (the Portscatho Society of Artists founded in

1984) and running a gallery, the New Gallery in Portscatho. The catalogue essayist, Sarah Drury, wrote for his exhibition of still lifes 'Paintings about Painting' at Falmouth Art Gallery in 2001 that the genre for Insoll 'is as much about formal innovation, subversion and playfulness as pictorial illusion'.(18) Insoll's formal innovation is however limited to a discrete play with those manifold domestic objects Drury calls 'the teeming carnival of the studio'. This historically-aware artist (he turned down the opportunity to study art history under Norbert Lynton at Sussex University in order to pursue the preferred option of painting) makes reference to past masters not stylistically – though what Drury describes as a 'sinuous, slightly nervy line' has, on occasion, yielded Braquian post-cubist compositions of spatially probing interplay between line and superimposed or interpenetrating planes of colour – but rather through the literal device of featuring postcards, prints or reproductions of their work as part of the richly detailed and ornate cornucopia of cluttered interior, window and still life subjects.

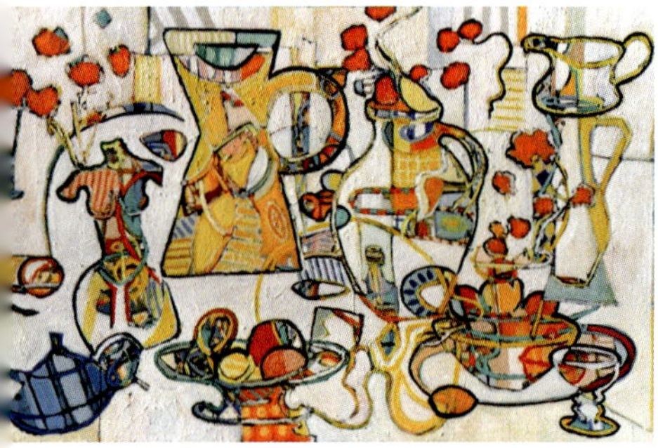

Chris Insoll
The White Still Life
2002/03, oil on canvas
courtesy of the artist

Insoll's rich colour and decorative verve lends stylistic kinship to John Bratby and Duncan Grant and there is something of both 'kitchen sink' and Bloomsbury tendencies in the frank everyday sumptuousness of his observations. Visits to John Piper and Henry Moore encouraged, rather than informed, the direction of work which benefited more from extra mural painting excursions with the Chelsea tutor Patrick Symons. The work of Picasso, Poussin, Phillipson and Braque are among those paraphrased and quoted. The English painter also paints 'plein air' landscapes on the Roseland coast, the St Ives painter and one-time harbour-master Eric Ward stopping over once a week to pursue plein air painting on the very different south coast near Portscatho. This informal, convivial interaction typifies the co-operative nature of the Portscatho enterprise and Insoll's 2006 book *Portscatho: Portrait of a Cornish Art Colony*(19) celebrated other working colleagues – among them Lynn Golden, Trevor Felcey, Grace Gardiner, Michael Stone as well as Ward – who have bought Insoll's dream of artistic kinship to fruition.

Chapter Six

GREAT ATLANTIC BLUES

It is well documented almost to the point of truism that the light of the Penwith peninsular contributed, among other factors, to the establishment of an impressionistic tradition of landscape painting. Endemic to this tradition was a use of 'plein air' techniques and 'realist' subjects. Seasonal contrast, climatic vicissitude and a changing economic infrastructure that saw traditional industries like mining and fishing replaced by tourism inspired varied artistic responses ranging from the tonal exactitude of the Newlyn School to the colourism of the inter-war St Ives painters. Anecdotal, picturesque or genre depictions of harbour bustle or beachside reverie reflected this economic shift. By the late twentieth century and beyond, however, a more generalised treatment using the 'pure' elements of sea and sky pointed to a new age transcendentalism appropriate to the post-industrial, post modern age. Artists sought solace from globalisation and other fin-de-siècle ills through another universal the natural sublime. These painters also betrayed the legacy of modernism in minimal canvases that, in terms of uniform areas of sublime or atmospheric colour, were almost abstract.

John Miller (1931–2002), a deceptively sophisticated landscape painter whose tranquil, monochromatic azure or ruddy depictions of St Ives Bay or the Mediterranean in high summer were made into best-selling poster prints in High Street art shops across Britain,certainly used landscape as a vehicle for the expression of tacit religious instincts. Studying after the war in Croydon and then central London, Miller worked as an architectural designer for Church architects. Later, in 1991, he became a member of Truro Cathedral Fabric Advisory Committee and became a Lay Canon there, duties that accompanied his chairmanship of the Newlyn Society of Artists in the 1960s and trusteeship of the Newlyn Orion Gallery during the 1980s. He submitted designs for the Passmore Edwards Gallery's first modernisation programme in 1968.

Moving with the potter Michael Truscott to Cornwall in 1958, Miller lived at Sancreed until a love of St Ives Bay took him, in 1995, to a house on the Hayle Estuary where he lived with Truscott for the remaining years. Here the impressive curvature of Hayle sands and the blue maritime expanses of the Bay inspired pictures built with subtle glazes of closely toned colour, often of a deep unfathomable mystery, that gave a contemplative stillness and depth to minimal-like canvases. Absorbed by the spectre of sunset over distinct yet intangible horizons, Miller produced symbolism of a personal or religious kind. After the death of his mother in 1988, for example, Miller produced an 'Interior Landscape' series in which a single diminutive figure floated like an apparition.

Frequent travels yielded Greek, Venetian, Tuscan, Egyptian and ultimately Goan motifs, his architectural interests surfacing again in accomplished compositions of San Gimignano's tall towers that contrast with the hazy indistinct atmosphere of Cornish, Scillonian or Mediterranean landscapes. Miller's changing output was the subject of thematic displays at Messums, his London dealers throughout the 1980s and 1990s. In 1999 he joined the Portland Gallery, London where he had two lifetime shows. A posthumous retrospective at Penlee, Penzance followed in 2005.

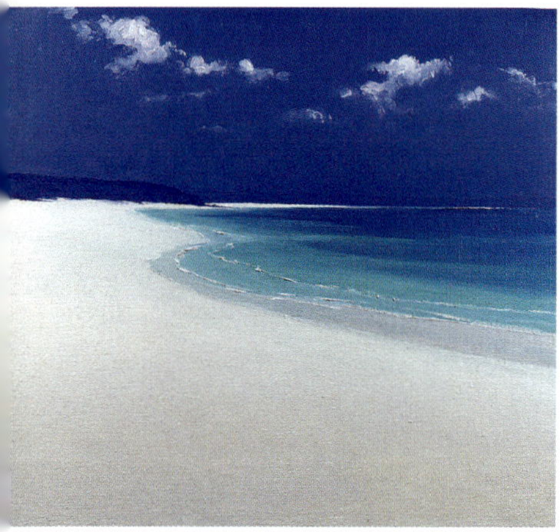

John Miller
Towards Trencrom - St Ives
oil on canvas
courtesy David Messum

Miller Blue also appears in the equally contemplative canvases of Tom Rickman (b. 1960), a Mousehole-based painter who trained at Epsom School of Art and came to Cornwall from Dorset in 1992. Rickman's preoccupation is unquestionably with that short time frame between sunset and nightfall when the dying light of dusk yields an array of deep dense colour. 'The air, atmosphere and space,' Rickman explains 'become charged with vibrant colour as the evening starts to merge towards nightfall'. The practical difficulty of painting in front of such dark and transitory subjects compels the artist to make rapid colour notes which, together with the faculty of memory, leads to studio compositions whose large scale enveloping abstraction is punctuated with vivid visual events such as sunsets, cloud bursts and the like, events that jolt the viewer back into a world of credible naturalisim.

The spiritual implications of Rickman's remark that in this 'external dimness there seems an internal clarity' speaks less of Millerian religiosity than of an introspective, even melancholic, temperament in tune with the silent but unlimited mystery of the Atlantic seaboard, the Scottish Highlands or Venetian lagoons that have inspired him. His numerous solo shows at such venues as Gallery Tresco, Scilly Isles, the Salthouse, St Ives, Thomas Henry Fine Art, London or the Great Atlantic Works Gallery, St Just, attest to thematic consistency within changing locations. The latter gallery produced a catalogue *On the Edge of Twilight* (2002) with a written endorsement by Miller of Rickman's preoccupations.

Neil Pinkett (b. 1958), a Penwith-born painter who, like Rickman, was commissioned to produce pictures for the Cunard liner *Q.M. II* and was similarly featured in the Great Atlantic Works catalogue series, prefers the elevated topographic viewpoint; he captures the play of light on the coves, rocks, inlets and small harbours of the Penwith coastline. A training in illustration saw several years in design and advertising in Bristol followed by a return to Cornwall. Several thematic exhibitions in St Just focused on specific places like Lamorna or the Scillies and see Pinkett's characteristic use of the palette knife to create iconic structures based on pier, cliff or tree motifs.

Mike Hindle (b. 1966) also creates contemplative images of Atlantic sunsets using Rickman's recurring low horizon to concentrate on spectrum-like skies; once again the inadvertent abstract implications of bands of prismatic colour invites comparison with Heron's stripe paintings of 1957–8. In a catalogue for a solo show at Great Atlantic Works in 2003 Chloe Wild spoke of 'quiet sobriety . . . a sense of calm . . . a response to slow down'.(1) A featured series based on Godrevy and Hayle sands was a reminder of Miller. Studying during the 1980s at art schools in Hastings and Farnham, Hindle went on to enjoy successful solo shows at Trelissick Gallery, Feock and at Gallery Tresco.

This gallery also features prominently in Richard Pearce's career. The 'John Miller of the Scilly Isles,' this native Scillonian took up the brush in the early 1990s going on to enjoy commercial success both at home, where his work provides holiday momentos for seasonal visitors to the Islands, and at the Great Atlantic Works on the mainland where a maiden solo show in March 2002 was a sell out. A lavishly illustrated catalogue *Island Dream* (2003) followed. Reproducing pictures like *Scilly Blue* or *Sansom Blue* the publication highlighted the way Pearce captures the timeless quality of the sub-tropical paradise in high summer. He subverted this Millerian theme in terms of textural embellishments like speckled overlays of light spots of paint or rolled 'ribbons' of white, the former describing the silver sunlight on the sea the latter shafts of light or wisps of cloud. The curved beaches, sand bars, broken islets, coves and promontories provide endless topographic variety.

Like Pearce Benjamin Warner (b. 1970) is native Cornish but exchanges the exposed Atlantic in intense summer colour for the sheltered tranquility of creeks, river inlets and meadows that abound between Truro and Falmouth. Warner's are tonally subdued pictures alert to subtle atmospheric effects or flashes of silver on the river during dimly-lit days. They possess the soft focus of the Welsh painter Harry Holland's interiors but are offset by tactile impasto in the muddy foreground. This region of 'wellies' and 'anoraks' is a Cornish world apart from the wet suits and wind breaks of the seaboard in summer. Trained as an illustrator at Falmouth, Warner worked in London as a

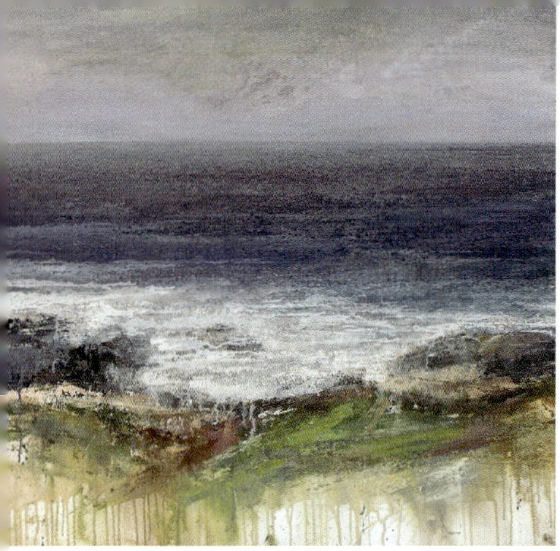

Benjamin Warner
Seaward
oil on board

designer in the 1990s before returning to Cornwall to paint full-time.

Associated with what was formerly the all-woman Art Space Gallery on the St Ives harbour front, a space founded in 2000, Helen Atkins, Lesley Ninnes, Annie Metcalfe, Angela Diggle, Chris Allen, Sadie Wyatt and Mike Hindle continue this exploration into the marine landscape. Though a native of St Ives Ninnes began painting while living in the Caribbean for a decade; her high-pitched naturalism focuses on St Ives Bay while Atkins employs the intensity of blues in sea and sky. Metcalfe betrays a Scottish robustness in rugged coastal landscapes. Here the violent interaction of sea and rock is evoked through vigorous expressionistic handling and sharp accents of colour.

Paul Lewin (b. 1974) was the Great Atlantic Works' first gallery director. He studied in Stockport and Bristol, lived in west Penwith throughout the 1990s and later moved to north Devon. Lewin's art resides, in the words of poet Christine Evans, 'where the frontiers between land and sea are blurred'. There is nothing blurred or mysterious in his creations that carry the vivid credence of protracted observation. Lewin's work is, therefore, subjected as much to the changing whims of natural light and weather as to the subjective and interpretative mood of the artist who frequently 'tidies' up 'plein air' work in the studio. Lewin's large, closely observed compositions celebrate the 'quiver of the moment' occasioned by the crash of wave or sudden shaft of light. He has also depicted coastal landscapes beyond Cornwall, painting on remote islands such as Nantucket (USA), Bardsy (Wales), Orkney (Scotland), Lundy (Devon) and Scilly (Cornwall).

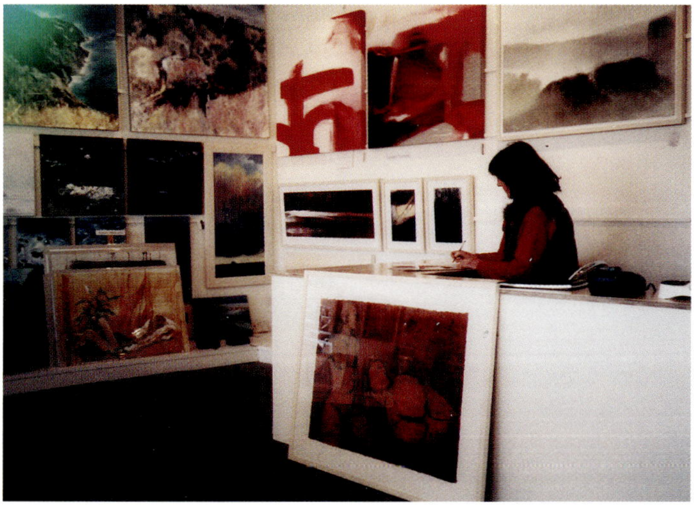

Lesley Ninnes at the Art Space Gallery, the Wharf, St Ives, 2007. Works by Ges Wilson, Annie Metcalfe and Ninnes are visible.
Photograph: Peter Davies

Robert Jones (b. 1943) depicts a choppier sea, its energetic and elusive movements often directly captured 'en plein air' from the deck of a ship several miles from shore. His is a more physical vision using expressive, thick and rapidly applied paint. Jones' unrelenting reportage, later subjected to studio revisions, yields an authentic seascape that links to a heroic tradition of Cornish maritime painting personified by Napier-Hemy, Moore, Olsson and Smart. In this context Jones' participation in historical surveys such as Truro Museum's 'A Century of Art in Cornwall'(1989) or the Tate's 'Porthmeor Beach, A Century of Images'(1995) seems entirely appropriate. Accompanying this body of work is the renowned topographic view capturing the play of light on mirror-like seas safely observed from elevated cliff-top vantage points around the Cornish coast.

The painter Robert Organ, a tutor at Falmouth College of Art where Jones studied during the early 1960s, wrote of a 'thrilling effusion of light, surging movement and flux' in the catalogue for Jones' large Penwith Gallery exhibition in 1997. This Newquay-born home-grown talent identified his Cornishness with Alfred Wallis whose work inspired Jones to write a book.(2) Like Wallis, Jones looked beyond Cornwall for subjects and so the pinks and browns of the Bristol Channel or the intense blues of the Mediterranean feature alongside the frothy green greys of the Atlantic. The occurence of tree or gorse bush subjects indicate a pantheism at the heart of Jones' vision which sees nature as an outwardly vital phenomenon calling for a descriptive, rather than analytical, naturalism.

A descriptive naturalism also characterises Kurt Jackson's coastal landscapes which add coarse materials like sand, grit, netting and other beachside debris as collage elements. Unlike Terry Setch in Cardiff, however, Jackson incorporates extraneous materials not for abstract ends but to enhance the descriptive 'realism' of the subject. While adding physical weight and literalness Jackson's collage does not gel; throughout modern art the 'objet trouvé' functioned as a conceptual or abstract device, mitigating the mimetic role of illusionist painting while promoting the physical autonomy of the art work as a constructed object in its own right. Jackson's use of collage for descriptive ends therefore adds a faint air of Disneyesque tinsel or trompe l'oeil gimmickry. Perhaps it is just this, as much as an obvious ability with drawing and tone, that led to spectacular commercial success. Like Miller Jackson was propelled by the Messum Gallery in London which provided the springboard for auxiliary solo shows in Cornish public museums in Truro, Falmouth and Newlyn.

Born in Dorset in 1961, Jackson studied zoology in Oxford before settling as a full-time painter in Cornwall. Inspired like his contemporaries by the Tate Millbank show 'St Ives 1939–64' in 1985, Jackson trod new ground with landscape painting that reinvigorated the conservative idea of representational literalism. In its large scale and textured impressionism Jackson's painting travels alongside the 'new' expressionism of the 1980s and beyond. The use of scribbled words is another contemporary affectation, a reminder of a poetic narrative or diary-like romanticism; the words 'catch a wave' appear in pencil in the picture of the same name made famous through its reproduction on the cover of Tom Cross' book on late twentieth century Cornish art.(3)

In Lieke Ritman's beachscapes and marine compositions collage – in her case sand and other thickening agents – is used as a discrete and endemic part of the painted surface. By using an area of ribbed sand or wind rippled water as subject-matter Ritman creates a composition of abstract, rather than topographic, pattern. The dry paint texture, evocative palette and rhythmic energy is however site specific. Born in Holland in 1942, she spent her childhood in Australia where interest in art was kindled through studying Interior Design. She visited Britain during the 1960s and, inspired by a friendship with Douglas Portway, settled in St Ives in 1969. Supporting herself during the 1970s by picture framing for St Ives artists, many of whom became friends, Ritman had, by the late 1980s, become a full-time painter, enjoying solo shows at the Penwith, Plumbline and Rainyday galleries. Through their physical execution, Ritman's pictures identify with the processes of nature and so become generic records of the interaction of sea and sand.

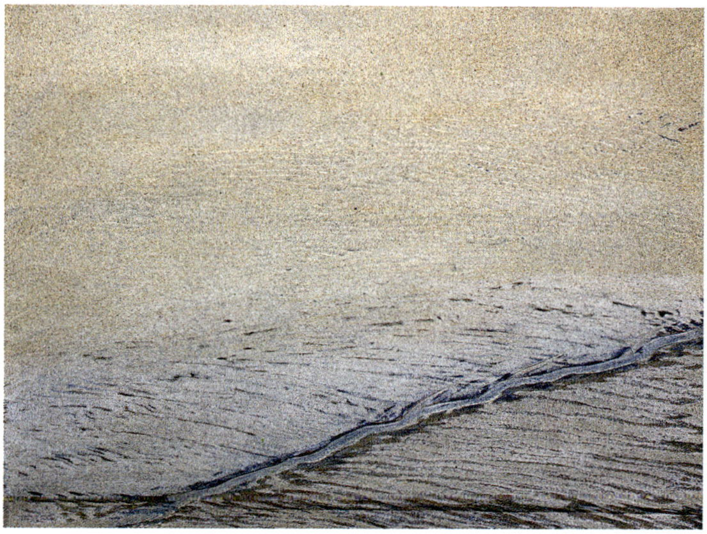

Lieke Ritman
Sand Channel, 2003
oil on board
courtesy of the artist

Where Ritman's beachscapes depart from the Boyle family's super real facsimiles of pavements and Holland Park Road surfaces by using 'real' rather than synthetic materials (in her case sand) Chris Hankey's animated paintings of turbulent seas in stormy weather use loaded pigment to express what he terms 'a deeply profound interconnection between consciousness and nature'. Hankey's gesturalism recalls Joan Eardley's late Catterline canvases and like Eardley Hankey paints the incoming sea head on. Winter skies with faint pinprick suns add to the desolate mood. Discriminating between the light of consciousness and that of nature Hankey expresses what he describes as 'the creative fluid interaction between light, sea, weather and mind'. Born in Lancashire in 1963 and trained in Wolverhampton and later Wales, Hankey moved to Cornwall only in 2003, his destiny as a Cornish-based painter established by solo shows at Rainyday Gallery, Penzance.

A more studied 'contre jour' impressionism characterises the beach scenes and harbour subjects by a much better known painter Ken Howard R.A. Howard captures the play of light on objects and from this tonal order he creates formal definition and credence. An Official War Artist in Ulster and Cyprus during the early 1970s, Howard is an experienced painter with the gift of the graphic gab. A Londoner with family connections to Cornwall, Howard acquired St Clements Hall, Mousehole in 1986 which he uses as a part-time studio alternative to William Orpen's former studio in Kensington. A retrospective at Plymouth Art Gallery in 1972 confirmed a westcountry identity. Since that time Howard's ubiquitous pictures at the Royal Academy in the summer, in the auction room or at solo shows with Richard Green, his main London dealer, have consolidated his reputation. The cluster of fishing boats in Newlyn harbour, the windbreakers at Sennen and other Cornish beaches in high summer and the figures playing beach sport have shown Howard's deft mastery of complex detail through a simplicity of painterly means. These subjects also contrast with the trademark studio interiors and nudes on draped furniture that issue from his London studio. Howard's high pitch retro impressionism brings a pre-war tradition into the modern era offering a popular and viable alternative to trendy contemporary imperatives.

The popularity enjoyed by Howard, Miller and several among the young generation featured here reflects the growing appetite for art among the public. The British taste for the romantic sublime is part fulfilled by these safe stylised images; the easy visual appeal of perfectly crafted, even virtuoso pictures whose impact is as immediate and captivating as it is unchallenging fills a gap left vacant by the avant garde awkward squad. The way many of these painters appease conservative taste is symptomatic of both strength and weakness. In the increasingly market-driven economy of the post 1975 world these painters have often enjoyed pronounced commercial appeal. Despite, or perhaps because of, this they have either dropped out of design and illustration careers in the city and set up as viable full-time painters in Cornwall or expressly sought an artistic style that in its homage to nature and the unbounded sublime accompanies an alternative lifestyle on the geographic if not cultural edge.

Chapter Seven

POTTERS SINCE LEACH

The development of studio pottery in Cornwall since 1920, when Bernard Leach and Shoji Hamada returned from Japan and set up a working pottery at the top of St Ives, has both conformed to, and diverged from, the anglo-oriental Leach tradition. By the outbreak of World War Two, when St Ives witnessed an international modernist influx of artists, sculptors as well as painters, this pottery had established itself as a productive workshop dedicated to traditional craft standards, to an aesthetic that merged indigenous country slipware with imported oriental influences and to a balanced output between functional ware and the rarified 'art' pot.

The art pot called into question the status of studio pottery as an art or a craft activity, a vexed issue that would come to the fore of post war debate in St Ives. During the inter-war years the Leach pottery functioned within a congenial, non-hierachical community, made up of late impressionist marine or landscape painters. This would change in the avant garde colony of the late 1940s, when the role of the artist potter suddenly became problematic to the extent that the newly formed Penwith Society of Arts introduced contentious selection criteria for exhibitions that discriminated between abstract and representational art and craft. Seen as divisive and prejudicial, the system contributed to the dissension and resignations that blighted the early history of the Penwith.

In many ways Leach himself was ideally suited to adopt an even-handed position in this debate. A temperamental modesty and affability, underscored by exotic religious convictions fitted well with the utopian or Christian Science beliefs of modernist artists like Nicholson, Hepworth and Gabo. During the 1940s he fraternised with them. Furthermore his employment of younger artists like Heron, Berlin, Mitchell and Leigh demonstrated the relevance of the ceramic object to both painting and sculpture. Heron's 1952 *New Statesman* essay *A Master Potter's Aesthetic* discussed these ties. Leach's Slade background, where he mastered etching and the watercolour sketch, made him the artist potter par excellence.

Consistent with his absorption into the cult of 'mingei', or the unknown master craftsman – a cult that perhaps sprung also from the notion of Zen selflessness – Leach did, on the other hand, resist grandiose and ego-driven claims about the 'high' art status of pottery. The critic Peter Fuller was, therefore, able to write in 1983 that 'the great strength of the Leach tradition was that it recognised that in the making of studio pottery, some sort of radical rupture with one-dimensional Modernism was essential'. Arguing that its enduring creative appeal lay in continued adherence to conventional function and traditional craft standard, Fuller went on to declare that studio pottery 'had constantly to proclaim its essentially conservative character'.[1]

From the vantage point of the Millennium, when the future of the Leach Pottery as a viable and ongoing educational and commercial resource is in the process of being secured, the legacy of Leach is one that transformed a historically and geographically disadvantageous region into a major centre for ceramic practise in Britain outstripping even more traditional and established locations such as north Devon or Staffordshire. The lack of trees or a Fremington like clay bed in south-west Cornwall was overcome, yielding generations of working potters who, in tandem with the painters, made up the majority of practising artists around St Ives.

Leach's last years, marked by dwindling production and attention to his legacy, were blighted by the onset of blindness in the mid-1970s. The small lidded pots with three feet, described by Emmanuel Cooper as 'finely balanced resonant forms'[2] were the last he made. After 1973 he turned his attention to travelling – a last trip to Japan would take place in June 1975 – writing, lecturing, attending conferences or communicating with students and potters, whom he often entertained in the evening in his beachside Barnaloft flat. Protecting his legacy clearly meant upholding values and defending principles; Cooper explained that Leach stressed 'the increasing need for potters to work 'from the heart'.'[3]

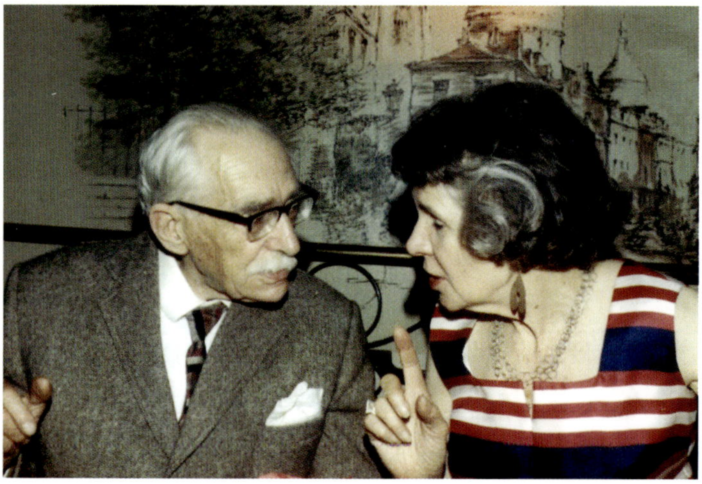

Bernard Leach
with Marjorie Parr,
Chelsea, 1972

During the 1970s, therefore, Leach was ideologically, if not productively, active, protecting and promulgating his vision of creative handmade wares. The publications of the period, such as *Drawings, Verse and Belief*, a limited edition book of poems, related sketches and pronouncements about his Baha'i faith, *Hamada, Potter* (1975), reprints of *A Potters Book* (1940) and *A Potters Portfolio* (1951) and most significantly *Beyond East and West* (1978), a collection of memoirs and essays, helped achieve these ends. Perhaps symptomatic of Leach's cerebral, intellectual side, the same care and attention was not given to the Stennack site whose financial history had been a precarious one.

Continuing throughout the 1980s and 1990s its fate fell into the hands of first Leach's widow Janet, then of her partner Mary 'Boots' Redgrave, both of whom were responsible for the short term folly of 'selling the family silver'. The property was sold by Redgrave to a local businessman Alan Gillam, whose commercial interests were tempered by a desire to safeguard the heritage status of the site. To that end The Leach Pottery Restoration Project was set up with the aim of 'rescuing the pottery and bringing it into public ownership'.[4] Chaired by Lady Carol Holland the project was led by Penwith District Council with support from many regional and national bodies. Over half the £1 million target was provided by a Heritage Lottery Fund Grant with a further grant, nearly £½ million, from the European Regional Development Fund in January 2006 securing the pottery's future.

Various attempts, some successful some not, were made during the late 1970s to kick start the workshop. Janet Leach, who installed a gas-fired kiln, continued working there. A showroom was created and Byron Temple was appointed manager and unsuccessful attempts to redesign Leach standard ware were made. Younger potters like Trevor Corser, Jason Wason, John Bedding and Nic Harrison were committed makers whose links to the Pottery would endure, Corser working on at the Stennack past the deaths of Janet Leach and Redgrave, Bedding later fundraising for the Restoration Project.

The Oldham-born Trevor Corser, who moved to St Ives in 1964 and worked part time at the Pottery after Bryan Illsley's departure, became sitting potter for the next forty years. Joining as an untrained assistant on standard ware production Corser learnt through trial and error and observing Tim Stampton, John Reeve, Elizabeth Heinz and others. Corser's education also included 'crits' from the man himself who visited the workshop most afternoons. By the late 1960s Corser, now full time, was making both standard ware and individual pots, among which were tea bowls and other small vessels. These have a firm unpretentious earthiness, the monochromatic celadon, tenmoku, ash or shino glazes enhancing the basic shapes and keeping decorative distractions to a minimum.

Another northerner, the Liverpudlian Jason Wason became a part time assistant at the Leach Pottery after moving to Cornwall in 1976. At this late stage Wason's dialogue with Leach, now blind, was restricted to weekly suppers at the latter's flat. This contact was as important as reading 'A Potters Book'. Wason's background was one of itinerant and pragmatic self sufficiency; he taught himself pottery during the years living on a Scottish commune. The forms his large and rhythmically handled mature vessels would take – Coperian sculptural shapes that in terms of a bold finesse depart from Leach's refined orientalism – reflected Wason's identification with the primitive shapes of ethnically diverse pots encountered during travels in Britain (for example ancient Celtic ironwork with intricate surface pattern) and in Africa and the Far East.

Wason's spacious vessels and square or round plates are decorated not with slips or glazes but with incised lines or snake skin textures; the dry metallic surfaces, which result from grogged recipes and unrefined metal oxide powders 'found' below Geevor near to his St Just base, impart a sculptural rather than ceramic feel. The interplay between smoothly burnished and incised surfaces or again between tapering or bulbous form promotes a feeling of classical balance. Dark carbonated surfaces are the outcome of 'raku', a process notable in a first exhibition with Austin/Desmond, his London dealers, in the late 1980s.

John Bedding, a Londoner, moved to Cornwall in 1967. He worked in a south London industrial pottery, an unsatisfactory and perfunctory beginning that required further studies at John Cass College where he learnt to throw. Bedding went on to St Ives, engaging in an eclectic set of ceramic practises. He worked at Anthony Richards' Arch Pottery in the Digey, moved on to the Troika pottery under Leslie Illsley and Benny Sirota and ended at the Leach Pottery where William Marshall 'taught' him. Like Corser and Wason he benefited from regular contact with Leach. In 1971 Bedding worked under Jean Tessier at St Aube in France where his knowledge of wood firing developed. Upon returning to St Ives Bedding became a full timer at the Leach Pottery until 1978 when, aided by money from sales, he was sent by the Pottery on an educational tour of Japan that lasted until 1980. A reaction against Leach orthodoxy characterised his work during the 1980s. Individual forms reflected non-ceramic influences like armour, textiles, gravestones and lacquer work all of which Bedding picked up on in Japan. Wheel thrown and hand-built forms were transformed into quasi sculptures which embodied subtle colour surfaces. A move in 1989 from Trencom into St Ives ushered in the era of Bedding's entrepreneurship when he opened first St Ives Ceramics (1990) then Goalyard Studios (1998), a centrally-placed multi-purpose studio complex.

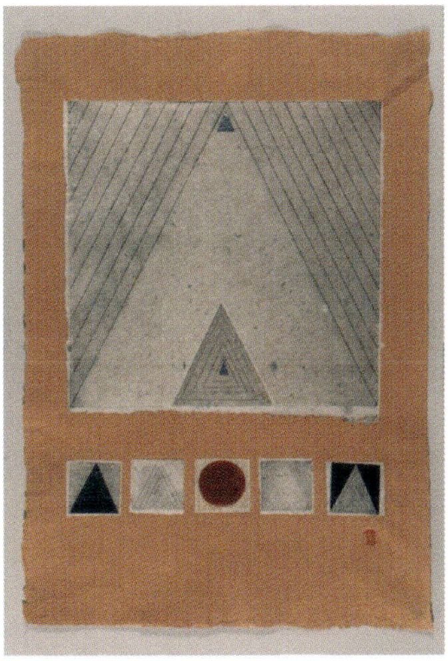

Denny Long
Inside the Mountain, 2003
courtesy of the artist

Denny Long (b. 1947) also brought an entrepreneurial zest to the St Ives art scene, developing with Jon Grimble a large gallery space near the St Ives Arts Club on the Warren. Also like Bedding, Long was affected by a visit to Japan made as early as 1966 while a student at the West of England College of Art, Bristol. Together with meetings with Hamada, Leach and Rie – a visiting tutor at Bristol – this formative experience was deemed by Marion Whybrow to 'have influenced her life's practise as an artist'[(5)] which saw subsequent diversification into different yet compatible areas of collage and intaglio printmaking. Reduction fired ash glazed slab dishes were shaped into geometric symbols, harbingers of later etchings on hand-made paper that transformed simple geometric shapes like triangles and circles into Buddhist-inspired symbols. Studying printmaking under Stephen Hawkins in Bristol during the early 1990s Long, by now separated from her husband Richard Long through whom she had built up manifold art world contacts, created mono-prints like the mystical part-etching-part-collage *Inside the Mountain II* (2003), a work reflecting an interest in Zen and the art of connecting the twain between ethnic and modern sources.

Potters like Joanna Wason (b. 1952), Nic Harrison (b. 1949) and Amanda Briers (b. 1978) who have persisted with Leach-derived ideas, have done so on their own terms. Wason, an art student from north Devon who went on to study in Exeter and then Liverpool, Jason Wason's home town, began as a sculptor who fired clay figures or heads. Through Jason she became Janet Leach's studio assistant gaining access to the latter's extensive collection of pots and books. Joanna's robust hand built or thrown stoneware vessels, notably squared bottle vases, were displayed in the Leach Pottery showroom from 1998 until its closure in 2005 for renovation. Harrison, who was working for a year at the Pottery at the time of Bernard's death in May 1979, also benefited from the tutelage and support of Janet. In 1981 he set up Trelowarren a workshop near Helston and worked there alongside his wife Jackie, a weaver. An earlier Leach student, Sylvia Hardaker (b 1930), who worked at the Pottery in the late 1960s, started the Kenilworth Pottery,

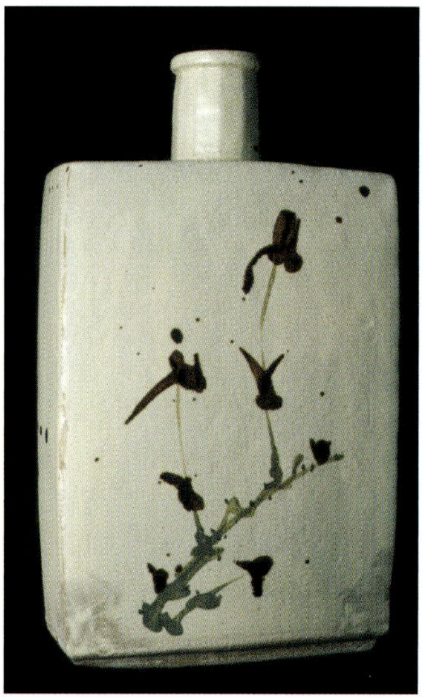

Bill Marshall
Rectangular slabbed bottle
photograph: Toni Carver

Warwickshire near her native Coventry. Since retiring to Cornwall in 1983 this Penzance-based potter produced individual stoneware pots. Amanda Brier trained at Portsmouth and Falmouth and worked alongside Corser and Wason at the Pottery from 2000, her delicate pots, bowls and tiles, in stoneware or porcelain, exhibited with theirs in the showroom. Together with John Rieve, Byron Temple, Warren Mackenzie, Jeff Oestreich, Jeff Larkin and Robert Fishman these later potters kept the Pottery open as a working and selling enterprise in the period after master thrower and potter William 'Bill' Marshall's retirement in 1977 and Bernard's death.

Younger or more recent potters such as the much exhibited and acclaimed Aki Moriuchi and Chris Prindl (b. 1968) have followed Japanese precepts beyond Leach Pottery orbit. They have alighted on an individual amalgam of sculptural and functional forms that never fully relinquish oriental principles thereby demonstrating diversification even within Leach-compatible aesthetics. Tokyo-born Moriuchi moved to Britain in 1971, studying ceramics in London in the early 1990s before moving to what she called 'the landscape of stones'(6) in Cornwall in 2000. Here an ancient rock-strewn landscape has made her into something of sculptor manqué, the former oriental tableware and ritual tea containers giving way to multi glazed objects of a surreal mystery. Their smooth or rough surfaces are the outcome of several stoneware firings, sandblasting and other sculptural finishing processes. What the potter described as capturing the 'essence of time contained inside the stones' enables the work to link the aesthetics of a pagan Cornish landscape on the one hand and the inscrutable Zen tranquility of the Japanese rock garden on the other. Emmanuel Cooper's estimation that Moriuchi integrates 'a Japanese sensibility . . . with western understanding'(7) is born out in ways that augment, indeed challenge, Leachian convention.

Chris Prindl, a German-born American who was educated in Sussex, spent the late 1970s in Japan where his mother was a silk weaver. At Princeton University a decade later, while studying Japanese, Prindl encountered Toshiko Takaezu, a Japanese Hawaiian potter in whose classes his life as potter commenced. Describing this as 'an art course rather than craft course' Prindl looked at sculptural ceramics, a pursuit that took him back to Japan and studies during the early 1990s with Takao Okazaki. He was introduced to anagama wood firing and later set up an anagama kiln in Pennsylvania. He moved to east Cornwall in 1996, acquiring a former forge near Lostwithiel in 2000. Tall, buckled

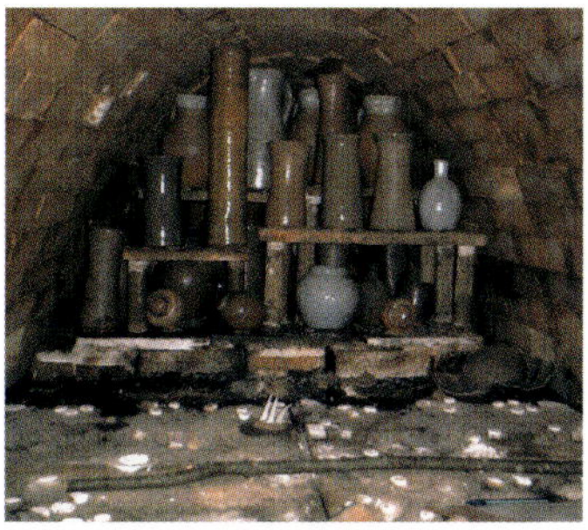

Peter Swanson pots inside his wood-fired Anagama kiln.

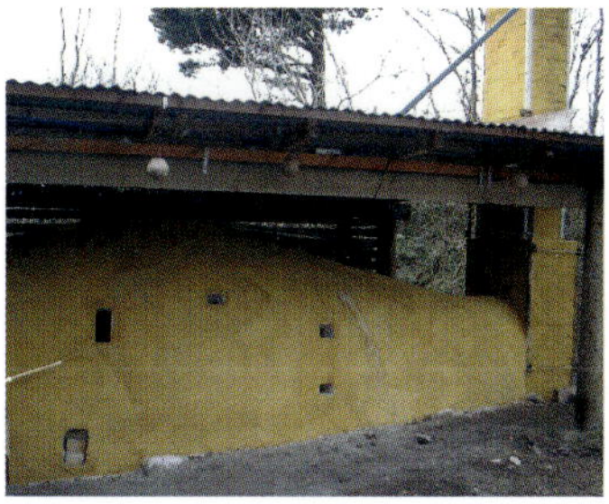

Peter Swanson's Anagama kiln.

pots are produced alongside emphatically thrown stoneware pots, Prindl developing a uniform copper-based purple glaze.

Peter Swanson (b. 1950), an independent, largely self-taught potter who abandoned a fashion design course in his native Southampton to learn pottery-making as he put it 'on the hoof,' also runs a selling workshop at a remove from St Ives and the Leach Pottery. Moving to Cornwall and setting up an earthenware pottery in the mid 1970s Swanson developed reduction fired stoneware and porcelain and employed plain and natural ash glazes. A Swanson pot is nothing if not well made. A highly productive workshop near Prussia Cove yields both standard ware and individual forms based on gently swelling vases, bowls and square bottle vases. Swanson also built an alumina brick Anagama kiln in the grounds of his Ashton home, using practical advice from the Devon-based Sven Bayer and from his visit to the ancient pottery village of La Borne in central France. The results are flame-licked pots of lustrous unpredictability and fortuitous mystery.

Andy Marshall developed a similar independence, in his case extending his father Bill's pragmatism to an almost ideological regard for humble 'folk' pottery, an interest stimulated by the Japanese Folk Craft Society's *The Mingei Magazine*. This informed non-intellectualism also led to an interest in unusual or lesser known figures like Rosanjin. He shared Bill's preference for old Korean peasant pots with hakeme glazes and for Medieval English slipware from north Devon. While living in Poland during the early 1970s, where he worked in a chemical factory, Marshall was moved by Moravian and German earthenware in which functional ware still possessed a charm and individual character based on robust shapes and vivid decorative schemes. Living near Truro Marshall alternated between working for Bill and creating his own standard ware in earthenware and stoneware.

The outcome of Anthony Richards' (b. 1924) long Cornish potting career took an even humbler turn, the former founder of Arch Pottery (1955–66) and Penerleath Pottery (1967–79) developing a lifelong interest in painting during his 'retirement' years. The painter's sensibility, rediscovered from his early studies at Kingston Art School, was evident in the decoration of ready-made earthenware garden pots and kitchenware bought in bulk from Brannams, north Devon. By this late stage bored with the disciplines and rigors of throwing, an art he had mastered during the 1950s, Richards indulged eye and hand in the decorative immediacy of Van Gogh-inspired colour relayed with black slips and lead, tin or cobalt glazes. Equally 'humble' was his manner

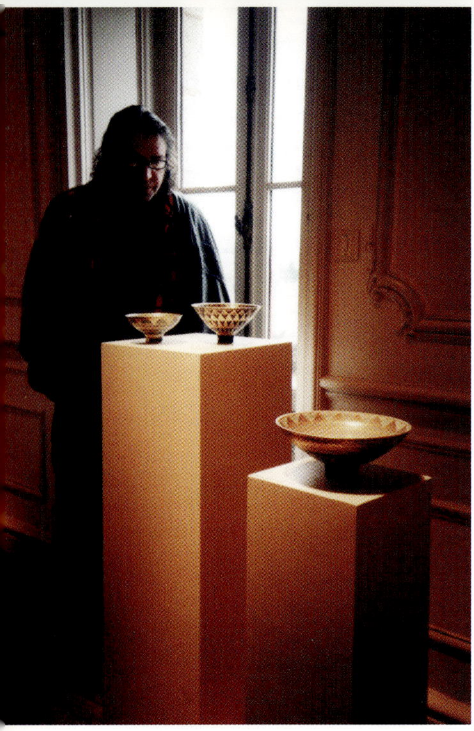

Mary Rich pots.
Peter Davies views her pots at Chateau Bressuire, France, Nov. 2004
Photograph: Ambrose Shere

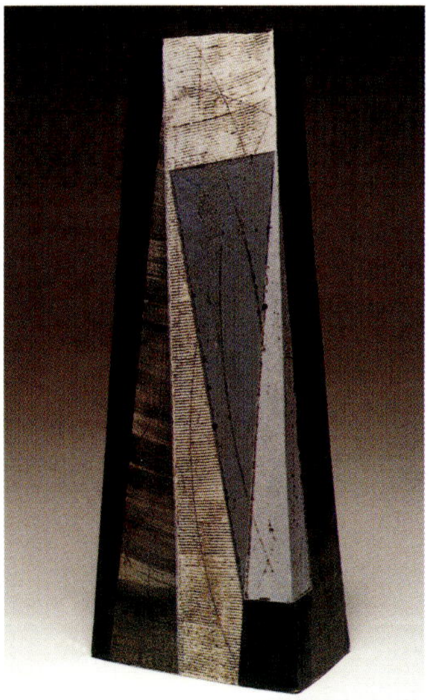

Bernard Irwin
Slabbed Pot
handbuilt oxidised stoneware with scraffito, coloured and textured with slips and oxides

of marketing his wares from his roadside house at Cockwells on the busy road into Penzance. Apprenticed at the Lamorna Pottery, Richards established his first venture the Penzance Pottery (1952–55) with Len Misen. With his French second wife, Christiane, Richards later produced slim and refined coffee and wine sets, jugs and dinner plates at Arch in St Ives.

Helston-born Mary Rich (b. 1940) also used an early training in painting to create a pronounced decorative and geometric vigour to refined, streamlined and often miniature pots. After studying at Portsmouth and later Bournemouth under David Valentine in the late 1950s Rich returned to Cornwall where, through a family connection, she worked at Harry Davis' Crown Pottery near Camborne. Later training under David Leach at Bovey Tracey, where she threw and experimented with clay bodies, led to her setting up on her own in 1969 at Cowlands Creek near Falmouth. Here she used salt glaze learnt from Valentine and later abandoned stoneware to concentrate on fine porcelain forms. While Rich's forms are, as she explains, 'a vehicle for decoration'[(8)] numerous unfinished or unglazed 'seconds' witness a sensitive feeling for tiny, miniature shapes. Influenced by the tall necks and fanned lips of Lucie Rie and the simple, neat, function-based shapes of David Leach, Rich's pots achieve creative individuality through the elaborate, ornamental and almost Islamic surface pattern for which she is known today.

Rich's lavish 'pictorial' embellishment, via lustre glazes and a painted gold 'enamelling,' is a reminder how creative studio pottery uses form for sculptural and surface decoration for pictorial effect. The Cheltenham-trained artist potter Bernard Irwin, for example, uses shape and surface in an ambiguous creative dialogue. A large ceramic pavement for the entrance to Weston College, W-S-M, for example, sees Irwin flatten both, the design becoming both function and environment. In the slim slab built column pots and asymmetric 'boxes', however, Irwin abandons function and utility to touch the purely visual, tactile and aesthetic realm of fine art. The Brancusi-inspired stacked wood columns Irwin made as a student – he went on to study sculpture in Holland in the early 1980s – influenced the upright, streamlined morphology of pots whose pinched elliptic compression reduced their role as containers while promoting the idea of a free standing painting in the round. Irwin's desire that the 'pictured space of the surface image collides with the real space occupied by the form'[(9)] is thereby facilitated by overlapping rectangles or truncated and interlocked squares of colour and smoothed sgraffito texture. The surface image is the outcome of stoneware-fired oxides and engobes that become a cross between the trompe l'œil or shallow space illusionism of Fritsch and Maltby on the one hand or of cubism on the other.

The collusion between space, form and colour in Irwin's ceramic work is, therefore, symptomatic of a broader interdisciplinarian collaboration between painting, drawing, sculpture and pottery. Moving to Cornwall from Bristol in 1996 – where he had spent his entire post-student career – heralded a new landscape-inspired phase. The resumption of painting in 1999, for example, represented the rediscovery of fine art roots albeit in a manner dictated by the peculiarities of ceramic process. Irwin's partner and fellow Cheltenham student Claire Edkins, who introduced him to many of these ceramic processes, also betrays in her work a fine art background. Her hand built, flattened orbs or narrow discs with fluted, ribbed or 'pleated' surfaces are sprayed with vivid 'mascara'-like colour in a way that seems to link sculpture with something more delicate like jewellery. This is consistent with the post student output of ceramic brooches and other fashion accessories with which Edkins made a vital income before moving to Cornwall. The recurring orbs have an art deco feel, the fanned linear rhythm's creating tactile as well as visual low relief patterns.

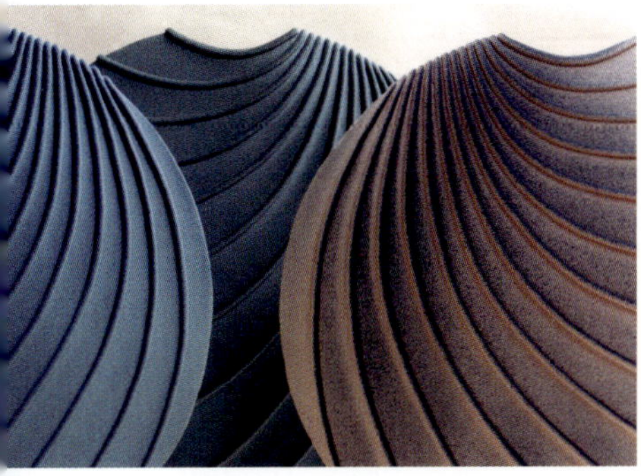

Claire Edkins
ribbed ceramic vessels

Delan Cookson's porcelain pots with slender necks and fanned lips also carry 'arty' associations, the blue surfaces originating from a copper carbonate glaze creating an IYKB uniformity. This artiness is even more apparent in earlier stoneware objects like the quasi sculptural *Squashed Tube* (1977), *Corset Pot* (1980) or the *Nut and Bolt* series. Parodying ready-made objects such as engineering tools or artist's materials these have a Duchampian wit that recalls the amplified 'pop' banality of Claes Oldenburg or Clive Barker. Studying at Bournemouth in the 1950s where, like Rich, he encountered Valentine, and then the Central School, Cookson later assisted in Ruth Duckworth's Kew studio. This, together with an admiration for Brancusi and the stainless steel sculpture of Bill Pye and the late David Smith, pressed him to make ceramic sculpture of a cerebral and conceptual though quirky and humorous kind. A year spent in Newquay as a child influenced the return to Cornwall in 1988 when he retired from teaching ceramics and glass at High Wycombe art school. During these 'retirement' years Cookson, based near Hayle Towans, increased the blue porcelain production in response to commercial success.

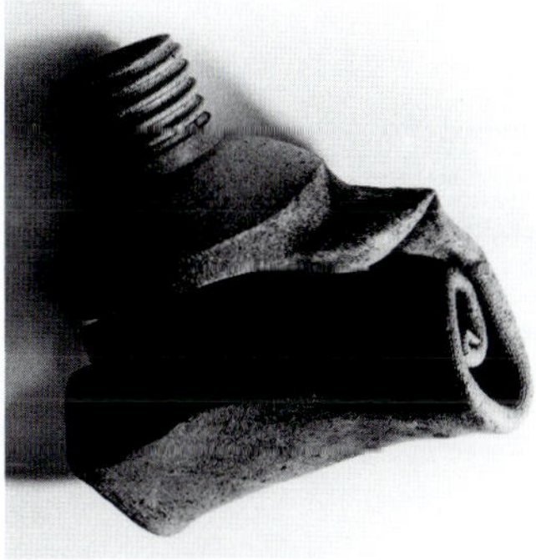

Delan Cookson
Squashed Tube, 1977
stoneware

Jon Middlemiss' wildly shaped thrown, cut or reassembled vessels share Irwin's intention to create dynamic interaction between form and surface decoration. The polymath Middlemiss, however, is even more eccentric in his conception of ceramic form as sculpture. The blurring of the distinction between the two originates from the student period of the early 1970s when the Yorkshire-born artist studied at Exeter College of Art. Again sharing with Irwin and other potters fine art origins Middlemiss all but ignored pottery as a student, only turning his hand to clay when he sought a creative alternative, indeed antidote, to what was perceived as unwelcome art world indoctrination and sophistry. Drawn also to the medium's vocational possibilities that nevertheless permitted wide-ranging scope for technical or creative experiment, Middlemiss ran a pottery in Devon between 1972 and 77.

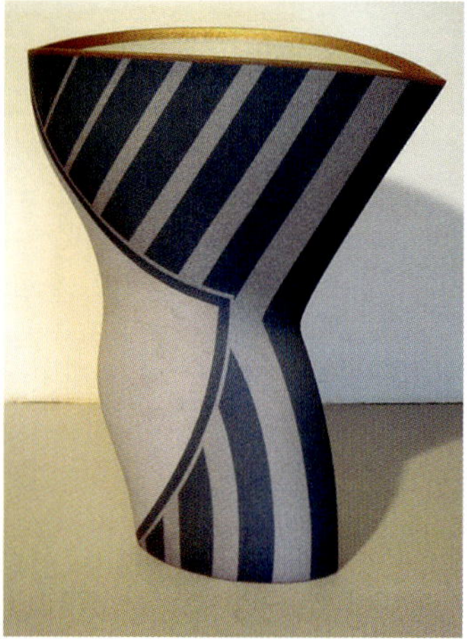

Jon Middlemiss
ceramic
Courtesy:
Katharine House Gallery, Marlborough

Middlemiss' delicate and cerebral ceramic work is stamped with the rigours of the designer; intellectually motivated Middlemiss avoids both 'folky' north Devon slip-ware and 'earthy' anagama-fired stoneware, venerable procedures with ancient provenance in the county and continued into the modern era by Svend Bayer, Clive Bowen and other followers of Michael Cardew. The ethnic and environmental concerns that drive Middlemiss are in fact general and global, rather than local, in character and reveal him to be as culturally inclusive as his work is interdisciplinarian in scope. The zigzagging, hard edged tableware designs of the so-called 'wide-flayed' dishes and Alison Britton-like 'cut and reformed' vessels of the 1980s or on the 'opening cone' and 'sphere and triangle' vessels of the 1990s recall early modern Suprematist or Bauhaus ceramics. While retaining semblance of the traditional pot what he calls his Teapot and Tableware prototypes – typically orbs with square, rectilinear or extruding handles – are contemplative rather than functional objects. Indeed Middlemiss' references to the Tree of Life, metaphysical symbolism and, at the other extreme, industrial ceramics makes him an artist of broad practical and philosophical significance.

By the early 1980s, domiciled in south west Cornwall, Middlemiss had relinquished stoneware with separated areas of ash or tenmoku glaze to alight first on delicate petal-shaped porcelain then on the above mentioned multi-facetted low temperature stoneware vessels. Two Salthouse Gallery exhibitions in St Ives in the early 1980s were followed by a working and teaching visit to California and successful forays into the German market. A decade-long teaching career ensued at Falmouth during which he enjoyed a successful exhibition at Hart Gallery, London. Middlemiss' interest in the interface between pots and sculpture led to the fin-de-siecle 'sectional sculptures,' wavy, upright ceramic forms that eschewed function while fulfilling a continuing intention to express the versatility of clay for which he used a combination of molochite grog and Devon ball clay. The sculptural work since 2000, which extended into dancing 'figures' fabricated with 'found' wood fragments and displayed at Trellissick Gardens in 2002, heralded a return to painting. Inspired by the formative years on a farm, Middlemiss' 'plein air' paintings of wild places like Dartmoor celebrate a pantheistic vision of nature.

The Scottish-born Waistel Cooper (1921–2003) was another potter whose early fine art training at Hospitalfield, Arbroath and Edinburgh College of Art set up an eventual return to art in terms of a late Cornish period dedicated to sculpture-like ceramics. Like W. Barns-Graham Cooper benefited from Edinburgh's awareness of St Ives and of Nicholson and Hepworth, the latter's sculpture inspiring Cooper's feeling for 'pure' formal rhythm and contrasting surface texture. Cooper spent the late 1940s as a portrait painter in Iceland, soon after turning to pottery as the 'perfect vehicle for my new found interest in form'.(10) The early Icelandic slip decorated earthenware pots were successful enough to finance a European tour, when he was inspired by Etruscan pots, and a return to England.

During the 1950s he potted at Porlock, north Somerset using contrasting surface patinas and oxide-treated (iron or manganese) engraved pattern for expressive effect. Cooper's 'sculptural' concern for 'pure,' as opposed to functional, form drew him to Rie and Coper, both of whom he met, and he resisted what he described as the over-subscribed 'Japonaiserie of the Bernard Leach school of pottery'.(11) Indeed, while learning much from Leach's *A Potters Book* Cooper followed the Dorset-based K. Pleydell-Bouverie's ash glaze experimentation. The 1960s and 70s were spent making slim and elegantly tapered ash glazed stoneware vessels at Culbone on the Exmoor coast, Cooper also practising as an art therapist in Taunton. After the death of his wife and working partner Joan, Cooper moved to Penzance in 1982 where he experimented with shape and entered into a Hepworthian dialogue between open and closed form and between white textured stoneware exterior and colour glazed interior surface.

The predominant effect of the Leach Pottery in St Ives was mitigated during the 1960s and 1970s by the Troika Pottery set up in 1963 by Leslie Illsley, Benny Sirota and Jan Thompson at Wheal Dream. A potent mix of artistic and business acumen created, against all odds, a successful twenty year enterprise. Notable for individual ceramic pieces based on the cube, cylinder and other basic geometric forms decorated with archetypal symbols, Troika was, in Harry Lyons' words, comprised of 'artists applying their skills to ceramics, rather than potters striving to be artistic'.(12) Successful commercial forays at Heals and Libertys in London notwithstanding, Troika specialised in rough textured vessels that allied a geometric late modernist formalism with 'pictographic' ethnic and neo-primitive imagery recalling the influential Paul Klee.

Relinquishing its St Ives working and selling premises, which was recalled by the Council for conversion into what is now the St Ives Museum, Troika moved to Newlyn in 1970 where it integrated with the existing Celtic and Tremaen Potteries. The weaver Stella Benjamin, sculptor Peter Ward, manager Roland Bence and later talented maker Julian Greenwood-Penny were notable among staff that, during Troika's peak in the mid 1970s, employed over half a dozen part-time decorators. Troika declined, however, in the late 1970s, Illsley returning to painting (he had studied at Kingston School of Art) and the business-minded Sirota opening a shop first in St Ives in 1980 then an art materials outlet in Wells, Somerset.

Peter Fuller's contentious, though probably just, estimation that 'To react against the Leach tradition absolutely is thus to reject the possibility of making good pots'(13) indicates the centrality of Bernard Leach to ceramic practise in Cornwall. While many of the discussed potters have reacted in myriad ways against Leachian orthodoxy, breaking down the vexed borderline between craft and art that had fired debate in post-war St Ives, there is constant tacit acknowledgement of Leach's importance. For that reason the apt securing of the future of the Leach Pottery, after years of decline and neglect, represents a situation where future generations of pottery students from Falmouth, Cornwall and beyond can study at, and benefit from, a site of singular importance in the revival of British Studio pottery.

Chapter Eight

THE BUILT ENVIRONMENT

Within the liberal climate of post-Coldstream Report art education during the 1960s and 1970s, where fragmentation between avant garde and traditional teaching methods helped slow down regimentation and new forms of conformity, there emerged individual tutors who proved to be charismatic and influential in spite – or perhaps because – of their going against the grain and remaining somehow outside the artistic mainstream. At the Central School of Arts and Crafts in central London, for example, there were the entirely different figures of Cecil Collins and David Haughton both of whom proved magnetic and gathered around them a committed group of like-minded students.

David Haughton (1924–91) provided a springboard at the Central – where he taught between 1951 and 1984 – for a recurring scrutiny of 'place'. His discovery in the late 1940s of the poor mining town of St Just near Lands End he described as an unforgettable, even life changing, visionary experience. It left in its wake a lifelong body of work that embodied both metaphysical atmosphere and a bricks – or rather granite – and mortar 'realism'. The Slade-trained Haughton's position in modern post-war St Ives art is secured through his contributions to the final Crypt exhibition in St Ives in 1948 and to the founding of the Penwith Society in 1949, at whose inaugural exhibition in June 1949 he showed. As such he was included in 'St Ives 1939–64' exhibition at Tate Millbank in 1985.

Ben Nicholson admired his draughtsmanship and, although he returned to London in 1951 where he remained for the rest of his life, he made almost annual 'pilgrimages' to St Just often with a group of fresh-faced Central students among whom were Noel Betowski (b. 1952) and Alex Lowery (b. 1957). One of Haughton's later apologists, the Newlyn Orion director John Halkes, who initiated a touring retrospective in 1979, wrote that such students 'perceived his fierce concentration and power of observation'.(1) Perhaps this intensity was indivisible from the Road-to-Damascus vividness he describes of encountering St Just with his companion Kit Barker:

> *"What happened to me on that spring day was inexplicable but once one has experienced anything of that nature it is impossible to forget it. And unless one is quite unworthy of one's human dignity one must live by it for the rest of one's life. I have no idea of what caused it whether it really was the divine and transcendent visitation that it so clearly seemed or*

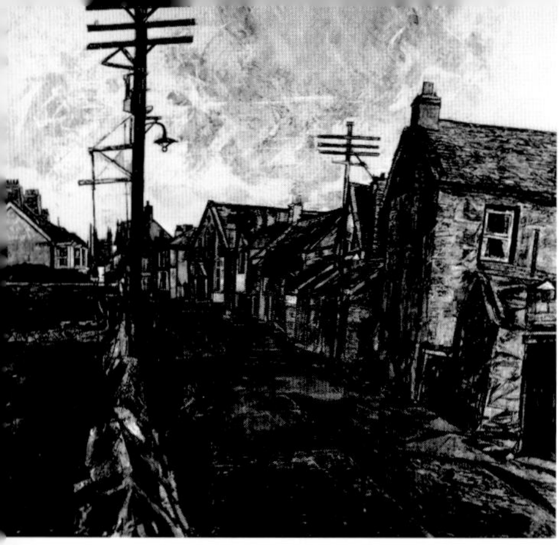

David Haughton
The Road to Cape Cornwall, St Just
1976, oil on canvas

merely a freak of one's chemistry. But I do know it was all important and unutterably beautiful, a trance that went beyond logic but never against it."

These definitive remarks are borne out in the consistency of a taut neo-romantic style where, as the artist explained, 'line is everything, without it imagination is confined to the material, without it colour becomes decoration, forms flat, and invention an impossibility'.(2)

Haughton possessed the temperament of the loner, a factor behind the attraction to the poignant obsolescence, abandonment or desolation of St Just. Whereas Lanyon's early *St Just* (1951) created symbolic metaphor for human tragedy (mining disasters) Haughton surveyed the topographic features to create a life-like 'genius loci'. Haughton highlighted such peculiarities as the sharp interface between industrial and rural, architectural and pastoral or redundant and regenerative factors. While the work was, according to Halkes 'packed with observation while briskly free of sentimentality'(3) it nevertheless provoked the poet Norman Levine to observe an art 'full of comment about human living'(4).

Haughton's aesthetic microscope was so acute that an independent hieroglyphic abstraction emerged that Halkes explained 'echoes the fall of light on quartz-veined granite'. This distillation of visual and tactile material represented a logical extreme against which the artist reacted to produce some major later topographic portraits of his favoured place such as *The Road to Cape Cornwall* (1976). His last years were spent refining these late canvases and other earlier ones salvaged from a disastrous studio fire (he was an habitual smoker) that destroyed much work. Blighted by ill health throughout his retirement period, Haughton lived in a Ladbroke Grove flat. Halkes' *Independent* obituary described correctly how 'waves of students became loyal friends and despite his self-centred needs they were able to give him companionship and hope in return for his undoubted gifts to them'.(5)

Noel Betowski, an Essex-born painter of Polish and Irish descent was introduced to Cornwall by Haughton and became one of those loyal friends. Studying at the Central School in the mid 1970s, where he experimented with abstraction, Betowski encountered the hamlets and villages around St Just during sketching trips the first of which was arranged by Haughton in 1975. Betowski's keen eye for detail led to similarly elaborate and often sizeable drawings made in situ at Kelynack near St Just where he focused on a cluster of roadside barns, farm buildings and houses surrounded by fields of long wind-blown grass. Working these up into large or, in the case of *The Kelynack Triptych* (1980), mural-sized canvases, Betowski eschewed the increasingly less fashionable trend of metropolitan abstraction. In its place he produced masterpieces of pale, atmospheric naturalism in which an obsessive graphic shorthand, always based on direct observation but in fact following an autographic trail of its own in the separate studio environment in Muswell Hill, was 'bodied up' with thin solutions of green, grey, ochre or rust paint. To this degree these paintings were essentially tinted drawings; even when, years later, Betowski returned to a kind of hieroglyphic or symbolic abstraction he did so using a graphic, rather than painterly, process.

A shy and self effacing 'craftsman,' Betowski was temperamentally suited to continue developing Haughton's legacy. There was, however, a generational difference in that the younger man, domiciled in Cornwall from 1987 onwards and without the benefit of Haughton's teaching income made possible by the once expanding art school support system, succumbed to the pressures of living purely from the sale of work with the inevitable commercial compromises that this entailed. Ironically, the years selling from a commercial premise in a Penzance back street were followed by the move into a Grade II Listed Manor style Farmhouse near Sancreed made possible by a family legacy. Spotlighted in the glossy *Cornwall Today* magazine, the house witnessed the gentrification of Betowski's standing if not in the London art world he left behind then at least in

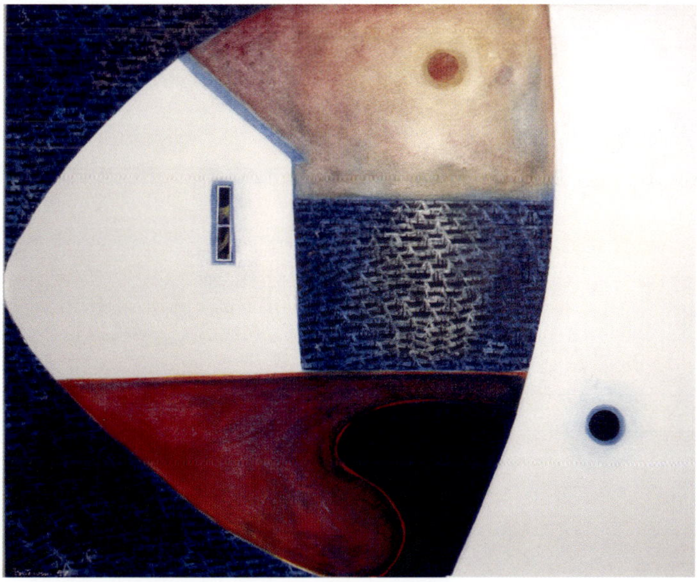

Noel Betowski
Harbour
1997, oil on canvas
courtesy of the artist

Cornish society. This was a far cry from 1982 when Betowski, an impecunious and tentative young painter, held his first solo exhibition in Cornwall. This took place at the Salthouse Gallery, St Ives, where the artist enjoyed two other solos in 1984 and 1991. The first vindicated the post-1975 work and was accompanied by an apt accolade from Haughton who described how his former student 'has to juggle with the tangible and the intangible'(6) in the paradoxically intimate or remote and immovable or fugitive qualities of the West Penwith landscape.

Alex Lowery's recurring pictures of West Bay differ from Betowski's St Just works not only in terms of using a different place, west Dorset, but also through substituting a stylised naturalism for a plastic reduction and reconstruction of 'reality'. Lowery succeeded Betowski as one of Haughton's last Central students (1979–82). Two student sketching visits to Forge Cottage, Kelynack in November 1980 and June 1981 introduced Lowery to the West Penwith landscape where his interest in iconic landmarks and man-made interceptions undoubtably took root.(7) Nevertheless, in the considerable critical literature to have accumulated around Lowery's art from an early stage no reference is made either to Haughton's early input or the student trips to Cornwall. Instead commentators like Ian Jeffrey, Andrew Lambirth, David Cohen and, most perceptively former Central student Merlin James,(8) spoke of more general traditions and widespread international sources (Marquet, Katz etc) to have impinged on Lowery's distinctive renditions of idiosyncratic West Bay features like E.S. Prior's out-size apartment block or the man-made harbour and sweeping low jetty.

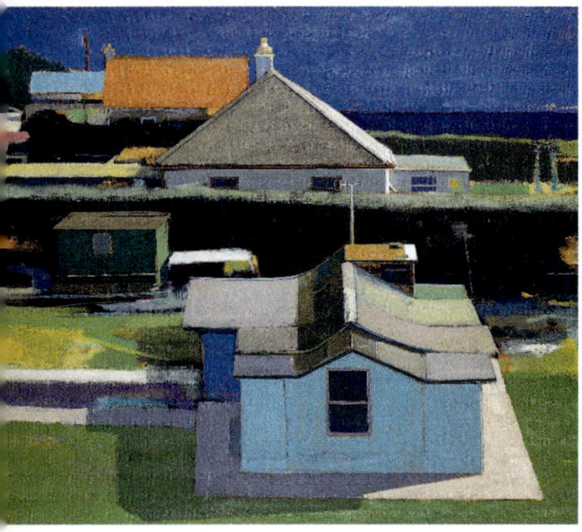

Alisdair Lindsay
Houses Above the Sea
acrylic on canvas
courtesy of the artist

Lowery's post student years were spent in Hackney where he worked for Momart removers. A move with Vanessa Gardiner in the mid 1990s to a family house near Charmouth, west Dorset triggered Lowery's long association with West Bay, the products of which were introduced to the world through the Devon-based dealer Gordon Hepworth. By 2000, however, Lowery's work had found itself into London's Cork Street where he enjoyed biannual shows with Art First. Both Merlin James and David Cohen referred to the 'synthetic' quality of Lowery's simplifications. This involved a transformation of a specific object – seafront buildings – into a series of toy-like scenarios.

Alasdair Lindsay (b. 1965), a Chester-born adopted Cornishman who studied painting at Falmouth between 1996 and 99, also uses architecture as a formal foil within landscapes habitually made up of compounded back garden and coastal views. Unlike the other painters in this discussion, in whose work observation plays a vital organic role, Lindsay improvises and 'improves' on nature through a range of abstract, second hand or popular culture devices. The paint handling too is deceptive, the architectural preciseness and look of photo accuracy belied by a discrete and controlled gesturalism in keeping with the artist's desire for the picture to be a record of its own process of creation. The influence of American photography, of jazz and soul album cover design[9] and of west coast painter Richard Diebenkorn's 'Ocean Park' series also makes its presence felt in canvases that subvert topographic naturalism.

Lindsay's noticeable attention to surface, which originated in student paintings based on the peeling, rusty hulls of container ships moored at Falmouth, created an ambivalence between abstract and representational orientation. An admiration for the Scottish 'colourists' also confirms the importance of the painted surface as a tactile and visual experience. Lindsay, who uses his father's boat at Oban every year to explore the Western Isles, likes to travel and a trip to San Francisco allowed him to see the revered Diebenkorn's work in the 'flesh' and to collect the soul records he later traded in. Lindsay's work subsequently echoed the American's move from topographic perspective to flat planarity, a tendency that, coupled with the introduction into Cornish landscapes of high modernist buildings gleaned from old *Architectural Review* magazines and other sources, resulted in significant synthetic overlay and thematic modification.

Danny Markey (b. 1965) also uses the natural and man made aspects of the modern environment in seamless, fluent pictures of cogent immediacy. If Haughton, Betowski and Lowery aim for a contemplative stillness then Markey's nirvana is an overview of unified kinetic energy. Markey's work has a greater air of impermanence, a feeling of the fleeting moment when the artificial light of motorways and of Falmouth or Caerphilly suburban streets at night provide what the singer Joni Mitchell once described as 'the mathematic circuits of the modern night'[10] Markey's rapidly sketched Whistlerian oil panels still trade in sublime naturalism – the smokey salmon skies of sunset for example – but the disarming subject-matter of housing estates, of Interstate freeways truncating a desert landscape or of Esso petrol stations bizarrely introduces consumer culture 'pop' imagery into late Victorian or Edwardian plein air impressionism.

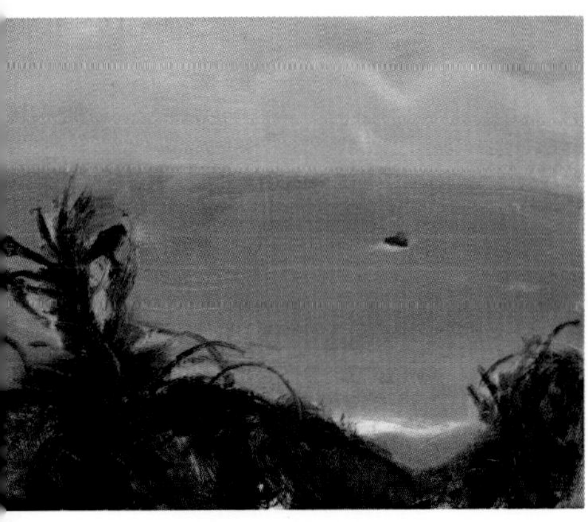

Danny Markey
A Boat Going out to Sea
1988, oil on board
courtesy: Redfern Gallery, London

Born in Falmouth, Markey went on from a Foundation Course at Falmouth to study at Camberwell School of Art between 1984 and 87. He won a major prize and had

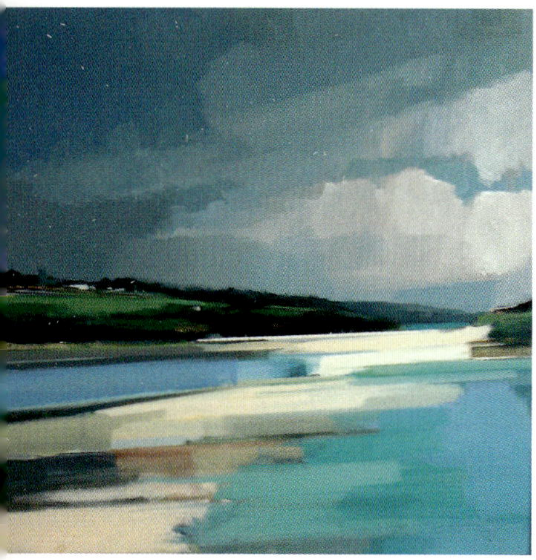

Myles Oxenford
Westerly Breeze,
Hayle Rivermouth
2006, oil on board
courtesy of the artist
and Cornwall Contemporary Gallery

Jonathan Miller purchase a picture for the South London Gallery adjacent to Camberwell art school. A few short years after graduating Markey began exhibiting at the Redfern Gallery in Cork Street where he enjoyed successful biannual solo exhibitions throughout the 1990s and beyond, a period that saw him move out of London to live first in Bristol and finally Cardiff. Markey's rapid impressionism uses a cheeky and clever tonality to capture the suburban environment in flux or at a junction between day and night. The subject-matter follows biographic threads in the sense that housing estates, motorways or Californian freeways reflect places where the artist lives or has visited. Indeed Markey's Cornish roots appear in recurring references to Falmouth, the artist explaining in the catalogue for 'Suburban Hymns', a solo Redfern show in 2002, that 'I have returned to Cornwall where I grew up and revisited subjects, '60's housing estates with ordered gardens, cars parked by the sea looking out to the horizon'. Like Lindsay and Lowery, therefore, Markey uses architecture as a formal foil to give weight, structure and foreground colour while providing pertinent thematic interplay between man-made or natural landscape elements.

Myles Oxenford (b. 1977), a Plymouth-born painter who, like Lindsay and Markey, studied at Falmouth also offsets architectonic and loose painterly elements. Raised in Scotland Oxenford developed both awareness of the inherent colour of the landscape north of the border and appreciation for the tartan colourist tradition. In common with his student friend Lindsay Oxenford also became interested in Diebenkorn, Wayne Thiebald and other Americans whose more conceptual approach to naturalistic imagery left its mark. A plein-airist at Falmouth Oxenford was guided back, albeit temporarily, to the studio. Staying on at Falmouth after graduating in 2000 Oxenford alighted on the subject of sweeping estuaryscapes around Helford. Partly through the influence of his partner Georgia, a florist, Oxenford also turned to still life in which jars of flowers and surrounding bric a brac become mini 'architectural' environments. In both the Cornish estuaryscapes and, further afield, the South African and Regents Park landscapes Oxenford employs broad gestural brush-strokes to capture the lyricism of fugitive light on water, passing cloud or the London skyline seen from Regents Park.

Devon-born Jason Lilley (b. 1966), who grew up in north Cornwall and studied art in Newcastle during the late 1980s, replaces the controlled gesturalism and flighty impressionism of Markcy, Lindsay and Oxenford with an architectural stillness that relies on compositional and textural editing for

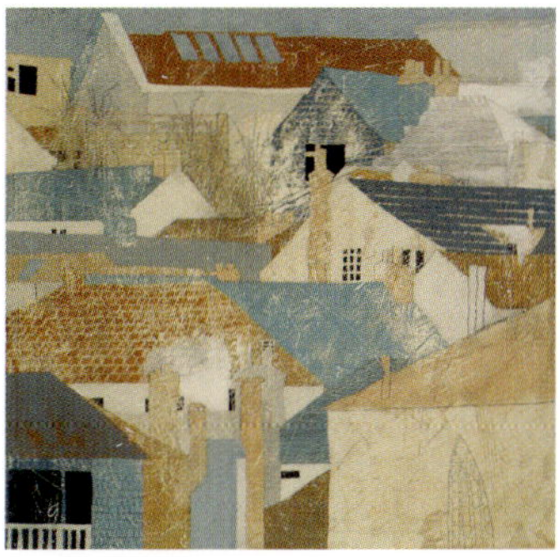

Jason Lilley
Cuckoo in a Western Town (St Ives) 2006
oil on board
courtesy: Belgrave Gallery, St Ives

an autonomous artistic effect. Lilley's built environment is a recurring and familiar one – the jumbled, lichen-coloured rooftops of St Ives in general and of 'Down'long' seen from Porthmeor or Barnoon in particular. The interlocking irregularity of Lilley's St Ives skylines, in taking Nicholson's or Haughton's mid-century rhythmic architecture into a new century, reveals artistic continuity and the safe-guarding of a townscape protected by restrictions of natural geography and local planning regulations.

Lilley's townscapes are thus both documentary and improvisatory in character, relying on a balance between naturalistic and plastic, descriptive and abstract factors. Lilley's stated intention that the picture 'goes through the same situation as the buildings' sees him attack the surface with a 'storm' of incised, abraded, sandpapered or collaged processes. Using 'plein air' drawings as starting points Lilley builds imagery through accretions of emulsion, acrylic and watercolour into which are registered linear or textural incident. The preference for hardy watercolour paper supports later attached to board is indicative of the completed works' umbilical link to drawing. But it is tinted drawing where selected zones of colour – the ink black of window, the acid verdigris of slate roof or ochre sliver of beach for example – impart pictorial completeness and definition.

Lilley's architectural profiles of St Ives recurs in Manx-born and Liverpool-trained Lil Elliot's sepia aquatint *St Ives.* Depicting a row of elevated houses behind her home near the Royal Cinema Elliot balances vernacular architectural detail with a simplified monumental treatment of light and shade. Learning her craft under Kevin Heffernan in Liverpool and Roy Walker in St Ives Elliot joined Porthmeor Printmakers after moving from Liverpool via Worcester to St Ives with her husband Arthur, an antiquarian book dealer, in 1997.

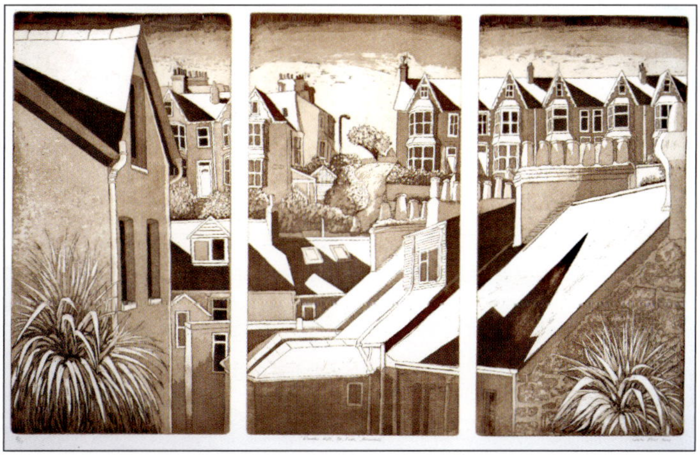

Lil Elliot
Windsor Hill, ***St Ives, 2001***
Sepia aquatint

Recurring studies of St Ives' unmistakeable skyline engaged St Andrews-born Wilhelmina Barns-Graham's talent for lyric precision. Edinburgh-trained, Barns-Graham (1912–2004) entered St Ives in 1940 as a pale but attractive 28-year-old in need both of a vital artistic milieu and a salubrious environment for fragile but retrievable health. Her arrival started a sixty year love affair with the town and her later status as post-war stalwart and survivor, upholding the principles of strong academic drawing based on landscape or townscape on the one hand and of non-figurative art on the other, ensured continuity between mid-century modernism and fin-de-siècle pluralism. Barns-Graham's art changed dramatically during the second half of the century, a formerly cool, analytic and linear language evident in the early Grindelwald Glacier masterpieces gradually giving way to a late colourism and gesturalism seemingly designed both to emulate late Frost and Heron and to acknowledge the traditional influence of France on art north of the border.

Despite the late foray into strong bright colour and loose energetic handling Barns-Graham's work eschewed the flamboyant expressionism of her better known middle generation colleagues for a more structured continental abstraction epitomised by Poliakoff, da Silva or Arp, artists she met on European travels. A Scottish relish for travel notwithstanding, and perennially dividing her time between Cornwall and a family home in St Andrews, Barns-Graham depicted St Ives in various stylistic guises. These ranged from the Ben Nicholson-inspired drawings like *Sleeping Town* (1987) – a late variation on the early drawings of St Ives front in which the interrelationship between linear and painterly elements questioned where drawing stopped and painting started – to 'faux naif' paintings such as the Wallis-influenced *Island Sheds* (1940) and finally on to undulating, tinted line drawings (1980s) based on the tides and moving ocean currents off Porthmeor.

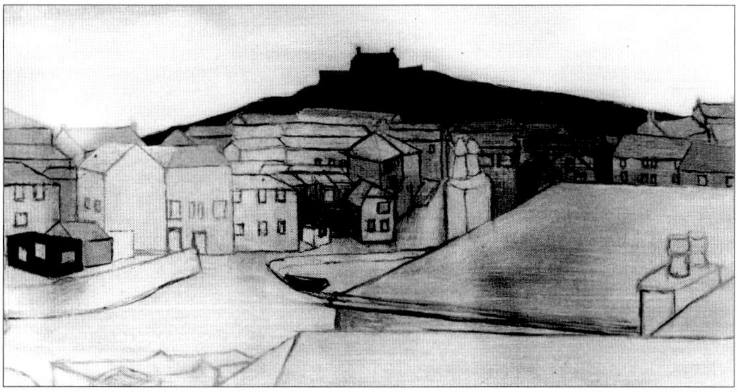

Wilhelmina Barns-Graham
Sleeping Town (St Ives)
1987
oil on board

Barns-Graham's penchant for drawing both man-made and natural structures motivated detailed, large scale drawings produced not only in Scotland and Cornwall but on her not infrequent travels to San Gimignano or Assisi in Italy, Spain, Lanzarote and France. Inspired by an early sketching trip to the Scillies with Ben Nicholson and her then husband David Lewis, Barns-Graham continued to depict churches or buildings of architectural interest. The fastidiousness of her enterprise led to the aptly-named valedictory Tate St Ives exhibition 'an enduring image' (1999) which was followed with a substantial publication, *A Studio Life* (2001) by Lynne Green and launched by the artist's London gallery Art First, events that helped mitigate her not altogether justified feeling of neglect at the hands of more boisterous, better known colleagues.

St Ives-born and Falmouth-trained Seb West (b.1968) creates a literal built environment, his tactile relief-like compositions focused on townscape. Using the novel technique of the painted linocut West gives palpable weight and texture to stylised and delineated man-made or natural landscape detail. Opening the Seb West Gallery, Fore Street, in 2006 this prolific artist communicates directly to pedestrians and informed passer-by alike.

Seb West
Island Chapel

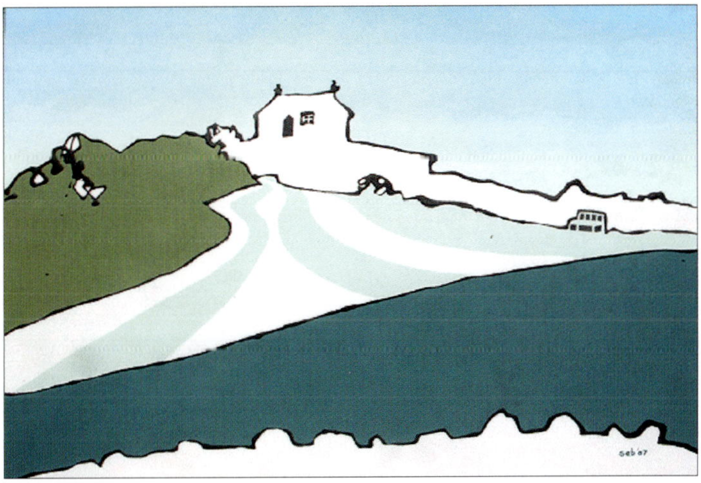

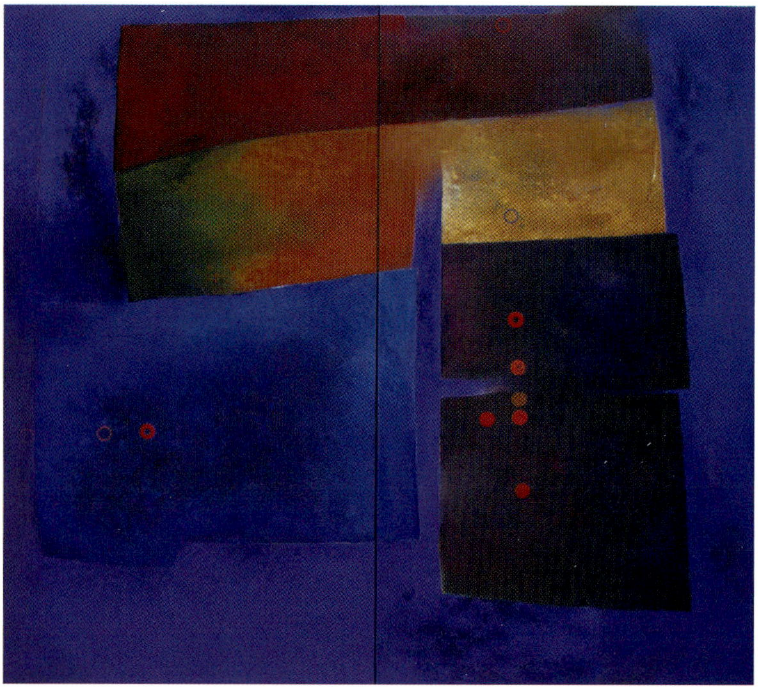

Lar Cann's *Quarry Series: Carbilly* exemplifies the modern Cornish School's investigation into the hidden structure of landscape. Influenced by his early mentor and teacher, Alexander MacKenzie, the underrated post-war St Ives Modernist 'par excellence,' Cann worked in discrete isolation 'up country'.

Pursuing the St Ives School's perpetual exploration of landscape as a repository of geological and social history, Cann brings a venerable tradition up to date with a contemporary relish for intense, saturated colour.

Chapter Nine

THE ANTHROPOMORPHIC LANDSCAPE

Alexander Mackenzie's central role in the Penwith Society, which he joined in 1952 after moving from his native Liverpool to Cornwall, made him a significant figure among his contemporaries. A distinguished teaching career at Plymouth College of Art, where he acted as Head of Fine Art between 1964 and retirement in the mid 1980s, also saw his influence extend beyond his own generation to form a 'following' of younger admirers some of whom had been his students and proceeded to create variations on Mackenzie's landscape theme of anthropological topography.

Landscape in Mackenzie's hands amounted to markedly individual topographic transformations based on lengthy observations of ancient places and notebooks full of on-the-spot graphic abbreviations. While adhering to the Nicholson-sponsored 'house style' prevalent at the Penwith Society in the mid 1950s, Mackenzie introduced a site specific anthropomorphism to the austerely reductive landscape approaches of the time. He was inspired by Welsh, Yorkshire, Dorset, Dartmoor and Mediterranean, as well as Cornish, locations. In his review of Mackenzie's maiden solo show in 1959 G.M. Butcher was thereby able to detect 'an ability to humanise Ben Nicholson . . . and to lend structural backbone to Peter Lanyon'.[1]

A tall, urbane and scrupulous man, Mackenzie's temperament was such that, as David Archer explained in the catalogue for his first solo show in the capital for thirty years, Austin/Desmond in 1999, he 'always maintained a dignified distance between himself and the fickle trends of the London art market.'[2] He also kept a sardonic and circumspect eye on the machinations of the art world around him. As a result of this integrity the aforementioned following was a particularly loyal and committed one including students or younger artists like Clive Williams, Lar Cann, his one-time son-in-law the Welsh-based Dick Chappell, Jeremy Gardiner, Patrick Haughton, Vanessa Gardiner, Vincent Wilson and others.

Mackenzie insisted on the uniquely visual nature of art. The catalogue statement for a spring 1975 exhibition, shared with John Wells and George Dannatt at the Orion Gallery, Penzance declared that 'my painting has its origins in visual experience, rather than in intellectual concepts, although a balance between intellectual and emotional demands must be resolved.'[3] He also spoke of an 'intuitive' process and of reaching 'an essence and imaginative synthesis . . . a struggle against one's stylistic tendencies and compul-

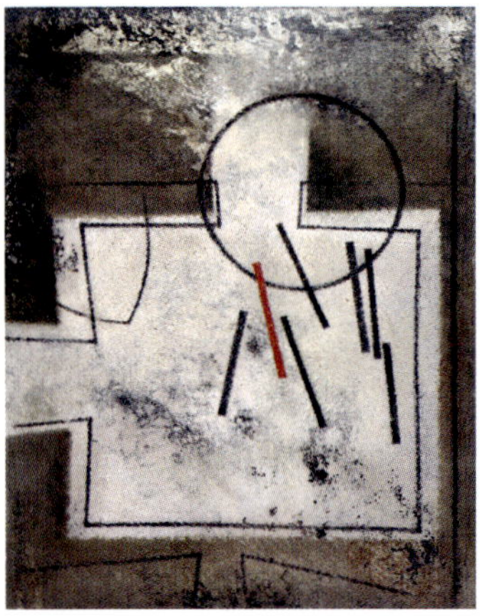

Alexander MacKenzie
Sacred Circle
1991, oil on card

sions'. This struggle gave Mackenzie's contribution, both as artist, teacher and man, its integrity, freshness and enduring relevance.

The Orion exhibition was accompanied in 1975 by another three-man exhibition at Plymouth City Art Gallery which Mackenzie shared with John Wells and Denis Mitchell. Consistent with being a sporadic exhibitor – throughout the 1970s Mackenzie's only other displays were a two-man with Bryan Wynter at Plymouth Art Gallery in 1970 and inclusion in 'Cornwall 45 - 55' at the New Art Centre, London in 1977 - was a slow, meticulous, craftsmanly output that put quality before quantity. A mere dozen works comprised Mackenzie's Orion output (Wells showed fourteen and Dannatt twenty-five works), ranging from the small-scale textured minimalism of *Hadrian's Wall* (1972) and *Askrigg Wensleydale* (1973) (from which he made an etching) to the large paintings on scraped board *Painting Drift/Wharnside* (1974) and *Yordas* (1975).

Mackenzie's three-man Orion show in 1975 was followed, in 1980, by a solo at the same gallery. A move to Penzance in 1981, where he would remain (using it as a base for many sketching trips in Britain and overseas), aligned him again with a local scene that, during the course of the 1980s and 1990s, was subject to a spectacular renewal of interest from the general public. Group surveys of the modern St Ives 'school' in which he featured included 'Cornish Art' at Cuxhaven, Germany in 1981, 'Looking West' in 1987 (both involving John Halkes' Orion Gallery) 'A Century of Art in Cornwall' in 1989 at Truro and 'Artists in Cornwall' in 1992 at the R.W.A., Bristol. 'St Ives 1939–64' at Tate Gallery, Millbank relaunched individual reputations. *Painting November 1960* was included, a horizorital, textured composition of interlocking rectangles that in the artist's words 'represented the worn granite landmass of Penwith and the hut circles and burial mounds of the ancient area'.[4]

Originally displayed in London in the middle of three solo Waddington Gallery exhibitions, the picture was commissioned by the architect John Crowther. Architecture interested Mackenzie and his peripathetic sketchbook delighted in the subtleties of buildings or natural landmarks from diverse times and places. A graphic interest in collage also surfaced and modestly-scaled works like *Domino* (1997), included in the 1999 Austin Desmond show, used musical scoresheets as calligraphic background texture against which were placed torn or cut paper fragments. The intimacy of the small-scale collages contrasted with recurring large horizontal landscapes such as *Pednvounder* (1993) and *Winter Estuary* (1992) which were more taut, rhythmic and defined variations on the early panoramas that established his credentials as a St Ives modernist painter in the 1950s and 60s.

Continuing a thread that invests landscape with a moral, as well as aesthetic, dimension, Clive Williams and Lar Cann developed Mackenzie's interests into an area of textural and chromatic autonomy. Perhaps more 'abstract' than Mackenzie their work speaks unequivocably about plastic equivalence between the materials of art and the physical processes of landscape evolution. Sharing remarkably similar professional backgrounds these Plymouth-born and trained artists, who pursued school teaching careers in Cornwall, shared regular group exhibitions with Mackenzie (and with other influential art tutors like Robin Plummer and Malcolm Carder) at Plymouth Society of Artists exhibitions held since 1944 at Plymouth City Art Gallery.

Williams' Devonian farming roots (extending back generations) provided an empathy with, and understanding of, the land as a vital and stratified repository, the process-based development of his layered, scored and rubbed canvases giving equivalence to this topographic accumulation. Working in his Penzance studio from in situ drawings and photographs Williams makes inadvertent reference to the classic technique of sgrafitto and to the faded tones of fresco painting. These qualities had, courtesy of Nicholson's influence on the younger post-war generation in St Ives (among whom was of course Mackenzie), characterised Penwith Society art during the 1950s, an institution in which Williams, as a Plymouth art student in 1963, exhibited an early aluminum collage on a white ground. The palette of Williams' mature pictures, however, favoured moss green, terracotta, ochre and other earth tones. The scratched delineations have the jagged edge of flint on a cave wall and anchor the eye on topographic markers like horizons or field patterns.

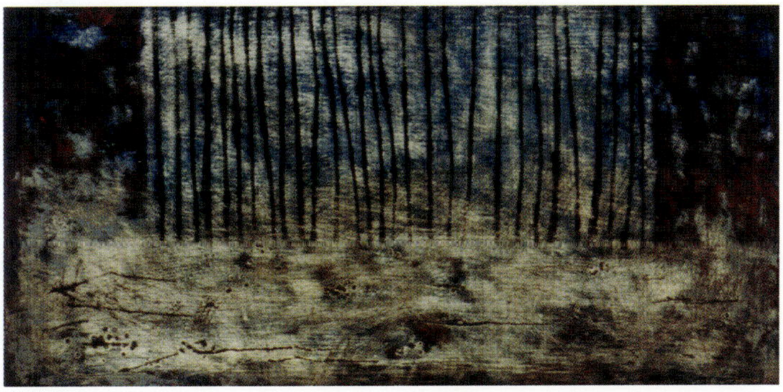

Clive Williams
Treva Croft Copse
oil on board
photograph by Simon Cook

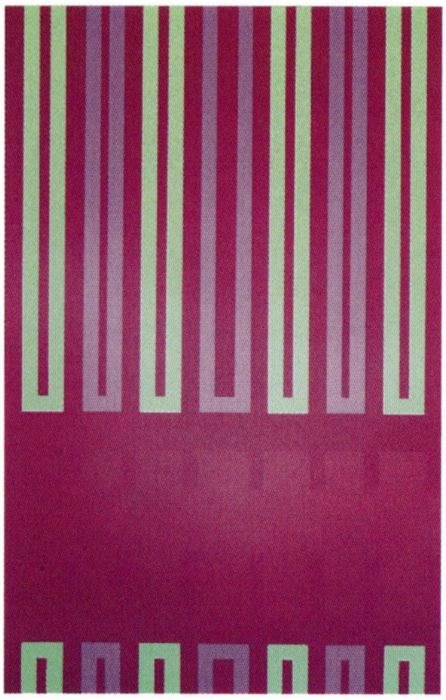

Lar Cann
Rising and Falling on Magenta, 1972
screenprint

Since retirement from teaching in 1996 Williams showed in various local galleries close to his Penzance base, with sorties to Brittany, Bath or London. A solo exhibition 'Overview' at Market House Gallery, Marazion in 2004 contained a coherent body of work described by Frank Ruhrmund as 'refined and reflective'.[5] Lar Cann also dedicated himself to full time painting after retiring from teaching and participated regularly in group exhibitions in Cornwall and beyond. Cann's exhibiting career, like Williams', began with the solitary early appearance of a constructed metal collage at a mid 1960s Penwith Society exhibition. Cann was not alone in finding the 1970s a transitory and uncertain decade; teaching, playing folk guitar and working in an industrial pottery between 1974 and 1979 distracted from painting. An unsuccessful phase experimenting with hard edge abstraction did, however, set the scene for later painting that used the scale and direct 'gestalt' of 'field' painting to present the incidental landscape themes that identify with the mining and quarrying domain around Bodmin Moor and north east Cornwall where he has lived since student days.

Large scale and pure 'Mediterranean' colour in Cann's later work derive from two visits in 1991 to the Midi, where deep azure skies, terracota terrain and orange tiled roofs suggested chromatic power in subsequent work. While Cann's primary intentions are structural and plastic, these landscape features, together with the drill holes on mined granite and the sub strata veining on quarry walls became important secondary elements. The red dots, for example, differ in intention from similar devices in Williams, which function more like cartographic markers. Cann's colour is achieved through glazed layers which give the surface a deep, mysterious lustre. The taut and frontal rectilinearity of many Cann compositions is inspired by both Mackenzie and Ben Nicholson. Cann encountered the former's work during his final student year in Plymouth and, while they never met, counted Nicholson as the earlier influence. Seeing Nicholson's 1963 exhibition of post-St Ives work at Marlborough, London proved revelatory, the younger man later speaking of Nicholson's 'direct and assured line'. While therefore sharing with Mackenzie and Nicholson a conception of landscape informed by both constructivist and romantic impulses Cann also veered in an entirely different direction with strongly designed figure paintings which have the stylised immediacy of fashion illustration.

Correspondences between the art object, as a transparently process-based medium and natural or man-made landscape evolution is also at the heart of Roy Ray's painting.

Ray too alights on ancient places where the scars of human activity provide evidence of distant civilisations. The stone circles or quoits across West Penwith inspired collages composed as flat, circular 'plans'. Developed from the late 1970s, when Ray relinquished deft small scale still life arrangements and 'plein air' oil sketches, these collages introduced extraneous material like grit, dust, cast paper, montage, photographs and acrylic paint. The roughness of these materials suggests an 'arte povera' bleakness but in what John Charles Clark has described as 'well crafted and physically sound' collages a neatness of finish, discrete symbolism and modest scale conspire towards a carefully wraught domestic object whose secrets are buried within multi-layered surfaces. Perhaps this neatness has as much to do with a 1960s career as a lampshade maker in London as with a sublimation of painful childhood experience of war-time chaos and dereliction in the capital. Like Mackenzie Ray's surfaces are often texturally explicit in a visual, rather than tactile, sense, the torn, jagged fragments or partial symbols (half circles, broken lines, dots, crosses or letters) hidden or 'varnished' beneath a final binding coat of oil paint. The uniform beige or off-white surfaces associate with the stone, rock or earth on which Ray's work is focused.

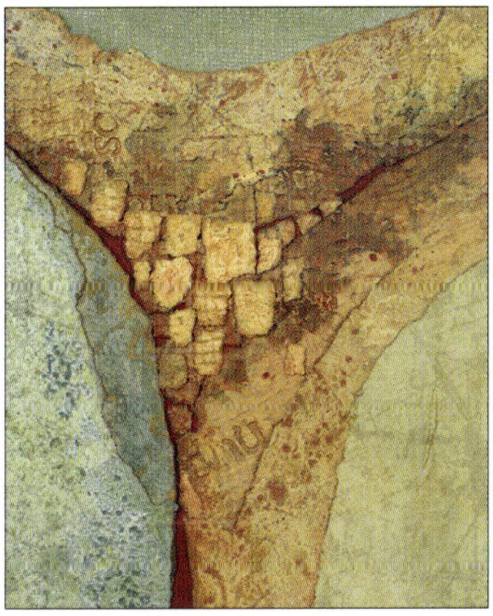

Roy Ray
Groundscape
Toni Carver collection

Ray's influential, almost 'establishment,' position within the St Ives art world is not based on a modest exhibition career but on his role as Principal of St Ives School of Painting between 1977 and 2000. Originally established in 1938 by Leonard and Marjorie Fuller, Ray turned around the dwindling fortunes of the school. A member of many committees concerned with initiatives and art causes in the town, his contribution has been low key but significant. Three solo shows at the Salthouse Gallery throughout the 1980s and a one-man exhibition at both Beaux Arts in Bath and the Penwith Galleries in 1984 were followed in 2002 with a solo display at Penhaven Gallery, St Ives which was accompanied by a publication *Breathing Life into Material* prefaced by Sandra Blow and written by John Charles Clark. The Penhaven works were considered by Frank Ruhrmund to 'come close to sculptures made from chains to chunks of harbour walls but are facsimiles of the raw material'.[5] Unlike the Boyle family's 'super-real' facsimiles of road surfaces Ray's collages are essentially post-cubist rearrangements of 'found' or concocted elements and as such stand in an abstracting St Ives tradition.

Within grander pictorial schemes Margrit Clegg also associates with the signs and textures of ancient places. In contrast to Joe Tilson and Tony O'Malley, however, Clegg reduces the form and colour to create earthy symbols of an austere mystery. David Falconer, the Director of the New Millennium Gallery, St Ives wrote in Clegg's 2003 catalogue how a 'connectness with the mystery of ancient history, whether in west Cornwall, in Andalucia, or in Morocco, has permeated . . . she is trying to communicate with these mysteries, not to interprete in a literal way, but to create a stairway to a world and time that has long gone'.

Bremen-born and Wimbledon-trained Clegg, who moved to St Ives in 1994, enjoyed a third solo at the same gallery in 2006 where the explicit source material of architecture, archaeology and geology informed axiomatically-titled pictures like *Facade and Portal, Strata, Orkney Field, Tablet,* and *Geological* respectively.

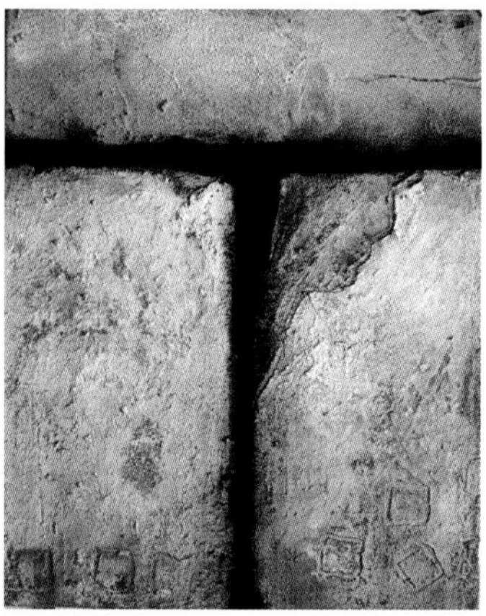

Margrit Clegg
Dolmen
oil and mixed media
courtesy of the artist

This exhibition, despite demonstrating what Falconer described as 'a strong desire to simplify'(6) in a modernist sense, extended these interests into the iconography of graffiti and calligraphy loaded with anthropological association. *Hyroglyphic* and *Cryptic Message* did, however, use the subject for purely visual and aesthetic, rather than ritualistic or literary ends, Falconer remarking that 'it is not the meaning of the language that inspires but the beauty of the many different forms of script'.(7) The dry, granular textures and limited palette – restricted to earthy brown, orange, ochre, white and a German predilection for black – conspired towards a confessed 'richness. . . faded with history'. These concerns revealed the influence of Tapies to whose work Clegg had been introduced as a student by Prunella Clough. *Dolmen and Ridge* (2004), informed by ancient burial chambers and Isles of Scillies rocks respectively and composed with a black and white palette, reveal a strength of composition based on beschaffenheit – form, texture and scratched mark – rather than on the easy seduction of colour.

Carole McDowell's collaged abstract paintings also use the automatic energy of gestural and calligraphic mark to register what she has described as an open-ended 'emotional/aesthetic journey'.(8) Similarly coloured with a dark, bleached or earthy palette, McDowell's (b.1944) work explores collage rather than thick paint texture and in so doing creates an airier, more atmospheric and improvised mood closer to late rather than early Lanyon. Even the artist's talk of a process that 'allows the work to float and drift into unsuspected areas' reveals imaginative abandon within the physical, plastic dictates of chosen media. Derby-born McDowell moved to Porthleven with her architect husband John in 1989 having studied at Putney and Sir John

Cass during the 1980s. Solo exhibitions followed at Rainyday (1993) and New Millennium and group displays with Belgrave in both London and St Ives.

Collage and a tactile earthiness also characterised the popular abstract paintings of Sandra Blow (1925–2006), a London-born and trained painter whose early year-long 'fling' with St Ives in 1957 was followed by a late, this time permanent, return to the town in 1994. The difficulties of maintaining a spacious South Kensington studio led to an exit to Cornwall where, after working from a Porthmeor Studio during the late 1990s, she finally realised the dream of building, owning and working from a large studio tailored to her unique, sometimes mural-sized, needs. Bullens Court, on the Stennack, although a short-lived enterprise, allowed an expansion of her language during fecund late years after the 2001 exhibition 'Space and Matter' at Tate St Ives.

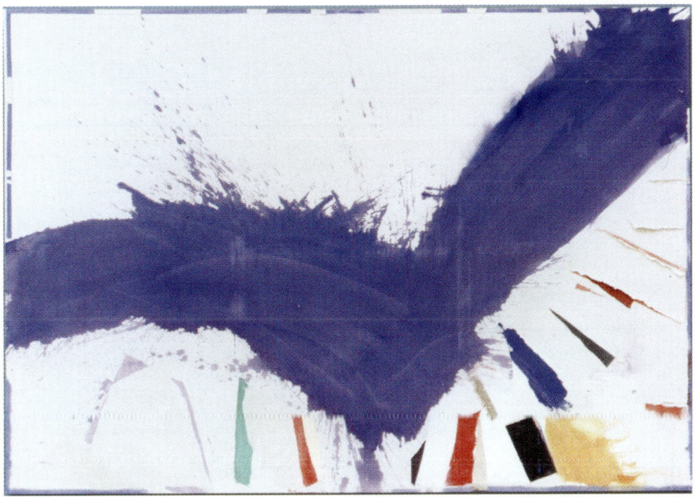

Sandra Blow
Glad Ocean
1989
acrylic and collage
courtesy of the artist

This title derived from the explosive gesturalism of a large 1959 painting whose palpable link to landscape was not topographic but elemental in nature. Typical of the expressive informality of the period's abstract art, Blow's early work utilised arte povera materials like sackcloth, sawdust or ashes alongside the more familiar material of paint. And while, in concert with the optimistic zeitgeist of the 1960s – a decade that began with a runners-up prize at the 1961 John Moores Liverpool exhibition and the embarking on a 15-year teaching career at the Royal College, London – Blow lightened her palette and constructed with easily manipulated collage materials like torn paper or canvas cut-outs, a seamless collaboration between the constructed and the freely painted took permanent root.

This collaboration made Blow's belated return to St Ives artistically appropriate and opportune, hastening what the

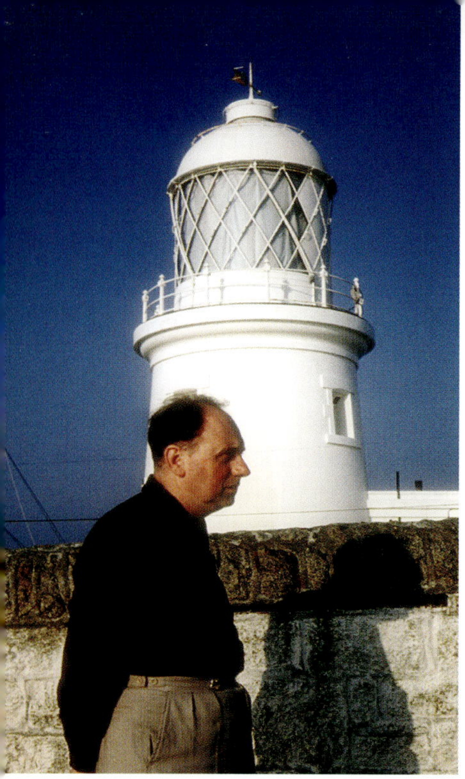

John Christopherson
at Pendeen Lighthouse, 1966.

abstract Scottish painter John McLean described as the 'rustic bravura' and 'stupendous late flowering'[9] of her post-1994 oeuvre. The large canvases *Vivace* and *Glad Ocean* announced this late vitality. The latter hinted also at the exhilaration of the great Cornish outdoors, an irresistible force which was effortlessly evoked in patterned compositions arguably reminiscent of windbreaks, kites or beach tents. Responding obliquely to environment Blow's work also continued its dialogue with the raw earth achieving a 'rustic bravura' through the Alberto Burri-influenced Matter Painting. Here the earth perceived as a collaged accretion of history was translated in a literal and direct way using the very matter excavated from landscape and given new form on the textured surfaces of the painting.

John Christopherson (1921–1996), a self taught London-based painter of Cornish descent, was also influenced by Matter Painting which for him, as his London dealer Jane England explained, created 'textures literally rather than by illusion'.[9] Christopherson was inspired by what he called 'the ambiguity between ancient and modern' and from 1950s artists associated with Art Brut – he corresponded with, and was encouraged by, Dubuffet. In Matter Painting and Informalism he found the confidence and means to create his own, rather idiosyncratic, modern art of decay, melancholy and anthropomorphic distance. Whilst never an expressionist Christopherson created plastic equivalence for archaeological accretion and landscape evolution through a patient, indeed obsessive, manner of working in which pictures were built up over long periods of time to create glazed lustre and jewel-like pictographic intensity.

At the start of the 1960s, when he relinquished his job at the Geological Museum, South Kensington to become a full time painter, Christopherson forged an immediately recognisable style that variously recalled the art of his 1950's heroes, surrealism and magic realism. In so doing he alerted the attention of fellow jazz buff George Melly who, as well as picking his work for the Arts Council exhibition 'A Cold Wind Brushing the Temple' (1979) described the poetic quietism of Christopherson's work as one 'worth listening to'. The authenticity of Christopherson's vision resides in its broad and enthusiastic range of ethnic interests and primitive sources. 'He was also interested,' England wrote, 'in ancient stones, pavements, mosaics, archaeological sites, walls and buildings which had been transfigured by time'.[10] He was also inspired by the built environment having a keen eye not only for the ancient but also for the vernacular idiosyncracies of architectural follies. Domes, towers or discordent decorative edifaces were portrayed in deserted

Chirico-like streets based not on Turin (though a Ventian subject did occur in Christopherson's largish oeuvre) but on Hampstead, Blackheath and Greenwich the domiciles for virtually his entire life. But he made annual pilgrimages to St Ives whose art he enthusiastically collected. Pendeen lighthouse, visited in 1966, was typical of the kind of landmark that stirred his imagination.

Irish-born Tony O'Malley (1913–2003), who lived in St Ives between 1960 and 1990, also saw landscape through the pagan eyes of a primitive celt. Essentially self-taught this former Irish bank clerk who became a full-time painter during the late 1950s drew much from the artists around him while never losing sight of visual sources in a landscape containing the scars and interception of man. O'Malley brought a note of Gaelic mystery to the landscape abstraction of St Ives art. The ancient symbols and hieroglyphics that marked the surfaces of his mature abstract pictures added a suitably celtic dimension to a school of painting that saw landscape as the outcomc of long, slow anthropologic evolution.

Treating St Ives as a spa town for fragile but retrievable health O'Malley also cut a popular figure across the whole artistic community from whom he in turn gained generous dollops of support. His friend Patrick Heron, for example sponsored his project while the wealthy artist Nancy Wynne-Jones who – like O'Malley – would later retire to Eire and develop a highly successful late career, offered him sanctuary at 'Trevaylor' her Charleston-like bohemian 'commune' near Gulval, Penzance. The theme of art as salubrious therapy did not hide a professional seriousness, a steady output leading to important exhibitions with Marjorie

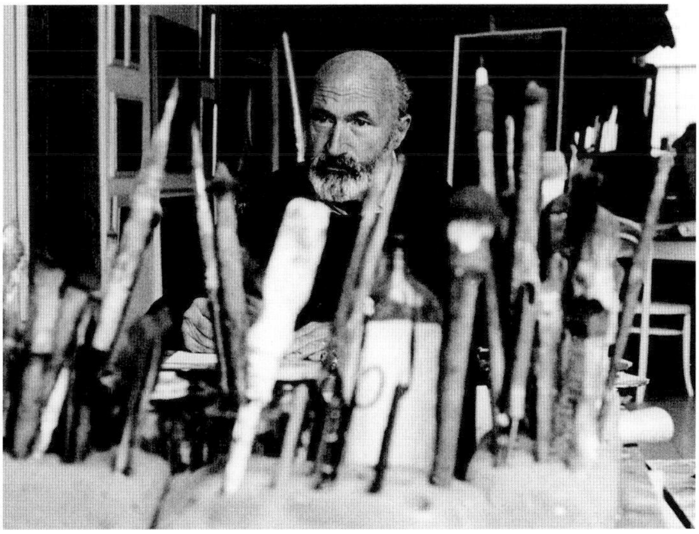

Tony O'Malley
in his Porthmeor studio, 1980s

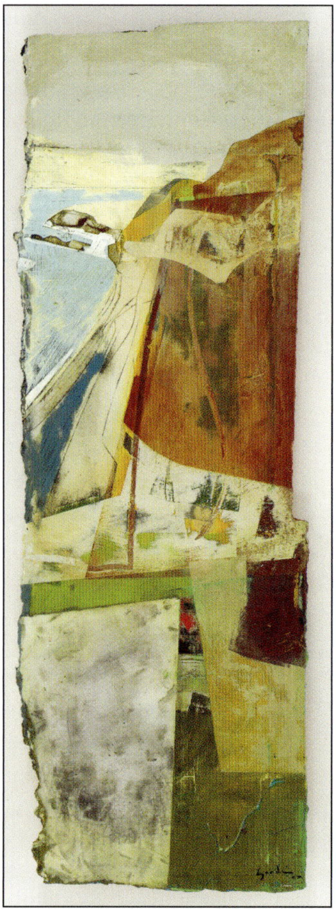

Jeremy Gardiner
Sandymouth, 2007
Acrylic & Jesmonite
on handmade paper

Parr, London (1966), Peterloo, Manchester, Compass, Glasgow and Taylor Galleries, Dublin.

Fascinated by ancient celtic ironwork and stone reliefs O'Malley incorporated cryptic symbols into the rhythmic patterns of his painting registered through razor incisions into the hardboard supports. Later, between 1974 and 1987, a change of environment - annual winter excursions from St Ives to the Caribbean where his Canadian wife since 1973 Jane Harris had relatives - yielded intensely-coloured pictures with a sub-tropical energy. *Island and Ocean:Bahamas*, a three-year touring exhibition initiated by John Halkes at Newlyn Orion in 1986, vindicated O'Malley's artistic responses to an exotic environment.

German-born and Dorset-raised Jeremy Gardiner (b. 1957) revisited the landscape of his youth - the Jurassic coast - because, rather than in spite, of a fifteen year teaching career in the United States from 1984. Despite teaching at the Pratt Institute, New York and in Florida, and meeting artists like Close and Haring, no discernible Americanisation of his work occured, Gardiner finding the flat, swampy landscape of Florida topographically uninteresting. He returned to Britain in 1999 with an enhanced feeling for the ancient landscape of southern England, his subsequent 'A Picture of Britain' using a mix of romantic and constructivist styles in the tradition of Lanyon, Ingham, Mackenzie and others. This reflected a long basic training at Newcastle University under Kenneth Rowntree in the 1970s and under Peter de Francia at the Royal College in the early 1980s.

Gardiner's exhibition 'Ballard Point' at Belgrave, London (2000) and 'Jurassic Coast' at Black Swan, Frome (2006) encapsulated his fascination with what he terms 'an imaginative travel into the distant past'. The conceptualisation of landscape as an ongoing archaeological process of erosion, weathering, human interaction and layered accretion took him beyond his native county to first Fernand De Noronha, a volcanic island off Brazil (his wife is Brazilian) whose unspoilt paradise echoed with the post-war Cornwall of the neo-romantics and then to Cornwall. Here, working on the granitic Lizard and Penwith peninsulars, Gardiner made rapid line drawings of place. These were worked up in his Bath studio on stiff handmade paper sheets where image formation was alternatively based on additions of collage or scraping back to reveal evocative under-layers and painterly substrata. The result is an anthropomorphic microcosm of natural landscape evolution at large, the sharp, jagged and fractured imagery of *Porthcurnow* (2006) or *Sandy Mouth* (2007) creating interplay between plastic and geologic process.

Chapter Ten

THE HARD EDGE

The tightly designed rectilinear geometry that characterises the post-1970 art of Paul Feiler (b. 1917) does not, in spite of appearances to the contrary, represent a fundamental change of direction from the gestural, impastoed landscape abstractions of the 1950s and 1960s. An implicit continuity between early and late work bears out Feiler's insistence that 'there has been no change of heart, no change of vision,' between the superficial dichotomy of these phases. In many respects the changes that did occur represent not only logical artistic progression, akin to Mondrian's march from naturalism to plastic and pure plastic art, but an expression of a post-swinging 1960's zeitgeist. The change from a post-war curiosity in nature and the landscape and in the underlying forces that informed it to a more general interest in the mystical or cosmological principles that took root during the hippie era is registered in Feiler's work. The *Adytum, Ambit, Sekos* or *Janus* series, the latter using gold or silver leaf paint, possess a sacred icon-like power. In this context it is no surprise that his daughter Helen, who enjoyed a small display of her work at Tate St Ives in Spring 2007, should make jewellry.

Identifying 'strong colour, interior framing and ambiguities of size and position'(1) as formal, architectonic factors common throughout, the critic Anthony O'Hear highlighted a will to order and a kind of Bauhaus rationalism at the heart of Feiler's project. The *Orbis* and *Lunatis* series pictures of the late 1960s establish an intermediate phase in which the sensual pigmentation of earlier work is combined with the cerebral – and perhaps even celestial – geometry of the late period. In spite of O'Hear's claim that *Orbis* and *Lunatis* 'have a lightness, even a jokiness unusual in Feiler's art' these paintings do in fact mark the start of a journey within, the images of discs and coloured circles embedded in areas of dense cream paint conjuring an astronimical symbolism inspired by the moon landings of the time.

The *Ambit* compositions of the late 1960s pioneered endless variations on the theme of diminishing squares or rectangles in stepped sequences leading to a suggested core or shrine-like spiritual centre, invariably circular in shape. The theological implications of these inscrutable rectilinear compositions relays themes of quietude, sacred enclosure and perfect order. Travel with his second wife, the painter Catherine Armitage, to sacred sites in the Mediterranean and Middle East reflected the esoteric interests that increasingly inspired his rigidly geometric but subtly coloured canvases.

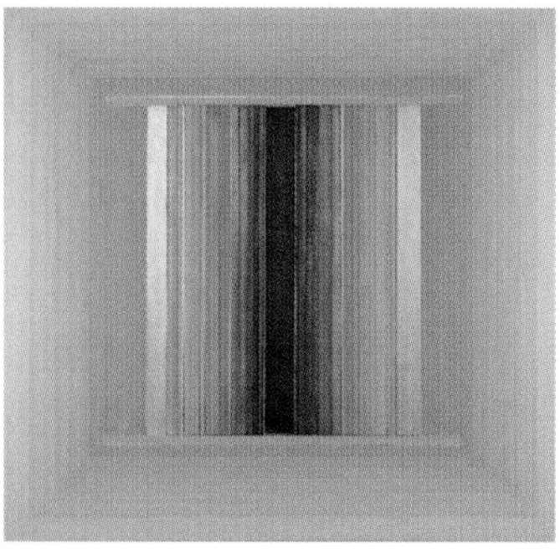

Paul Feiler
oil
courtesy: Redfern Gallery, London

The landmark group exhibitions that established Feiler's reputation during the 1950s included 'The Mirror and the Square' (1952), the I.C.A.'s 'The Unknown Political Prisoner' (1953), the Redfern Gallery's 'Metavisual, Tachiste, Abstract' (1957) and the Tate's 'Religious Theme' (1958). In their different ways these pertinently reflected important features of Feiler's career, among which was an outlook consistent with being a German emigré and wartime internee, the development of a richly allusive abstraction and an underlying transcendentalism. Three successive appearances in John Moores biannual exhibitions in Liverpool confirmed a niche within contemporary art. Between 1963 and 1975 he was Head of painting at the West of England College of Art, Bristol, where he continued to teach until final retirement in 1984. Exhibiting with mixed fortunes at the Redfern Gallery, London throughout the 1950s, Feiler's exhibiting career came full circle when he returned to the gallery in 1993 after an hiatus of nearly thirty-five years. Thematic solo shows there included: 'Janus'(1998), 'Orbis' (1999) and 'Connections' (2002). A 1995 retrospective at Tate St Ives aptly titled 'Form to Essence' defined the seamless interplay between formal and religious intentions.

The search for essences achieved through simplified formal means also characterised the work of Keith Leonard (1921-1993). Like Feiler, Leonard was Slade-trained and exhibited in 'The Religious Theme' show in 1958. The progressive reductionism to which his drawings, paintings and sculptures were subjected matched Feiler in retaining a linear and planar language of precision and purity. Like Michael Finn, Leonard was a modest, religious man whose equally influential teaching career (he was Head of sculpture at art schools in Sunderland and Farnham) and devotion to family came before the pursuit of an artist career. He saw no conflict between the modernity of his artistic project, in the tradition of Mondrian, Malevich and Kandinsky, and established religion. The minimal, rather than symbolic, abstraction of his work precluded conventional ecclesiastical commissions. In spite of the figurative disciplines learnt at the Slade under the sculptor Alfred Gerard Leonard divined from human activities like dance a feeling for balletic movement, postural poise and versatility which was expressed through simple and taut means. Leonard's minimalism was not puritanical, but rather inclusive and interdenominational, an interest in Christian Science linking him to the Nicholsons in St Ives as well as more generally to that long standing accord between modern art and science.

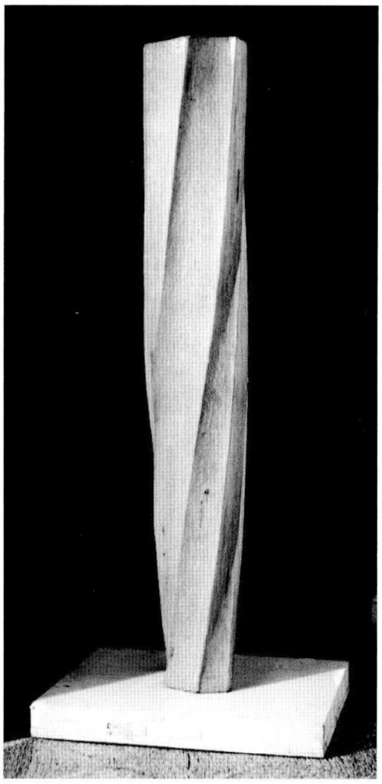

Keith Leonard
wood

During the 1950s Ben Nicholson told the critic Herbert Read that he 'couldn't resist' Leonard's drawings. These were blueprints for large paintings like *Burning Bush* (1956), exhibited in 'The Religious Theme,' *Evening Star Bush* (1957) and *Sky Forms*, compositions whose centrifugal lines or wave-like patterns were akin to cosmological diagrams or neo-religious metaphor. This culminated in *And the Morning Stars Sang Together* (1964) where the theme of unity-within-diversity was achieved through a myriad of white intersections gathering into a constellation of nodal points across a large blue surface. Leonard's return to St Ives after retirement in 1984 saw him perfect a vision in terms of white fibreglass sculptures like *Reclining Youth* (1992), a simple planar form in straight and curved undulations, or the weaving *Monument to Pavlova* (1992.) Leonard's final decade in St Ives led to a memorial show at the Penwith Galleries in 1994. David Brown's catalogue Introduction paid tribute to an unjustly neglected artist of formal and conceptual integrity.

Michael Finn
Falmouth Art Gallery
oil on canvas
courtesy: Brian Stewart

The art of Michael Finn (b. 1921-2002) produced mainly after retirement from a long and distinguished teaching career, operated within a late modernist space in which painting as a concrete wall-bound object competed with other objects – such as sculpture, architecture and even furniture – in the real world. This factor was a pertinent feature of Finn's later oeuvre in that he extended a near pictorial minimalism into the third dimension through constructed wall-bound reliefs and later through freestanding 'sculptures' based on the universal Christian icon of a Crucifix. These two categories remained for Finn fairly distinct. Unlike the art of Noland, Stella or Kelly in America or of R. Smith in Britain, Finn did not move into the adjacent area of sculpture merely through the formalisation or shaping of the painting as object but through a thematic transcendentalism, in his case an obligation to express deeply-held religious conviction. Finn's cruciforms achieved the theme of transcendental certainty through an appropriate concretisation of aesthetic means. His complex hand-painted wood or bronze-cast crucifixes are late, not post, modernist forms, their static monumentality not contingent upon kitsch or ironic paraphrase but rather the outcome of handicraft and devotional abstract symbolism.

The wholly serious tenor and religious purpose of Finn's work, therefore, belongs to a line of transcendental modernism from Malevich and Mondrian to Rothko and Newman. John Golding's exemplary study *Paths to the Absolute* (1999) described this tradition as one where the progressive reductionism of modernist painting chimed with the Zen notion that 'less is more'. The theme of timelessness in both Finn's two and three dimensional work, therefore, cohered perfectly with the premise that the painting, relief or sculpture capture a pure and essential moment of 'being'. Using means that were non-figurative but visibly hand-made Finn's art represented a formalism that stood in opposition to the secular materialism of Minimalist art on the one hand and the dematerialised mode of Conceptual art on the other.

The modest Finn acted as Principal of Falmouth College of Art between 1958 and 1972 and Bath Academy, Corsham between 1973 and 1982. During this time he effectively placed the educational priority of helping others over pursuit of his own creative impulses. This contrasted with the egoism of many contemporaries. During his teaching career Finn settled for exhibiting still life and landscape pictures in group shows at the Royal West of England Academy, Bristol, then at the Penwith Society and Newlyn Art Gallery. Born in Surrey the son of an architect, Finn seemed predestined to pursue a visual art career which was realised slowly after studies at Kingston were interrupted by wartime service in the RAF and concluded at the Royal College of Art, London, after the war. Starting a family in 1945 can only be said to have imposed teaching as an essential component of his future survival and development.

During the decisive last twenty years Finn's work witnessed a 'micro climate' of minute, yet significant, shifts involving scale, format, colour and spatial divisions between horizontal (landscape) or vertical (architectural) axes. Format, though always rectilinear, varied to accomodate single, diptych or triptych arrangements. The latter engaged real physical wall space as an active compositional component which formed white bars linking vertical single colour canvases. The serialised units of Minimalist sculpture (D. Judd and R. Morris) or Keith Milow's late 1970's relief 'crosses'[(2)] are echoed by Finn's triptychs and wood or bronze crucifixes[(3)]. A solo exhibition curated at Newlyn Orion Art Gallery in 1989 by John Halkes (who later became a priest) was a prelude to a valedictory lifetime retrospective in 2001 split between Newlyn and Falmouth art galleries[(4)]. A degree of commercial success beyond Cornwall was belatedly afforded through exhibitions with David Messum Fine Art, London.

By contrast, the sensual hedonism of the art of the sixties and beyond swung to a busier visual beat in which form and colour re-asserted themselves as active, inter-related and decorative components on the picture plane. While uncompromising in its hard-edged compositional clarity Roy Conn's art entered a limited dialogue with both 'pure' forms of abstraction and with romantic notions of the sublime and spiritual. In this the prime inspirational power of Barnett

Newman and Mark Rothko – who visited St Ives at about the time Conn moved there – proved equally relevant to both Finn and Conn. London-born Conn (b. 1931) studied structural engineering, a discipline that informed the work of a mainly self-taught painter unencumbered by academic convention. Early achievements in London before moving permanently to St Ives in 1958 included being selected by Anthony Blunt and Herbert Read for the '*Daily Express* Young Artists Exhibition'[(5)] in 1955. Appearances in London Group shows and in a pertinent theme show 'Form +Experiment' at the New Vision Centre, London followed.

The bracing air of Cornwall made a difference in that, while his post-painterly mode was at variance with the obligatory landscape expressionism of late fifties St Ives art, Conn's membership of the Penwith Society (his later partner Kathy Watkins would become a longstanding Penwith curator) offered a springboard from which his art fused with the burgeoning style and spirit of 1960's abstract painting. Inclusion in the 1961 and 1965 John Moores Liverpool Exhibition was a case in point, *Domino (Twin Reds)* being shown at the Walker Art Gallery in 1965, the year Michael Tyzack won the main prize with a wavy colour field painting similar in kind to Conn's work. Michael Kidner, Robyn Denny, John Edkins and Terry Frost, among other prizewinners, confirmed the current pertinence of systematic or hard edge abstraction. The former category included the 'Systems' artists like Gillian Wise, Peter Lowe and Jeffrey Steel who promoted geometry and expunged romantic associations. The latter, in contrast, developed from the pictorial culture of abstract expressionism. Conn's solo exhibitions at the Rowan Gallery, London in 1966 and Arnolfini Gallery, Bristol in 1969 – incredibly his last solo exhibition – consolidated his position as a notable contemporary painter.

The Bristol exhibition included eleven canvases, among them two from the *Kodak* series. Unusually, Conn reconstructed from his geometric repertoire imagery close to old cameras, a 'subject' that clearly interested him – and would later inform his art – in the sense that he became an intrepid landscape photographer. This activity yielded many of the basic shapes, undulating forms and compositional ideas that would subsequently lead to the 'organic' softening of rigid symmetries and formats. Unlike Paul Nash, who also took landscape photographs in Dorset and elsewhere, Conn used this process for formal rather than romantic ends. Indeed, in *Porthmeor* (1981), a gouache and photo-collage, Conn introduced a photograph he had taken of the former Porthmeor gas works where Tate St Ives was later built. This was included in the Tate's 1995 'Porthmeor Beach: A Century of Images'.

While Conn's art of the 1980s and 90s did convey pebble-like or topographic shapes the suggestion of landscape was subliminal rather than literal. The introduction of collage fragments or of conic areas of graphic shading added textural interest of an associative kind, a feature augmented by a restricted palette based on the primaries with black and white that introduced an air of naturalism. From the vantage point of the millennium such 'impurities' did not represent a loss of faith in an uncompromising mode of painting, as old as modernism itself, which the critic Robert Melville described in 1968 as expressing 'the mood of their generation,and the mood is cool and relaxed'.[(6)]

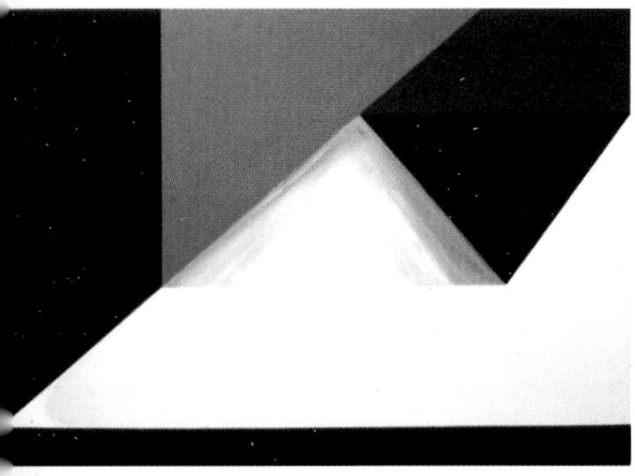

Roy Conn
Cone of Silence, 1972
oil on canvas
courtesy of the artist

In common with many contemporaries Conn taught on a part time or visiting basis at art schools, principally Plymouth in the mid and Falmouth in the late 1960s where he encountered Alexander MacKenzie and Michael Finn respectively. Another teaching colleague, Justin Knowles, used hard edge abstraction to different ends but revealed an admiration for Conn's work which he often bought for his art collection. Appealing to artists like Knowles, architects and to an informed audience, Conn's pictures acquit themselves commercially within the milieu of the group show. The 'localisation' of his reputation as a seasoned and reputed – if discrete and retiring – St Ives artist has militated against participation in mainstream surveys like David Mellor's 'The 60's Art Scene in London' at the Barbican, London in 1993 or 'Formal Situations: Abstraction in Britain 1960–1970' at Tate, Liverpool in 2003. Given his Merseyside profile during the 1960s Conn was a notable absentee from an inevitably incomplete exhibition.

Justin Knowles (1931–2004) a polymath whose exhibition 'From Nature to New Nature' was staged by Michael Wood Fine Art in conjunction with Plymouth City Art Gallery in 2003, applies the discipline of plastic abstraction to the contingencies of mixed media experimentation. The fluid and empirical nature of Knowles's work integrates an inclusiveness of working materials and varied processes into an hermetic corner of geometric abstraction. Important differences of intention notwithstanding, the art of Knowles overlaps with that of Finn and Conn in terms of its later production of Crosses and Altar Groups for churches (using in commissions for Winchester Cathedral in 2001 and Exeter Cathedral in 2002 the technically innovative material of cast cerulean optical blue glass) and of annotated landscape photographs. The latter overlay Conn's investigative use of the camera with a conceptual dimension based on simple line drawings in ink, provisional and hypothetical in nature, drawn onto the gelatin print surface. While resolutely individual in its relentless search for the purest formal solutions to free, random and intuitive impulses, Knowles' art unintentionally overlaps with artists as diverse as the American minimalists or Caro, Pye, Jules de Goede or Michael Kenny in Britain. Eschewing both dialetical aestheticism and metaphor or extraneous symbolism, Knowles' art in two or three dimensions can seem blandly akin to technical drawing exercises. The multi-part 'oeuvre,' however, places the individual work, regardless of its scale, material or fabrication method, within a broad, coherent context in which the essential and integral theme is purely visual in nature. A busy and successful solo exhibiting career during the late 1960s and early 1970s was followed by a long 'silence,' his solo exhibitions at the Serpentine (1970), Arnolfini (1971) and Waddington Galleries (1973) the last until the exhibition at the Royal Albert Memorial Museum, Exeter in 1997.

The 'early' work, encompassing the 'dimensional' paintings (shaped, free-standing, quasi-sculptural canvases included in the Whitechapel 'New Generation' exhibition (1966)) and the low-lying stainless steel floor pieces painted in enamel integrated painting and sculpture. This interdisciplinary osmosis extended to kinetics and to the synaesthesia of the stainless steel Forms/Sounds pieces (1966–68) shown at the Whitechapel 'Interim' exhibition in 1968. The later work replaces the asymmetry of the pre-1973 work (in 1973 a disastrous studio fire destroyed much of the early work) with a rigorous, post-diluvian symmetrical order using sequences of modular units in industrially fabricated materials. These included perspex and resin wall panels which allowed a pictoriality to re-emerge but on ambitious architectural or environmental scales.

Described by the critic Mel Gooding as 'a knowing and highly intelligent beginner'[7] Knowles was from the outset determined to establish an individuality. In distinction to the Systems artists, announced in Lawrence Alloway's 1966 'Systemic Art' exhibition at the Guggenheim Museum, New York, and in the 'Systems' show at the Whitechapel in 1972, Knowles eschewed the cerebral for the sensuality of the declaratory and visual. Knowles's art hides neither implicit mathematical structure nor unstated geometric order. 'The conceptual aspect of my art,' he declared, 'is not mathematical it is mystical,'[8] a factor literally evident in the 'primitive' stack of several sculptures in Dartmoor Granite. A Devon-based artist whose work has broad St Ives 'school' relevance, Knowles exhibited in a solo at the Lemon Street Gallery, Truro and in Exeter City Art Gallery's 'Artists of St Ives' in 2002

The diversity of Knowles' approach to geometric abstraction contrasts with the singularity of Bob Crossley's career-long adherence to the activity of easel painting. Crossley's four year adventure into printmaking between 1968 and 1972, in departing from random painterly expressionism, used the hard-edge order of geometry with which to investigate the chromatic effects of superimposed or interacting inks. Crossley's activity as printmaker, which saw him produce as many as fifty sets of limited edition screenprints using the hand cut stencil technique previously employed to make Xmas cards, proved a suitable vehicle for exploring the opaque and transparent properties of colour. The impersonal, flat surfaces of the prints relied for their effect not on handmade mark or material texture but on the psychological and even spiritual charge of alternatively deep, sombre or bright colour.

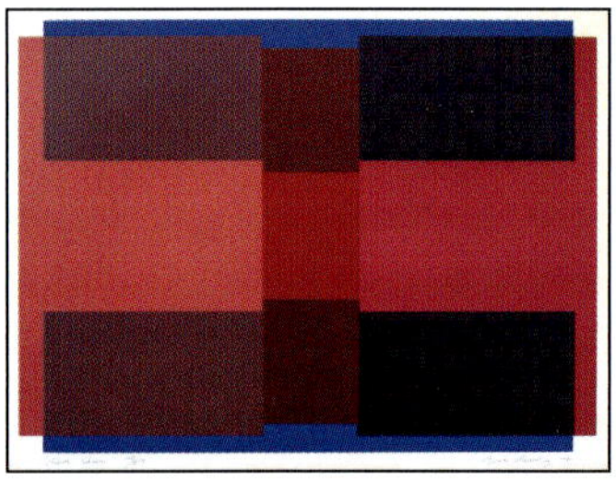

Bob Crossley
Red
silkscreen print
Toni Carver collection

The printmaking phase coincided with a decade-long urban interlude in Crossley's long St Ives career, when he lived in southwest London between 1963 and 1972. These prints sold well in many prominent London galleries. Reviewing his Curwen Gallery show in 1972 the print critic Pat Gilmour described an artist 'playing geometrically with illusory spatial recession and advance'[9]. In *Trapezoid Umber*, however, the geometric symmetry of diminishing rectangles was disrupted in a way that complemented the unpredictable procession of opaque or transparent colour. The main legacy of the printmaking phase, informing his subsequent painting in fast-drying acrylics, was to push his work towards a more symmetrical ordering of the gestural mark, strongly-accented colour and a pronounced interaction between surface and depth.

The contemplative Rothkoesque paintings of Royal College-trained Robert Culwick (b. 1926) use vaporous colours that appear at one and the same time to float free of the boundaries of the picture plane and to draw the onlooker into a deep illusory space. This is aided by thin, slit-like bars of luminous colour that function both as formal devices on the surface and illusionistically as glimpses of something behind the picture plane. First encountering Rothko's work at the Whitechapel Art Gallery, which he regularly visited during the early 1960s and where he showed early abstract paintings in open submissions, Culwick developed delicate, atmospheric colour fields after leaving school teaching in London and moving down with his family to St Ives in 1967. Here the commanding, uninterrupted views across St Ives Bay from his studio home provided a cue for an emerging style notable for its sense of sublime natural space.

Robert Culwick
Au Revoir
oil on canvas

A quietism residing at the heart of Culwick's artistic endeavour sees a modest, even self-effacing, artist limiting his exhibiting career to Penwith Society group shows. The dark subtlety of his paintings appeal directly to the eye and the spirit and require extended looking, the barely perceptible movement of veiled colour and light emerging slowly. The same was true of a small Rothko exhibition at Tate St Ives in 1998, mounted to celebrate the American's visit to St Ives forty years previously, a display Culwick enjoyed for its intimacy and discretion. Perhaps Patrick Heron's reticense towards Culwick's work (they had minor social and professional involvement through the Penwith) reflected a critical ambivalence towards Rothko, which oscillated from the perceived pre-eminence of the American in 1958 to a situation in 1989 where the English painter/critic posed the question 'Can Rothko Survive?'(10)

Culwick's retinal envelope is replicated in Luke Frost's monochromatic expanses of colour divided by thin razor-sharp lines, or 'volts' of contrasting hue. Frost's painting has the hard edge precision and mechanical anonymity of minimal or post painterly abstraction and as such draws on the more recent hard-headed notion of the concrete art object. This distinguishes Frost from both the transcendentalist intentions of New York 'field' painters Newman and Rothko and from the lingering pastoral landscape content of post-war 'middle generation' abstraction in St Ives. Cornish-raised and Bath-trained Frost (b. 1976) follows family precedent in a meticulous professional, not to say commercially expedient, body of work painstakingly executed from a studio complex in central Penzance.

Despite its blank physicality and intense gestalt,the product of as many as fifteen acrylic layers, Frost's painting carries a fathomless mystery, an enveloping mood and atmosphere that speaks of an unfolding temporal, as well as spatial, experience. Certainly the paintings are slow in the making, built with the perfectionist's eye for facture, pitch and colour saturation. In the *Volts* series (2006) comprising low key colour – metaphors for night or for the infinitude of cosmic space perhaps – subtle chromatic intonations emerge from within the paint layers. Variety from across a span of work is a function of colour, scale, format and linear placement, plastic features that impart differing spatial sensations both in relation to the composition and beyond to the environment. The lines also vary from central to peripheral elements in the *Supervolt* and *Chromavolt* series respectively and carry singular or compounded colours.

Frost, a child of the 'high tech' age, collaborates on public or educational projects. These include fibre-optic

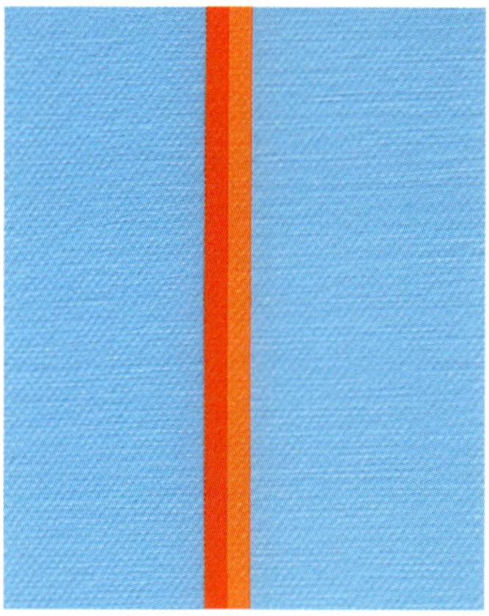

Luke Frost
detail of *Chromavolt 22*
2004, acrylic on canvas
courtesy: Paul Somerville, Plymouth

installations with architects or building contractors in London and a six-month residency at Tate St Ives in 2007 which coincided with inclusion in Tate St Ives's controversial and partial exhibition 'Art Now Cornwall,' outgoing Tate director Susan Daniel-McElroy's parting shot. Since the millennium Frost exhibited with increasing regularity both locally and in the metropolis, a sell-out exhibition at Somerville Gallery, Plymouth in November 2006 announcing the arrival of a significant new abstract painter branching out from family tradition on his own hard edge terms. Frost's explorations into the world of light and colour belong to the tradition of Goethe and Chevreul, the colour theorists, and Seurat and the Divisionists, linking his late modernist project with their proto-modern spirit of scientific discovery.

The older John Charles Clark, who freelanced on Tate St Ives' Education programme, used hard edge abstraction not as a singular formalist statement but as part of a multi-facetted enterprise comprising experiment with soft focus abstraction, writing, concrete poetry, events and what he terms 'proto language images connected with the 'word' work'. Moving to St Ives in 1965 as a kinetic sculptor Clark 'succumbed to the Hard Edge School' as he put it.[(11)] A graphic designer and illustrator by day Clark had, by the mid-1980s, moved on to part-time teaching; both activities, however, put him in touch with other artists and galleries and as such 'helped keep me in touch with other artists, processes and thinking,' a factor that, for better or worse, no doubt influenced divergence from the straight and narrow - or straight and wide - disciplines of formal abstraction.

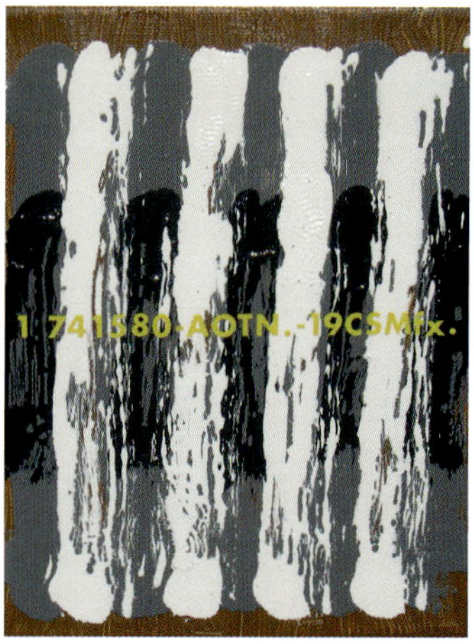

John Charles Clark
courtesy of the artist

Appendix I

ACKNOWLEDGEMENTS

This study of St Ives art since the 1970s, a demanding and tricky subject due to the pluralistic and populous circumstances of the fin-de-siècle and post-millennium Cornish art scene, is a mixture of recent art history and contemporary criticism. Having lived through and directly experienced the late 20th century art colony I have attempted to temper objective scrutiny with more personal feelings of time and place. Artists are grouped, for the most part securely, according to formal or thematic considerations. Otherwise very different artists are, therefore, threaded along such concerns as still life, the figure, various interpretations of landscape and approaches to abstraction.

I acknowledge a debt to Toni Carver who has not only published this much-needed critical insight into recent Cornish art but consistently showed faith and offered a platform for my writing on the current St Ives art scene in his newspaper *The St Ives Times and Echo.* Thanks to his family and staff in all stages of preparation and to Simon Bishop for designing the cover and consulting on the layout. Very many thanks to Brian Stewart for contributing the Foreword. Thanks also to the many artists and galleries who co-operated by answering my questions, provided archive material and/or sponsored colour reproductions. I owe a particular debt of gratitude to: Belgrave Gallery, London and St Ives; Redfern Gallery, London; Katharine House Gallery, Marlborough; Stour Gallery, Warwickshire; England & Co, London; Whitford Fine Art, London; Somerville Gallery, Plymouth; Thompsons', Marylebone; Morley Contemporary, Sheviock and David Messum.

Artists who have offered hospitality and practical or moral help include: Geoffrey Robinson, Linda Weir, Vincent Wilson, William Bolger, Clive Williams, Lar Cann, Patrick Haughton, Edward Lewis, Bob Osborne, David Hampton, Chris Insoll and Peter Swanson. Trevor Barratt, Rosa Keith and Andrew Stewart were also indispensible as were Ben Harcourt and Maggie Davies on the home front. Yankel Feather and Jeremy Gardiner of Hove and Bath respectively and Chris Gange of Katharine House, Marlborough and Richard Selby of the Redfern Gallery, London, were hugely helpful. John Rastall of the Harlequin Gallery vetted the Potters Since Leach chapter.

Appendix II

FOOTNOTES

Chapter One : Introduction

1. Lawrence Alloway. 'Nine Abstract Artists'. p.3 Tiranti, London 1954.
2. F.A. Halliday. 'Barbara Hepworth of Downalong, St Ives.' *St Ives Times & Echo.* 23/5/75.
3. See: 'Barbara Hepworth Sculpture Garden'; Chris Stephens and Miranda Phillips. Tate Publishing 2002.
4. Peter Davies. 'Nasty, Cynical and Self-Indulgent: Real Life at Tate St Ives'. *St Ives Times & Echo,* 10/1/03.
5. Waldemar Januszczak. *The Guardian,* March 1985. See also Peter Davies' 'Letter to the Editor' in *The Guardian* taking issue with Januszczak's dismissal.
6. Waldemar Januszczak. *The Sunday Times,* 13/6/04. Januszczak wrote: 'St Ives is an offensive parody . . . a momentously false experience, with only the Tate enclave offering any serious aesthetic resistance to the relentless gale of tat'.
7. *St Ives Times & Echo,* 18/6/04. 'Snide remarks lead to Mayor's invitation to real St Ives'.
8. Charles Harrison. 'The Place of St Ives,' *Art Monthly,* p.9–12. March 1985.
9. Peter Fuller. 'St Ives at the Tate'. *Artscribe,* Spring issue 1985.
10. Iain Gale. 'Led by Kindly Light'. *The Independent,* 11/8/92.
11. Leigh wrote to ICI about the tensile strength of nylon and read on aerodynamics, a subject that formed part of his architecture training.
12. Lane made a T.V. programme on Leigh. The outdoor exhibition, which ran June 1 – Sept. 30, also included Tom Bates, Hubert Dalwood, Warren Davis, Justin Knowles, Roger Leigh, Denis Mitchell, Nicholas Monro, William Pye, Peter Startup, Peter Thursby, Brian Wall and Richard Willis, Leigh's interest in structures in landscape and in new developments in sculpture saw him later acknowledge Richard Long, P. Randall-Page and Andy Goldworthy, a poster of whose work he hung in his Carbis Bay holiday cottage.
13. Sara Hughes. Denis Mitchell: 'Ascending Forms'. p.24 Tate St Ives, Jan–May 2005.
14. John Milne moved into Trewyn House, acquired for him by his friend and patron Cosmo Rodewald, in 1957. In 1965 he sold the bottom part of his garden to Hepworth who needed more space for the display of outdoor work. Money from the transaction enabled Milne to erect a garden studio away from social distractions of the main house. Cordial, neighbourly relations extended to Hepworth's encouragement and a visit by the elder artist to Milne's solo Marjorie Parr show in April 1972.
15. J.P. Hodin. Latimer Press, London 1977. This was the only lifetime book on the artist. It was followed by 'The Sculpture of John Milne' (Belgrave Gallery, London 2000) by Peter Davies.
16. E.H. Ramsden. *The Times,* 3/7/78.
17. Anna Britten. 'Bodies in evidence' p.25 Review of Edgarmodern Christmas show, Bath. 'Metro'. 4/1/07.

Chapter Two : After the Middle Generation

1. Lawrence Alloway, 'Nine Abstract Artists.' Pg. 12 Tiranti, London, 1954.
2. Adrian Heath, 'Recollections and Movements.' From the exhibition 'Painting in the 1980's.' University of Reading, 1986.
3. Alloway. p.4, Tiranti, 1954,
4. Chris Stephens. 'Terry Frost.' P.62, St Ives Artists, Tate Publishing, 2000.
5. Heath. Reading, 1986.
6. Stephens. p60, Tate Publishing, 2000.
7. Nick Hackworth. 'When Abstract Becomes Domestic.' *Evening Standard*, 2/4/03. This caustic review of Frost's exhibition at Beaux Arts, London, featured a colour reproduction of *Central Rhythm*, a painting that it was alleged in the caption could be, '. . . Mistaken for a tea towel commissioned to reflect the spirit of the Caribbean.'
8. Patrick Heron. 'A Kind of Cultural Imperialism?' *Studio International*, p.62 - 64, Feb. 1968. *The Guardian* articles ran for three days, Oct. 10 - 12, 1974.
9. Peter Fuller. 'The Innocent Eye' *Artscribe* no. 54, Sept. 1985. See also Fuller, 'Art Monthly' no.50, Oct. 1981. Review of Heron exhibition at Riverside Studios, Hammersmith.
10. Alan Bowness. Catalogue introduction for 'Patrick Heron: Recent Paintings and Earlier Canvases,' Whitechapel Art Gallery. June/July 1972.
11. Fuller. 1985.
12. Alan Gouk. 'Recent Paintings.' Patrick Heron exhibition catalogue, Barbican Art Gallery, London, 1985. See also Gouk *Artscribe* no. 34, March 1982.
13. Andrew Wilson. 'Early and Late Garden Paintings.' Tate St Ives exhibition catalogue, 2001.
14. Stephens. 'Reintroducing Trevor Bell' Modern Painters. See also catalogue essay 'Beyond Materiality' (paintings and drawings 1967 - 2004), Tate Publishing, 2004.
15. Alex Kidson. *The Burlington Magazine*, 2000.
16. Emily Ash. 'Viva Blues.' Newlyn Art Gallery, 1996. The exhibition toured to the Midland Art Centre, Birmingham and Darlington Arts Centre. Ash's introduction was accompained by Mike Venning's essay, 'They Had to be Done.'
17. Sheila Oliner. 'Anthony Frost talks to Sheila Oliner.' *Printmaking Today*. 2001.
18. Mary Rose Beaumont. 'Neil Canning.' New Millennium, St Ives, 2002. In the same catalogue was an essay by Michael Bird, 'Neil Canning in St Ives,' and a short Mel Gooding piece.
19. Rachael Kantaris. *Printmaking Today*.
20. Richard Blackborow. Catalogue introduction for 'Tuath' Belgrave Gallery, St Ives. 2006.
21. Maurice Cockrill. 'Mark Surridge: Recnt Paintings.' New Millennium, St Ives 2001.
22. Liam Hanley. 'Land Veils' 2003. Breadsmore Gallery, London, 2003.
23. Ryya Sanders. Exhibition catalogue for 'Idiom.' Lemon Street Gallery, Truro. 2005.
24. Des Hannigan. Catalogue note for Rainyday Gallery, Penzance, 2006.

Chapter Three : Landscape Pure & Simple

1. Peter Fuller. Letter to Phil Whiting. 13/4/90.
2. Jeremy Le Grice. 'At Seventy'. Royal Cornwall Museum, Truro. Autumn 2006.
3. William Packer. Catalogue Foreword for 'At Seventy'. Truro 2006.
4. Lorraine Craig. *Arts Review*, April 1974.
5. Daphne McClure. 'Cornwall to Connecticut'. Badcocks, Newlyn 2006.
6. Robert Clark. *The Guardian*, 31/12/91.
7. Mike Venning. 'Inside Looking Out and Outside Looking In.' Catalogue essay for 'Bob Bourne Goes Solo'. Rainyday, Penzance. May 2002.
8. John Branfield'. 'Tony Giles: a personal memoir'. Mingoose Books 2005.
9. Murray Milgate. 'Fragmented Landscapes'. Belgrave Gallery, St Ives. 2001.
10. John Martin. 'Simon Averill: recent painting'. John Martin London Sept. 2006.
11. ibid.
12. 'Images of London'. Michael Strang. The Gallery. Virginia Water.
13. Eric Ward. *Eric Ward's St Ives*. Halsgrove, Tiverton. 2003.
14. Larry Berryman, *Arts Review*, 27/3/87.
15. Toni Carver, *St Ives Times & Echo* April 1992. Carver wrote that in Wilson's etchings: '. . . lines twist and turn, winding through form and figure in a continuous metamorphosis with their ancient landscape.'
16. Lucie Bray. Rainyday exhibition catalogue, Penzance, April 2004.

Chapter Four : The Figure

1. Edward Lucie-Smith. *Studio International*, London commentary, 1967.
2. Conroy Maddox. *Arts Review*, Vol XIX No. 9. 13/5/67.
3. Maurice Sumray. 'Reflections of the Work of Sheila Oliner,' *St Ives Times & Echo*, 4/10/2002.
4. Wyndham Lewis. *The Listener*, 1950.
5. Anne Tuckwell. *Arts Review*, 1984.
6. William Feaver. 'Ray Atkins' Exhibition catalogue for 'Painting of the Figure from London, Reading and Cornwall.' Royal Cornwall Museum, Truro, 1999.
7. Tom Cross. *Catching the Wave*, Pg. 83, Halsgrove, 2002.
8. Richard Blackborow. 'Boats, Birds, Boys and Beats,' Exhibition catalogue, Belgrave, St Ives, 2006.
9. Letter to the author, 2000. See *After Trewyn,* 2001.
10. Brian Fallon. *Breon O'Casey*, Scolar Press, Aldershot, 1999.
11. Ibid.
12. Peter Fox. Statement from privately published, hand printed document, (edition 100 copies), 1995.
13. John Lane. Easter Sunday 1994. Quoted in above.
14. David Archer. 'Michael Rees: Trace Elements,' Austin/Desmond, London.
15. ibid.
16. See William Packer. Exhibition catalogue from Lisa Wright, Beardsmore Gallery, London Oct/Nov 2005 and Virginia Button, catalogue essay for 'Lisa Wright – Night Paintings.' Lemon Street Gallery, Truro, Oct. 2006.
17. Frank Ruhrmund. *The Cornishman*, 13/7/89

Chapter Five : Still Life

1. Alan Bowness. Catalogue note for Bryan Pearce exhibition, MOMA, Oxford, 1975.
2. Conversation with the author, St Ives. May 15 2005.
3. Letter to the author. 3/6/05.
4. Artist's statement for Mullan Gallery catalogue. Oct. 2003 (Introduction by Professor Alan Livingston).
5. From Jessica Cooper lecture to R.W.A. Friends at the Fedden Gallery, Royal West of England Academy, Bristol, 6/6/05.
6. Alice Mumford. Catalogue note (Feb. 2004) written for Badcocks exhibition. April 2004.
7. 'Intimate Interiors and Favourite Objects'. Julian Lax. June 2003.
8. Ibid.
9. Christopher Turner. 'Looking Awry'. Redfern Gallery, London. July 2005.
10. Julia Paton Walsh. Catalogue essay for Rachel Nicholson exhibition 1997.
11. Ibid
12. Ronald Gaskell. 'June Miles: A Retrospective'. Nancherrow Studio, 2001.
13. Pat Gilmour. 'Three Etchers'. 'Arts Review'. 12/7/74.
14. Mel Gooding. 'Symbolic liaisons' Feb. 1995. Francis Graham-Dixon Gallery, London. March/April 1995.
15. Bryan Ingham interview with Sheila Oliner. 'Printmaking Today' Vol.6. No.3. 1997.
16. Patrick Hughes with the author. Jan 2006.
17. 'Behind the Rainbow: Prints 1964 - 83'. Paradox Publishing, London, 1983.
18. Ruth Jones, *The Path of the Son* (1976). Marion Whybrow, *Bryan Pearce: a private view* (1985) Janet Axten, *The Artist and His Work* (2004).
19. Sarah Drury. Catalogue Essay, 'Painting about Painting'., Falmouth 2001.
20. Chris Insoll. Halsgrove, Tiverton. 2006.

Chapter Six : Great Atlantic Blues

1. Chloe Wild. 'Mike Hindle,' 2003, Great Atlantic.
2. Robert Jones. *Alfred Wallis, Artist and Mariner*, Halsgrove, Tiverton, 2001.
3. Tom Cross. *Catching a Wave*, Halsgrove, 2001.

Chapter Seven : Potters Since Leach

1. Peter Fuller. *The Proper Work of the Potter.* See *Images of God.* p.235. Chatto and Windus, 1990.
2. Emmanuel Cooper. *Bernard Leach:Life and Work,*Y.U.P. Spring 2003.
3. Ibid.
4. See *St Ives Times and Echo.* 9/1/04. Headline 'A million pounds needed to save pottery'.
5. Marion Whybrow. *Leach Pottery St Ives.* p.188. Beach Books, 2006.
6. Quoted from *Harlequin* Gallery News broadsheet. No.55. Oct. 2004,
7. Emmanuel Cooper. Review of Aki Moriuchi exhibition at Crafts Council 1998.
8. Mary Rich with the author, Cowlands Creek Nov 04.
9. Bernard Irwin statement written for author.
10. See Lesley Jackson *Waistel Cooper: forty years of individual pottery.* Manchester City Art Gallery Oct 1993. I am grateful to John Rastall of Harlequin Gallery for drawing attention to the catalogue.
11. Ibid.
12. See *Troika — A Brief History.* Intro, by Harry Lyons.
13. Fuller 1990.

Chapter Eight : The Built Environment

1. John Halkes, *Independent* obituary 24/6/91.
2. David Haughton quoted in above.
3. Halkes 24/6/91.
4. Norman Levine quoted in above
5. Halkes 24/6/91.
6. Haughton catalogue note for Noel Betowski solo exhibition, Salthouse Gallery, 1982. See also *Noel Betowski* (1998).
7. Lowery was accompanied by his future partner the painter Vanessa Gardiner on these trips. Haughton conducted crits of students work in the evening based on day-time 'plein-air' sketching. Lowery recalls Haughton demonstrating how to draw an hydrangea still life and remembers the St Ives art scene scarcely entered the conversation. This probably held true where his London tutorials were concerned. A graphically talented Central School student from the early 1970's, Peter Curran (died Bristol 2006) adapted Haughton's obsessively-worked draftmanship to arch-tectural depictions of church interiors or castles in Gloucestershire and south-east Wales.
8. See Andrew Lambirth *What's On* 4/10/95, Merlin James' *The London Magazine* Dec/Jan 96, David Cohen *Modern Painters* vol 8. No 4. 1996 and Ian Jeffrey catalogue essay for 'Art First' exhibition 'Unchartered Edges' Feb-April 2002. A Lowery painting illustrated the cover of *The London Magazine*.
9. See for example Aaron Siskind's 'Abstract Expressionist' photographs of peeling sections of wood. Lindsay is also drawn to the way the American photographer and graphic designer Reid Miles crops images and designs the covers of American jazz albums.
10. Joni Mitchell, *The Jungle Song* from 'The Hissing of Summer Lawns' (1975).

Chapter Nine : The Anthromophic Landscape

1. G.M. Butcher.
2. David Archer. Austin/Desmond, London, 1999.
3. Alexander MacKenzie. Newlyn Orion, Penzance, 1975.
4. Alexander MacKenzie. *St Ives 1939-64*, Tate Gallery, London, 1985.
5. David Falconer. *Margrit Clegg*, New Millennium Gallery exhibition catalogue essay 2006.
6. ibid
7. Statement for Carole McDowell solo exhibition, New Millennium Gallery.
8. John McLean. Sandra Blow obituary, *The Guardian*, 23/08/06.
9. Jane England. *John Christopherson: Silent Worlds*, p.3, England & Co, London, 1997.
10. Ibid.

Chapter Ten : The Hard Edge

1. Anthony O'Hear. 'Paul Feiler'. *Modern Painters* Summer 1999.
2. Milow exhibited these at the Rowan Gallery, London in Nov. 1979. See Peter Davies review *Arts Review* Nov. 1979.
3. Cast by Michael Werbicki in Bristol who also cast many Paul Mount sculptures.
4. Curated by Elizabeth Knowles and Brian Stewart respectively, the exhibition of recent paintings at Newlyn and of constructions and sculpture at Falmouth celebrated Finn's 80th birthday. A catalogue essay was written by Knowles. A Foreword by Knowles and Stewart referred to the 'inveterate modesty' of Finn.
5. New Burlington Gallery, London. In this debut Conn showed *Suspended Forms* alongside Heron and Mackenzie.
6. Robert Melville *Why I Chose these Pictures.* Catalogue note for the Ind Coope Art Collection. May 1968.
7. Mel Gooding. *The Work of Justin Knowles.* p.9 Bovey Art Books 2002.
8. Justin Knowles. 'Notes on Artform'. p.171. Bovey 2002.
9. Pat Gilmour. *Arts Review,* 29/1/72.
10. Patrick Heron wrote in *Arts (N.Y.)* in May 1958 that Rothko was: 'the best of living Americans'. In the summer 1989 issue of *Modern Painters,* however, his article 'Can Rothko Survive?' marked a startling shift of position.
11. John Charles Clark. Handwritten notes to the author. undated.

Appendix III

INDEX